Reading Literacy in an International Perspective

Editors:

Marilyn Binkley
National Center for Education Statistics

Keith Rust
Westat, Inc.

Trevor Williams
Westat, Inc.

Collected Papers from the IEA Reading Literacy Study

U.S. Department of Education
Office of Educational Research and Improvement

NCES 97-875

U.S. Department of Education
Richard W. Riley
Secretary

Office of Educational Research and Improvement
Sharon P. Robinson
Assistant Secretary

National Center for Education Statistics
Pascal D. Forgione, Jr.
Commissioner

The National Center for Education Statistics (NCES) is the primary federal entity for collecting, analyzing, and reporting data related to education in the United States and other nations. It fulfills a congressional mandate to collect, collate, analyze, and report full and complete statistics on the condition of education in the United States; conduct and publish reports and specialized analyses of the meaning and significance of such statistics; assist state and local education agencies in improving their statistical systems; and review and report on education activities in foreign countries.

NCES activities are designed to address high priority education data needs; provide consistent, reliable, complete, and accurate indicators of education status and trends; and report timely, useful, and high quality data to the U.S. Department of Education, the Congress, the states, other education policymakers, practitioners, data users, and the general public.

We strive to make our products available in a variety of formats and in language that is appropriate to a variety of audiences. You, as our customer, are the best judge of our success in communicating information effectively. If you have any comments or suggestions about this or any other NCES product or report, we would like to hear from you. Please direct your comments to:

National Center for Education Statistics
Office of Educational Research and Improvement
U.S. Department of Education
555 New Jersey Avenue NW
Washington, DC 20208–5574

December 1996

The NCES World Wide Web Home Page is
http://www.ed.gov/NCES/

Suggested Citation

U.S. Department of Education. National Center for Education Statistics. *The Schools and Staffing Survey: Recommendations for the Future,* NCES 97–875, by John E. Mullens and Dan Kasprzyk. Project officer, Mary Rollefson. Washington, DC: 1996.

Contact:
Mary Rollefson
(202) 219–1336

For sale by the U.S. Government Printing Office
Superintendent of Documents, Mail Stop: SSOP, Washington, DC 20402-9328
ISBN 0-16-048957-1

FOREWORD

The National Center for Education Statistics has a continuing interest in understanding new and evolving analytic methods as well as thoroughly understanding the data we collect. During the course of its participation in the International Reading Literacy Study, it became apparent that a number of researchers from other countries shared common interests with the U.S. National Research team. Consequently, a collaborative effort to further analyze specific portions of the data was undertaken with the intent of learning more about both the particular issues as well as research methods. The papers presented here were commissioned by NCES to promote the exchange of ideas among researchers; as such, they do not all adhere to standard NCES practices. Because the views and the analytic methods represent a variety of research traditions, we expect that they will provoke discussions, replications, replies, and refutations. If so, the publication will have accomplished its task.

Jeanne E. Griffith
Associate Commissioner
Data Development and Longitudinal Studies

Eugene H. Owen
Director
International Activities Program

ACKNOWLEDGMENTS

This volume is the fourth to be released by the National Center for Education Statistics (NCES) concerning the IEA Reading Literacy Study. The contributions to this present volume have cumulated the efforts made nationally and internationally in connection with the study as a whole and the previous NCES reports. The following contributions are of special note in connection with this volume.

The International Reading Literacy Study, which provided the basis for this report, was conducted under the auspices of the International Association for the Evaluation of Educational Achievement (IEA). The International Steering Committee, the International Coordinating Center, and the National Research Coordinators of each of the participating countries developed the assessment instruments, assessment procedures, and scaled scores used to report the results and oversaw the conduct of the study internationally.

Within the United States, the research reported in this volume was initiated, encouraged, and sponsored by the International Activities Group of the Data Development Division of NCES. Marilyn Binkley was the U.S. National Research Coordinator and convener of the working group of National Research Coordinators, whose deliberations gave rise to much of the research reported in this volume. Overall direction for this activity was provided by Jeanne Griffith, Associate Commissioner for Data Development throughout most of the life of the project, while Eugene Owen, Chief of the International Activities Group, provided constant support and wise guidance.

A number of individuals contributed significantly to the various chapters of this report. Stephen Roey and Marianne Winglee of Westat, Inc., provided considerable analytic and technical contributions to chapters additional to those that they authored. Christina Yen and Paul Zador, also from Westat, also provided considerable analytic and technical assistance on the project.

Stephen Norris and Linda Phillips of Memorial University, Newfoundland, Canada, provided expert review and advice for the chapter Teaching Reading in the United States and Finland.

Strong and supportive overall technical review and guidance was provided by Susan Ahmed and Mary Frase of NCES. Their efforts provided some measure of consistency and quality of technical approach across this diverse set of manuscripts. They also provided detailed reviews of each manuscript individually.

Each of the authors received funding support from his/her institution of affiliation. In addition, Rainer Lehmann's contribution was supported in part by a grant from the German Federal Ministry of Education and Science. In no case are the views expressed in this report necessarily those of the sponsoring institutions.

Expert technical editing was carried out by Carol Litman at Westat and Anita Wright of the Educational Statistical Services Institute. Document preparation was the conducted by Gil Leigh and Sylvie Warren of Westat.

TABLE OF CONTENTS

INTRODUCTION

The IEA International Reading Literacy Study was initiated in 1988 as a comparative study of the reading literacy of 9- and 14-year-olds in the schools of 32 nations. The main assessments were administered during the period October 1990 through April 1991, and the results were reported in 1992 and thereafter in several international and national reports.

Over the several years that separate designing such a study from reporting about it, the principal investigators within the various nations meet to discuss the form and content of the study as a whole and to comment on the findings. During these meetings, they will often raise issues of importance to themselves as researchers and more generally to education within their respective nations. Inevitably, informal groups coalesce around common interests and problems. The papers in this volume arose in such a situation, and since they contribute toward meeting one of the aims of the United States' study—placing the U.S. results in an international perspective—the National Center for Education Statistics provided support for the development and publication of the analyses.

The nations of primary focus here are Denmark, Finland, France, the former West Germany, Italy, Spain, Sweden, Switzerland, and the United States. The papers that emerged from the work of this group of researchers address issues in three broad areas: factors related to variation in literacy outcomes, both across and within countries; the teaching of reading; and the quality of life in schools. The papers in this report are organized into three sections along these lines.

The first paper in the report presents an analytic approach that cuts across the group of countries that participated in the Reading Literacy Study. In this paper, Raudenbush, Cheong, and Fotiu of Michigan State University develop a statistical model and its application simultaneously to investigate the effects on literacy of social inequality manifested within societies, schools, and individuals. They use data from 22 countries to investigate these issues, focusing their conclusions on the place of the United States among the nations in terms of the level of social inequality identified on these dimensions and its effects on reading literacy. A second paper to focus on issues of inequality is by Taube and Mejding, the national research coordinators for Sweden and Denmark, respectively. They explore the data from all nine nations listed above in an attempt to answer one of the central issues in schooling—what it is that distinguishes low-performing students from their high-performing age peers.

Lehmann's paper on aspects of literacy outcomes is a comparison of the reading literacy of immigrant students in the United States and in the former West Germany, as well as the source of differences between immigrants and nonimmigrants. The focus is on immigrant students whose first language is not the language of their adopted country (English and German, respectively). Lehmann finds persistent differences arising from particular aspects of family and schooling—differences that are greater in Germany than in the United States. The Gil, Rust, and Winglee analyses address questions about the literacy level and its correlates of three regional languages among Spanish students. Through the use of linear regression models, literacy in each region in the regional language is compared with literacy in the national language, Castilian. In general, the authors find that proficiency in the national language is much more strongly associated with student individual and family background characteristics measured in the study than is proficiency in each of the regional languages.

The second section on instructional practices in reading contains two papers. The analyses by Binkley and Linnakylä address the extent to which reading teachers, and the teaching of reading, varies between the United States and Finland. They focus on the origins of these differences in the nature of the

1

reading theories teachers hold. The authors develop this theoretical basis in some detail and link it to teachers' beliefs and instructional practices. The paper by Barrier and Robin of France addresses the extent to which the teaching of reading varies within and between all nine countries. They extend these analyses to identify the dominant teaching styles in the various nations and the commonalties across nations.

The focus of the final three papers is the quality of life in schools. While this matter almost certainly has some bearing on reading literacy, the authors examine the subject as an educational issue in its own right, taking advantage of the fact that a multi-item scale was included in the student questionnaire for 14-year-olds. Williams and Roey explore the latent structure of the measure in eight nations, concluding from their analyses that students in Denmark, Finland, France, Germany, Italy, Spain, Switzerland, and the United States perceive the qualities of schooling in much the same way. It appears that some aspects of schooling elicit the same kinds of affective responses in students no matter what the country. Linnakylä and Brunell explore the quality of school life in each of Finland's two school systems, one serving the Finnish-speaking majority and the other catering to the Swedish-speaking minority, generally seen as the socioeconomically advantaged group. The authors make comparisons between the two school systems, with other Nordic countries, and with United States and German schools to arrive at the conclusion that student dissatisfaction may be a problem in the Finnish-speaking school system. This finding is of particular interest given the high achievement of Finnish students relative to those in the other participating nations. Finally, Gil focuses on whether cultural differences between the four language groups in Spain are reflected in different patterns of affective responses to schooling. His basic conclusion is that, in general, all Spanish students have similar reactions to what is good and bad about life in schools.

In all, the nine papers provide an interesting view of issues regarding reading literacy that are of concern to all nations engaged in the teaching of reading and in the amelioration of persistent inequalities in literacy. These papers also provide a view of the statistical complexities that are required to mirror the substantive complexities of cross-national analyses. Finally, they show the results of a mutual interest in the affective outcomes of schooling, an interest that arose serendipitously during the course of collaboration in this cross-national study of reading literacy.

SECTION A. OUTCOMES IN LITERACY ACHIEVEMENT

- **Social Inequality, Social Segregation, and Their Relationship to Reading Literacy in 22 Countries**
  Stephen W. Raudenbush, Yuk Fai Cheong, and Randall P. Fotiu

- **A Nine-Country Study: What Were the Differences Between the Low- and High-Performing Students in the IEA Reading Literacy Study?**
  Karin Taube and Jan Mejding

- **Reading Literacy Among Immigrant Students in the United States and the Former West Germany**
  Rainer Lehmann

- **Comparison of Reading Literacy Across Languages in Spanish Fourth Graders**
  Guillermo A. Gil, Keith Rust, and Marianne Winglee

Social Inequality, Social Segregation, and Their Relationship to Reading Literacy in 22 Countries

Stephen W. Raudenbush, Yuk Fai Cheong, and Randall P. Fotiu
Michigan State University, USA

1. Introduction

1.1. Home and School Sources of Social Inequality in Literacy

Social inequality in educational achievement has been a subject of sustained debate and research in the United States (cf., Ryan 1971; Jencks et al. 1972; Kenniston 1977; de Lone 1979; Grubb and Lazerson 1982; Kerckhoff 1993). Controversy has tended to focus on two institutions: the family and the school.

Home Environmental Effects. Families have long been known to vary substantially in their capacities to provide educational environments that foster school readiness and reading literacy (Fraser 1959; Wolf 1968). Linguistic input from parents, the availability of books in the home, and early reading experiences predict vocabulary development and early reading proficiency (Huttenlocher et al. 1991; Rutter and Rutter 1993). Such differences in family environment are linked with social status indicators, including income, parental occupation, and parental education (Coleman et al. 1966; Peaker 1971). Parents of high social status are more likely than parents of low social status to have the resources and skills needed to foster reading literacy in their children. Although debate persists about the use of social policy to modify the unequal distribution of wealth or to intervene to provide enhanced educational opportunities for poor children, there is little doubt that the social status of a child's family is linked to the home educational environment and to educational achievement. This link between social background and achievement, mediated by the home environment, is believed more pronounced for reading literacy than for mathematical literacy (Bryk and Raudenbush 1988).

School Contributions to Social Inequality. Although few would deny that families vary in their capacity to educate children, many commentators have emphasized the school as the key institution translating inequalities of social origin into inequalities of educational and social attainment (Bowles and Gintis 1976; Edmonds 1979; Rutter et al. 1979; Kerckhoff 1993). Children of diverse social status vary in the schooling environments they experience. In the United States, for example, local control and funding of schooling are linked to residential segregation by social status, apparently increasing the chances that children of high-status families will attend schools with other "high-status" children while more disadvantaged children will likely have relatively disadvantaged classmates. And many studies indicate that the social composition of a school predicts that school's mean achievement, even after adjusting for the effects of individual student background (see Willms' 1986 review). Thus, if two children with similar family backgrounds attend schools of different social composition, the child attending the more advantaged school can be expected to achieve more than the child attending the less advantaged school. This pervasive effect has been labeled the "compositional" or "contextual" effect of social background (Firebaugh 1978; Burstein 1980). What is less clear is the cause of this difference. The mean social background of a school is undoubtedly correlated with a variety of ecological factors that might predict school learning, including, for example, community expectations, peer influences, norms, resources, and effective practices. Bryk and Thum (1989) were able to account for the substantial compositional effect of U.S. high schools by identifying and specifying in their statistical model aspects of school climate and organization correlated with school mean social class and predictive of achievement.[1]

---

[1]Hauser (1970) has cautioned that inadequate specification of student-level predictors can inflate the estimate of the school compositional effect.

The Compositional Effects Model. The contributions of the individual and compositional effects of socioeconomic status (SES) on achievement can be understood by referring to a regression model that decomposes the effect of SES into its within- and between-school components:

$$E(Y_{ij}|X_{ij}) = \alpha + \beta_w(X_{ij} - \overline{X}_j) + \beta_b(\overline{X}_j - \overline{X}) \tag{1}$$

where

Y_{ij} is the measure of educational achievement for student i in school j,

X_{ij} is the indicator of SES for student i in school j,

$\overline{X}_j$ is the mean SES of school j,

$\overline{X}$ is the grand mean SES,

β_b is the between-school effect of SES on achievement, and

β_w is the within-school effect of SES on achievement.

Figure 1 depicts this relationship in a hypothetical society with three schools: school 1 is a low-SES school, school 2 an average-SES school, and school 3 a high-SES school. Within each school we see a weak positive relationship between SES and achievement characterized by the within-school regression slope β_w. *Ceter paribus*, this slope represents the strength of association between the social status of the child's home and that child's achievement. Specifically, β_w is the expected difference in achievement between two students who attend the same school but differ by one unit in SES. The between-school regression relates the three school means on SES to the three schools' mean achievement and is characterized by the larger regression slope, β_b. The compositional effect of SES is then defined as the discrepancy between the between-school and within-school effects, that is, $\beta_c = \beta_b - \beta_w$. This is the expected benefit of attending a school with a mean SES one unit higher than average, holding constant the SES of the student.

One can also consider the overall association between SES and achievement, as indicated by the regression coefficient β_T. This is the slope of the regression line that would best fit the entire scatter of points, ignoring the clustering of students within schools. For the example shown in Figure 1, β_T is neither as steep as the between-school slope, β_b, nor as flat as the within-school slope, β_w. In fact, the overall slope β_T is a weighted average of the other two:

$$\beta_T = \eta_x^2 \beta_b + (1 - \eta_x^2) \beta_w \tag{2}$$

where η_x^2 is the proportion of variation of X that lies between schools (see review in Burstein 1980), that is,

$$\eta_x^2 = \frac{SS_{bx}}{SS_{bx} + SS_{wx}} \tag{3}$$

where SS_{bx} and SS_{wx} are the sums of squared deviations between and within schools, respectively, on the SES indicator. The quantity η_x^2 may be viewed as an index of segregation of schools with respect to X

Figure 1: Compositional effect model

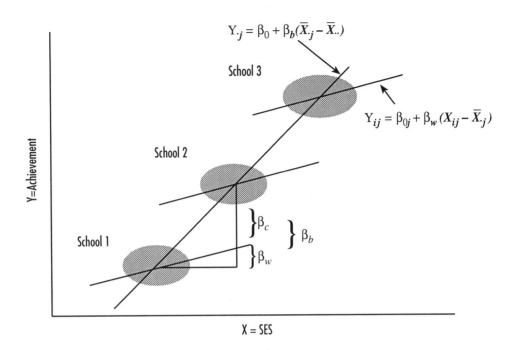

$$\beta_c = \beta_b - \beta_w = \text{``Compositional effect''}$$

$$\beta_T = \eta_x^2 \, \beta_b + (1-\eta_x^2) \, \beta_w$$

$$= \beta_w + \eta_x^2 \, \beta_c$$

$$\eta_x^2 = \frac{SSbetween, \, x}{SStotal, \, x} = \text{``Segregation index''}$$

(Willms and Paterson 1993). The more segregated the schools in a society, the more heavily dependent is β_T on the between-school slope, β_b.

This reasoning leads directly, then, to an expression for the overall effect of SES as a function of the within-school effect and the compositional effect:

$$\beta_T = \beta_w + \eta_x^2 \beta_c. \tag{4}$$

As Equation 4 shows, the overall effect of SES depends on the within-school effect, β_w; the compositional effect, β_c; and the degree of segregation of schools by X, η_x^2. This decomposition of the SES effect will prove useful in cross-national comparisons of educational achievement.

1.2. Cross-National Studies of Educational Achievement and Inequality

As concern for improving educational effectiveness has intensified during recent years, policymakers in many countries have demanded better information about the outcomes of schooling (Willms 1992). Governments in a number of countries have recently developed performance indicators for the purpose of monitoring levels of achievement, often with the aim of holding national, provincial, or local officials accountable for the productivity of schools under their supervision (cf., Fitz-Gibbon 1991; Bosker and Guldemond 1991; Wheeler, Raudenbush, and Pasigna 1992). The policy of using better information to guide educational improvement poses, within each country, a series of methodological issues and dilemmas discussed in detail by Willms (1992).

The policy environments impelling governments to monitor learning within each society have also inspired a need to synthesize information about educational outcomes across societies. It is widely held within many countries that improved educational achievement is a key to improved global competitiveness. Thus, it is natural for policymakers within a country to inquire about the standing of their country relative to other countries with respect to educational achievement, and a finding that one's country is faring poorly in the educational competition becomes the occasion for intensified efforts to improve schooling within that country.

Our purpose now is apply the logic of cross-national comparison to the study of social inequality in reading literacy. Rather than asking how societies vary in mean literacy, we shall examine the extent to which they vary in the social equality with which literacy is distributed. This work follows in the tradition of Heyneman and Loxley (1983), who synthesized data from 29 countries with the aim of discovering the extent to which countries vary in the socioeconomic inequality of educational outcomes. They found socioeconomic status to be less important for predicting educational achievement in developing than in developed countries. However, our purpose is to achieve a more fine-grained analysis by exploring the within-school and between-school components of social inequality across 22 countries. The magnitudes of these components have potentially different implications for theory and policy.

To modify the effect of individual social background on literacy (β_w in model (1)), policymakers in the United States have developed compensatory education programs such as Head Start and Chapter I. A potentially different set of policy options may be relevant to modification of the school compositional effect of social background (β_b in model (1)).

First, social status compositional effects can occur only to the extent that educational organizations are segregated with respect to social status. The more segregated are a society's schools with respect to social status, the more potentially influential are social status compositional effects as determinants of social inequality in achievement in a society. Hence, social status desegregation represents one option for reducing such social inequality. McPherson and Willms (1986) reported that by moving from a selective to a comprehensive secondary school system during the 1970s, Scotland reduced social class segregation and increased the achievement of poor children, resulting in an overall increase in educational attainment across all children.

The influence of school composition on social inequality depends, however, not only on segregation by social status, but also on the distribution of resources as a function of school composition. Controversy and litigation have arisen in a number of states in the United States concerning the causes and consequences of educational funding differences between school districts varying in the social status of their students. Holding constant the level of social status segregation in a nation's schools, it is reasonable to conjecture that a large positive relationship between school social status composition and school resources will result in a comparatively large compositional effect of social class. Of course, such school compositional effects may arise for other reasons including, for example, peer interactions and normative environments that condition parental expectations and pupil achievement motivation and may be related to social composition.

There are two reasons, then, to believe that social composition effects may be large in the United States as compared to other middle- and high-income countries.

1. Between-school segregation by social status may be comparatively large. The local control and funding of schooling encourages a degree of residential segregation, with wealthier families moving into districts with favorable funding. To the extent parents understand the importance of the school social composition effect, they have another incentive to compete for housing in districts with favorable composition. Such incentives for residential segregation by social status may be weaker in societies with centralized control and funding of schools.

2. The local control and funding of schools leads to substantial variation in school resources across U.S districts. Holding constant the level of between-school segregation across a set of countries, this inequality in resources may lead to magnified social compositional effects (see Equation 4).

2.   The Anatomy of Social Inequality in Literacy

Our analysis is based on the reasoning that the social inequality of educational outcomes (and literacy achievement in particular) has four sources. These become clear if we use Equation 4 to define the expected increase in achievement associated with a one standard deviation increase in X, our indicator of SES:

$$Social\ Inequality\ in\ Achievement = \beta_T S_x$$
$$= (\beta_w + \eta_x^2 \beta_c) S_x. \tag{5}$$

Equation 5 shows how the overall level of social inequality in achievement depends upon four factors:

1. The overall degree of inequality in SES in the society, as indicated by S_x, the standard deviation of SES in that society;

2.   The degree of segregation of schools by SES, η_x^2;

3.   Within each school, the importance of student SES in predicting the outcome, β_w; and

4.   Holding student SES constant, the importance of the social composition of the school in predicting achievement, β_c. [2]

The first two sources are displayed in Figure 2. Overall inequality in SES varies on the vertical axis and is measured by S_x, the standard deviation of the SES indicator within a given country. The degree of SES segregation between schools varies on the horizontal axis and is operationalized by η_x^2, the proportion of variance in SES that lies between schools. The expected mean SES of the school attended by a student of SES = X_{ij} is approximately[3]

$$E(\overline{X}_{\cdot j} \mid X_{ij}) = \overline{X} + \eta_x^2(X_{ij} - \overline{X}) .\tag{6}$$

Thus, in a society with no segregation ($\eta_x^2 = 0$), the expected mean SES of the school attended by any student is the grand mean of X, while in a society with complete segregation ($\eta_x^2 = 1.0$), the expected mean SES of the school attended by each student is the same as that student's SES. Thus, for any society, $\eta_x^2 S_x$ is the expected gap between the social composition of the typical school attended by a student who is one standard deviation above average in SES and the typical school attended by a student who is of average SES.

The upper right quadrant of Figure 2 gives the expected social composition gap for a society characterized by high inequality in SES and high segregation. The lower right quadrant gives the gap for a society with low inequality in SES but high segregation. The egalitarian ideal is found in the lower left quadrant—low inequality, low segregation.

Associated with the four sources of social inequality in outcomes are different sets of social and educational policy options. One might attempt to reduce the overall level of inequality in SES, that is, reduce S_x by income redistribution, for example. One might reduce social status segregation between schools as occurred, for example, in Scotland during the 1970s. Alternatively, one might attempt to reduce achievement gaps between more and less advantaged students attending the same school (determined by β_w) by compensatory education policies or by early intervention into the home environment. And one may attempt to reduce the impact on achievement, β_c, of school segregation by equalizing school funding or other resources or by intervening to improve the climate of schools attended disproportionately by socially disadvantaged students.

Our analysis is not sufficiently fine-grained to evaluate the potential efficacy of such interventions. Instead, we aim to explore the anatomy of social inequality in reading literacy in 22 countries to the extent feasible given the limited data available and, by doing so, to clarify research issues and data quality requirements that must be faced in future cross-national research focused on such inequality. We shall examine not only the anatomy of social inequality in reading literacy within each country, but also the

---

[2]Clearly, points 2 and 4 could be expanded to include effects of segregation between classrooms within schools and ability groups within classrooms. For simplicity we restrict the current discussion to segregation between schools.

[3]In fact, the regression coefficient for predicting X_j from X_{ij} is $J/(J-1)\eta_x^2$ where J is the number of schools.

Figure 2: Extent of social status (SES) variation and school segregation

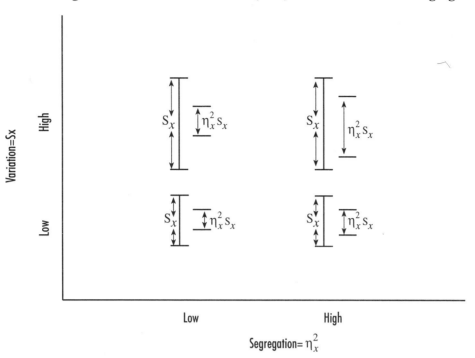

$$\text{Predicted } \overline{X}_{\cdot j} \approx \overline{X}.. + \eta_x^2 (X_{ij} - \overline{X}..)$$

Inequality in Outcome Index:

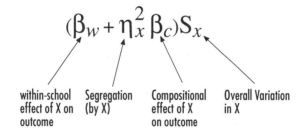

$$(\beta_w + \eta_x^2 \, \beta_c) S_x$$

within-school effect of X on outcome   Segregation (by X)   Compositional effect of X on outcome   Overall Variation in X

mean level of reading literacy in each. This will enable exploration of whether equity is purchased only at the price of excellence.

3.   A Primary Analysis and a Series of Sensitivity Analyses

Data were collected as part of the IEA Reading Literacy Study. Unfortunately, the number of variables measured on commensurate scales across all countries is quite limited, leaving statistical models underspecified. To cope with this problem, we conducted a single primary analysis followed by a series of sensitivity analyses seeking to assess the robustness of the findings from the primary analysis.

Our initial interest was at the primary school level, so our primary analysis uses the fourth grade (Population A) data. Unfortunately, only one indicator of home environment—number of books available at home—was measured on a commensurate scale across a large number of countries in the fourth grade data. While certainly related to the social status of the child's family, this indicator is better viewed as an indicator of home literacy resources. Our primary analysis examines the variation of this resource across societies, the extent to which assignment to schools tends to segregate children on the basis of this resource, the relationship between this resource and literacy within schools, and the compositional effect of attending a school with other students who are more or less disadvantaged with respect to this resource.

While providing a first approximation to a portrait of home environmental inequality in literacy across countries, the primary analysis, based only on one home resource indicator, undoubtedly underspecifies the relationship between home background and literacy. Such underspecification may have a variety of negative effects on the validity of the results, including the artifactual inflation of estimated compositional effects (Hauser 1970; Hutchinson 1992). Therefore, we turned to a second data source—data from ninth graders (Population B)—for which a second home environmental indicator becomes available in most countries participating in the IEA Reading Literacy Study: years of maternal education. A variety of sensitivity analyses, using availability of books and maternal education separately and together, provided a basis to assess the robustness of the Population A results.

Even on the basis of the primary analysis and a series of sensitivity analyses, however, the essential conclusions of the study must be viewed as quite tentative. Our main purposes are to establish a methodological framework for comparative research on social inequality in literacy and to establish new data quality standards so that future international literacy surveys can provide better answers to these questions.

Data and results for the primary analysis are considered in detail in the text of this paper. Results of the secondary analyses are then summarized in the text with details about the data described in the Appendix.

4.   Data for the Primary Analysis

Twenty-seven countries of the 32 that participated in the Reading Literacy Study are predominately high-income countries, mostly in Europe. Not all of these countries were used in the analysis. Two low-income countries were excluded because their income levels were substantially different from those of all other countries. (If there had been a larger number of low-income countries, they would have been retained.) Two other countries were excluded because of apparent irregularities in test administration. One other country was excluded because of insufficient data on key predictor variables. Thus, the analytic sample included the 22 countries listed in Tables 1-7, which give descriptive statistics for each country on each variable.

Within each country, schools were selected at random. Within most countries, one fourth grade[4] classroom was selected at random, although some schools had only one fourth grade class. In a few countries, two classrooms were selected per school. We view the design as a two-stage cluster sample within each country having students clustered within classrooms/schools and classrooms/schools clustered within countries. Note that because in most countries only one classroom was selected per school, we cannot distinguish between school and classroom effects. Our analysis was conducted using classrooms as the clusters. As mentioned in Section 5 of this paper, we view the countries as exchangeable (conditional on the model at hand), so that we conceive of three levels of random variability in the data.

As indicated in Tables 1 through 7, the analytic sample includes 2,908 classrooms and 55,951 students, an average of 132 classrooms and 2,543 students per country and 19 students per classroom. School and classroom variables include urban versus nonurban location, school size, class size, and classroom mean availability of books in the home. These are described in Tables 1 through 4. Somewhat more than half of the classrooms are urban (Table 1), though all classrooms in Singapore and 94 percent of the classrooms in Hong Kong are urban. In contrast, fewer than half the classrooms in France, the Netherlands, Portugal, and Switzerland are classified as urban. Average school enrollment (Table 2) is 416, with Singapore having exceptionally large schools (mean enrollment of 1,261) and France having the smallest schools (mean of 112). Class sizes (Table 3) average 24 overall, with the largest classes found in Singapore (mean of 37) and the smallest classes in Iceland (mean of just under 15). After transforming to the logarithmic scale (described below), the overall mean of the classroom means of the number of books at home was 4.31 (this corresponds to a figure of 73.4 books in the home, by taking the exponential). The greatest mean was found in Sweden (4.94, equivalent to 138.8 books) and an extreme low mean was found in Hong Kong (2.80, equivalent to 15.4 books).

Table 1. Distribution of urban versus rural location of Population A classrooms: IEA Reading Literacy Study, 1991

Country	Proportion urban	Standard deviation	Number of classrooms
Entire sample	.64	.48	2,908
Belgium (French)	.55	.50	113
Canada (British Columbia)	.88	.33	123
Finland	.55	.50	67
France	.35	.48	108
Germany East	.61	.49	82
Germany West	.60	.49	89
Greece	.76	.43	141
Hong Kong	.94	.23	124
Hungary	.63	.49	135
Iceland	.59	.49	153
Ireland	.54	.50	114
Italy	.52	.50	105
Netherlands	.33	.47	77
New Zealand	.81	.40	176
Norway	.51	.50	158
Portugal	.26	.44	124
Singapore	1.00	.00	206
Slovenia	.65	.48	138
Spain	.80	.40	232
Sweden	.52	.50	118
Switzerland	.35	.48	173
USA	.80	.40	152

---

[4]The grade selected actually varied across countries. Population A consists of the grade with the greatest number of students aged 9 at the time of the assessment. This was grade 4 in the United States and several other countries, grade 3 in a number of other countries, and grade 5 in New Zealand.

Table 2. Distribution of school enrollment of Population A classrooms: IEA Reading Literacy Study, 1991

Country	Mean	Standard deviation	Number of classrooms
Entire sample	416.47	394.78	2,908
Belgium (French)	241.31	137.37	113
Canada (British Columbia)	327.46	147.09	123
Finland	271.58	145.99	67
France	111.99	85.42	108
Germany East	382.55	153.09	82
Germany West	293.12	146.69	89
Greece	249.27	163.94	141
Hong Kong	696.73	352.84	124
Hungary	560.13	249.63	135
Iceland	215.71	233.29	153
Ireland	285.93	215.89	114
Italy	470.38	277.16	105
Netherlands	178.13	78.97	77
New Zealand	288.56	135.94	176
Norway	156.55	129.08	158
Portugal	168.02	167.53	124
Singapore	1,261.22	489.50	206
Slovenia	701.03	365.86	138
Spain	597.33	409.39	232
Sweden	233.75	161.37	118
Switzerland	196.34	276.06	173
USA	505.93	306.60	152

Table 3. Distribution of class size of Population A classrooms: IEA Reading Literacy Study, 1991

Country	Mean	Standard deviation	Number of classrooms
Entire sample	24.04	8.34	2,908
Belgium (French)	20.21	4.47	113
Canada (British Columbia)	23.33	3.19	123
Finland	24.48	5.08	67
France	21.34	6.03	108
Germany East	20.42	3.46	82
Germany West	22.20	4.31	89
Greece	23.59	5.40	141
Hong Kong	36.38	6.47	124
Hungary	23.39	4.68	135
Iceland	14.84	6.46	153
Ireland	29.71	8.86	114
Italy	16.36	5.17	105
Netherlands	24.29	5.75	77
New Zealand	29.75	7.35	176
Norway	15.52	6.46	158
Portugal	20.90	5.62	124
Singapore	36.83	5.22	206
Slovenia	24.65	3.91	138
Spain	27.91	7.12	232
Sweden	19.98	4.07	118
Switzerland	18.41	4.25	173
USA	23.94	5.55	152

Table 4. Distribution of number of books at home, with logarithmic transformation (classroom means): IEA Reading Literacy Study, 1991

Country	Mean	Standard deviation	Number of classrooms
Entire sample	4.31	.74	2,908
Belgium (French)	4.54	.60	113
Canada (British Columbia)	4.70	.46	123
Finland	4.62	.30	67
France	4.28	.57	108
Germany East	4.23	.50	82
Germany West	4.15	.42	89
Greece	3.72	.65	141
Hong Kong	2.80	.65	124
Hungary	4.51	.49	135
Iceland	4.86	.37	153
Ireland	4.27	.58	114
Italy	3.84	.58	105
Netherlands	4.69	.49	77
New Zealand	4.58	.63	176
Norway	4.75	.50	158
Portugal	3.39	.99	124
Singapore	3.89	.54	206
Slovenia	4.37	.41	138
Spain	4.32	.58	232
Sweden	4.94	.35	118
Switzerland	4.54	.55	173
USA	4.53	.54	152

Student-level variables include overall reading literacy, gender, and books in the home (Tables 5-7). Overall reading literacy (Table 5) is the average of three test scores, each of which indicates proficiency in reading a different type of text (narrative text, expository text, and documents). Country sample means range from 484.06 in Portugal to 569.11 in Finland, with standard deviations ranging from 68.10 in Hong Kong to 91.34 in Sweden. As one might expect, every country shows nearly equal proportions of males and females (Table 6).

Availability of books at home (Table 7) was measured as a six-category variable, with categories 1 = none, 2 = 1-10, 3 = 11-50, 4 = 51-100, 5 = 101-200, 6 = more than 200. We initially coded these by assigning the midpoint of each interval to that category (the highest category was set to 250). A preliminary analysis indicated that within each country, the relationship between this indicator of book availability and literacy had a positive linear component along with some evidence of negative curvature (i.e., a diminishing positive effect of book availability). This result suggested a logarithmic transformation (after adding 1 to avoid an argument of 0 for the log function). The resulting variable displayed an almost entirely linear relationship to literacy in each country. Descriptive statistics (Table 7) indicate a mean of the new books variable of 4.28, equivalent to about 71 books. Mean books ranged from 2.81 in Hong Kong (about 15 books) to 4.90 in Sweden (about 133 books). The standard deviation of this variable ranged from 0.84 (Sweden) to 1.56 (Hong Kong).

A number of variables we had hoped to use in the analysis were found unusable or unavailable. These included a home possession score and a student possession score. These were measured on different metrics in different countries with different types of possessions and commodities listed in different countries and no attempt to equate the scales. The variable years of maternal education was unavailable for Population A, though it was available for Population B. Our sensitivity analyses include analysis of Population B data using maternal education in addition to books at home.

Table 5. Distribution of overall reading literacy of Population A students: IEA Reading Literacy Study, 1991

Country	Mean	Standard deviation	Number of students
Entire sample	516.55	78.54	55,951
Belgium (French)	510.37	72.91	1,924
Canada (British Columbia)	504.87	74.93	2,035
Finland	569.11	69.37	1,377
France	533.54	69.49	1,460
Germany East	500.99	81.28	1,448
Germany West	511.93	81.07	1,621
Greece	512.56	73.59	2,837
Hong Kong	524.24	68.10	2,415
Hungary	503.53	75.39	2,705
Iceland	517.77	85.51	1,739
Ireland	509.13	76.63	2,402
Italy	538.45	77.30	1,476
Netherlands	487.02	71.93	1,341
New Zealand	532.30	83.49	2,920
Norway	528.89	86.68	2,017
Portugal	484.06	70.22	2,124
Singapore	513.48	72.01	7,286
Slovenia	500.09	77.92	3,200
Spain	510.68	77.12	5,827
Sweden	538.87	91.34	2,084
Switzerland	509.53	80.51	2,430
USA	546.25	74.30	3,283

Table 6. Distribution of gender of Population A students: IEA Reading Literacy Study, 1991

Country	Proportion male	Standard deviation	Number of students
Entire sample	.51	.50	55,951
Belgium (French)	.49	.50	1,924
Canada (British Columbia)	.52	.50	2,035
Finland	.52	.50	1,377
France	.49	.50	1,460
Germany East	.49	.50	1,448
Germany West	.52	.50	1,621
Greece	.50	.50	2,837
Hong Kong	.54	.50	2,415
Hungary	.50	.50	2,705
Iceland	.51	.50	1,739
Ireland	.49	.50	2,402
Italy	.52	.50	1,476
Netherlands	.48	.50	1,341
New Zealand	.52	.50	2,920
Norway	.49	.50	2,017
Portugal	.51	.50	2,124
Singapore	.52	.50	7,286
Slovenia	.51	.50	3,220
Spain	.49	.50	5,827
Sweden	.51	.50	2,084
Switzerland	.52	.50	2,430
USA	.50	.50	3,283

Table 7. Distribution of books at home, with logarithmic transformation for Population A students: IEA Reading Literacy Study, 1991

Country	Mean	Standard deviation	Number of students
Entire sample	4.28	1.28	55,951
Belgium (French)	4.54	1.18	1,924
Canada (British Columbia)	4.72	1.05	2,035
Finland	4.62	.89	1,377
France	4.28	1.20	1,460
Germany East	4.22	1.08	1,448
Germany West	4.16	1.19	1,621
Greece	3.84	1.29	2,837
Hong Kong	2.81	1.56	2,415
Hungary	4.53	1.06	2,705
Iceland	4.85	.86	1,739
Ireland	4.31	1.20	2,402
Italy	3.88	1.31	1,476
Netherlands	4.71	1.11	1,341
New Zealand	4.62	1.15	2,920
Norway	4.80	.95	2,017
Portugal	3.57	1.44	2,124
Singapore	3.92	1.39	7,286
Slovenia	4.39	1.11	3,200
Spain	4.35	1.19	5,827
Sweden	4.90	.84	2,084
Switzerland	4.60	1.05	2,430
USA	4.52	1.17	3,283

Histograms of all candidate variables and scatter plots between pairs of variables were examined for each country's data. These analyses led to the exclusion of some variables as mentioned above and informed choice of metric for those variables that remained. Small numbers of anomalous cases (at the student level) were removed within several countries. These included students who achieved the minimum on all three tests, likely indicating that they had not tried to respond to the test. Two countries having large numbers of such cases and, as a result, displaying unexpectedly low mean overall literacy, were also excluded.

5. Statistical Methodology

5.1. Overview

A number of inferential problems arise in synthesizing results from multiple countries. First, within each country if data are collected via a two-stage cluster sampling procedure (as they were for this study), it is important that model estimates appropriately reflect uncertainty associated with the clustering of students in classrooms. Two common approaches are used to incorporate the clustering effect: resampling approaches such as the bootstrap or jackknife; and model-based approaches. To cope with effects of clustering, we have opted to use a hierarchical linear model (Raudenbush and Bryk 1986) within each country. Effects of clusters are represented via random effects, the variance of which is incorporated into standard error estimates for means. Although the resampling approaches might be viewed as more robust than the model-based approach, the model-based approach extends better to the more complex estimation tasks described below.

Second, an unknown degree of heterogeneity between countries will exist on mean literacy and quantities like β_w and β_c. The magnitude of such heterogeneity is interesting in itself and also has consequences for inferences about cross-national differences in outcomes. However, estimating the extent of between-country heterogeneity is nontrivial statistically because each country's coefficients are estimated with different precision. Thus, an iterative computational procedure is needed to estimate the between-country variance. More important, given a modest number of countries (n=22 in the analyses below), a point estimate of the between-country variance will be imprecise. A confidence interval is needed, but large sample confidence intervals based on the asymptotic normality of maximum likelihood estimators will often be inappropriate in this small sample setting.

A more profound conceptual problem is in interpreting a measure of between-country variance. In what sense are countries random? For example, the countries in the Reading Literacy Study volunteered for the study, and so they cannot constitute a random sample.

To address the problems of estimating and interpreting between-country heterogeneity, we adopt a Bayesian approach with estimation via Gibbs sampling (Fotiu 1989; Gelfand and Smith 1990; Seltzer 1993). In the Bayesian framework, the between-country variance represents the investigator's uncertainty about the degree to which countries vary in their effects. Thus, we need not assume countries to have been sampled randomly. We postulate a relatively noninformative prior distribution for the between-country variance components. Then the posterior distribution of a variance gives us a range of plausible values of the extent of between-country heterogeneity and, for each value, a degree of plausibility (technically the posterior density).

Below we briefly illustrate the logic of our modeling procedure in the simple case of comparing country means. We then extend the approach to a more general model that incorporates country differences in social inequality and between-school segregation.

5.2.   Testing Hypotheses About the Relationship Between Country Characteristics and Mean Literacy

Though comparing country means is a plausible use of cross-national literacy data, many researchers would seek to account for the variability among country means. For purposes of illustrating the methodology, we consider the simple hypothesis that the level of development of a society, as indicated by its gross national product (GNP), will be positively related to the level of reading literacy of its children. Efficient estimation requires that the varying precision of the country means be taken into account via weighted least squares (Seber 1978). However, the precision of the country mean (the inverse of its variance) depends not only on the data within each country but also on the variance between countries. Let b_k denote the estimated mean outcome for country k and let β_k denote the true mean. We may write

$$b_k = \beta_k + e_k, \quad e_k \sim N(0, v_k) \tag{7}$$

that is, e_k is the error by which b_k estimates β_k and v_k is thus the sampling variance of b_k. However, the true means β_k, k = 1,...,K are themselves viewed as randomly varying about their predicted values. For example, using GNP as a predictor, we have

$$\beta_k = \gamma_0 + \gamma_1 (GNP)_k + u_k, \quad u_k \sim N(0, \tau) \tag{8}$$

where u_k is the unique effect associated with country k assumed normally distributed and τ is the between-country variance. Combining Equations 7 and 8, we have

$$b_k = \gamma_0 + \gamma_1 (GNP)_k + u_k + e_k, \quad u_k + e_k \sim N(0, \tau + v_k) . \tag{9}$$

Under the model of Equation 9 and with τ and v_k known, the maximum likelihood estimator of the GNP coefficient and its variance are given by weighted least squares with weights $\omega_k = 1/(\tau + v_k)$ according to the formulas

$$\hat{\gamma}_1 = \frac{\sum \omega_k (GNP_k - \overline{GNP})(b_k - \overline{b})}{\sum \omega_k (GNP_k - \overline{GNP})^2} \tag{10}$$

and

$$Var(\hat{\gamma}_1) = \frac{1}{\sum \omega_k (GNP_k - \overline{GNP})^2} \tag{11}$$

where

$$\overline{GNP} = \frac{\sum \omega_k * GNP_k}{\sum \omega_k} \quad and \quad \overline{b} = \frac{\sum \omega_k b_k}{\sum \omega_k} .$$

When the data are balanced, the weights ω_k are equal for every country, and Equation 10 reduces to ordinary least squares, eliminating dependence of the coefficient estimate on τ. Moreover, Equation 11 simplifies and an exact t test becomes available, eliminating dependence of hypothesis testing on τ (see Raudenbush 1992 for detailed applications in the balanced case).

However, when the data are unbalanced, which will generally be the case in international studies, Equations 10 and 11 will depend upon τ via the dependence of the weights ω_k on τ, and τ will not be known.[5] When τ is not known, the maximum likelihood estimates (mle's) of γ_1 and its standard error are Equations 10 and 11 with the mle of τ substituted in the construction of ω_k. These mle's will be sensible when τ is estimated with reasonable precision. However, this precision depends heavily upon the number of countries, which will tend to be limited (K=22 in our case). When the precision is poor, Equation 11 will underestimate the uncertainty associated with the mle of γ_1.

Our strategy for coping with the small number of countries and the consequent limited precision of the mle of τ is to employ a Bayesian estimation strategy. Using this approach, the posterior distribution of γ_1 gives a range of plausible values for that parameter and, associated with each value, its degree of plausibility (posterior density). This posterior density fully incorporates the uncertainty about τ. An important by-product of this analysis is a good approximation to the posterior density of τ itself, which indicates the range of plausible degrees of heterogeneity in country means that remains after controlling for the effects of GNP.

---

[5] The sampling variance v_k can be precisely estimated and assumed known given the large amount of data typically gathered within countries in international educational surveys.

19

5.3. Studying Cross-National Differences in the Equity of the Literacy Distribution

The approach we have adopted for studying equity differences has the same structure as the model for mean achievement described above. The model has the following elements:

- A two-level hierarchical model is first estimated for each country's data separately. Estimation is via restricted maximum likelihood. The output for each country is a set of regression coefficient estimates and their variance-covariance matrix. These separate analyses are highly efficient because data are summarized within each classroom so that, for each country, the effective sample size for the computations is the number of classrooms rather than the number of students.

- A multivariate Bayes regression model is formulated to describe variation between countries. The input data are the vectors of regression coefficients and associated variance-covariance matrices from the separate countries. The output is constituted by estimates of the posterior densities of all quantities of interest.

- Bayesian computations are achieved via Gibbs sampling as described in detail in Raudenbush, Cheong, and Fotiu (1994). This approach avoids the need for difficult numerical integrations and produces an empirical representation of the relevant posterior distributions.

The structure of the analytic model and assumptions are described in more detail in the next section.

5.4. The Model

The choice of variables for the model at each of its levels was made after extensive exploratory analysis of the data country by country. Many potentially relevant predictors were rejected—because they were clearly not measured on comparable metrics across countries, because of missing data, or because of anomalous features of their distributions. As a result, the specification of the model is quite thin. For example, our sole indicator for the social status of the students is the availability of books in the home. While related to social status, this indicator better reflects the literacy environment of the home. Our sense is that this variable is a better indicator of the social status composition of a classroom or country at the aggregate level than of the child, implying that the estimate of compositional effects will be biased away from zero (Hauser 1970).

Because the model is underspecified, substantive conclusions are made with extreme caution. Later we consider a series of sensitivity analyses designed to check the credibility of these findings.

We formulate a within-country model having two levels. At level 1—the student level—overall reading literacy is predicted by the logarithm of the number of books at home (log-books) and gender. This model defines, for each classroom, three quantities of interest: a) the adjusted overall reading literacy mean for the class; b) a regression coefficient indicating, for that class, the strength of association between log-books and literacy; and c) a regression coefficient indicating, for that class, the gap in overall reading literacy between males and females. These three quantities in essence define the distribution of literacy within each class in terms of the average level of literacy and the equity of distribution of literacy with respect to social status and gender. At level 2—between classrooms within each country—these three quantities become the outcome variables. We use the class mean of the variable log-books at home, school size, the class size, and the urban versus rural location of the school to predict the classroom means. This level-2 model defines a vector of regression coefficients for each country that become outcome variables at the country level. Key country-level outcomes of interest[6] are

The country's mean overall reading literacy;

- The effect of student-level log-books at home on overall reading; and

- The compositional effect of log-books.

Each of these is adjusted for the other variables in the model, including urban versus rural location, school size, class size, log-books, school mean log-books, and gender. Variation in these outcomes across countries is then studied by means of a multivariate Bayes regression model. We now turn to specification of this model in detail.

Level-1 or Student-Level Model. Within each classroom j of country k, we formulate a model to predict the overall reading literacy of fourth grade student i:

$$Y_{ijk} = \pi_{0jk} + \pi_{1jk}(books)_{ijk} + \pi_{2jk}(gender)_{ijk} + e_{ijk} \qquad (12)$$

where

Y_{ijk} is the combined reading literacy outcome for child i in classroom j of country k;[7]

π_{0jk} is the mean outcome for class j, country k (assuming books and gender are scaled as deviations about their country means);

$(books)_{ijk}$ is the log of books at home for student ijk; so that

π_{1jk} is the expected increase in literacy per unit increase in log-books for students within classroom j of country k;

$(gender)_{ijk}$ is an indicator for males (1 = male; 0 = female) that has then been centered about its country mean; so that

π_{2jk} is the mean difference between males and females within classroom jk, adjusted for the effect of books; and

e_{ijk} is a within-classroom random error assumed normally distributed with mean zero and a country-specific within-classroom variance, that is, $e_{ijk} \sim N(0, \sigma_k^2)$.

---

[6] See Raudenbush, Cheong, and Fotiu (1994) for a discussion of country differences in gender effects on literacy.

[7] The outcome Y_{ijk} is the simple average of the narrative, expository, and document reading subtest scores for student ijk.

21

Level-2 or Classroom-Level Model. The level-1 model defines three quantities (the π's) as characterizing the distribution of overall reading literacy within each classroom. These now become the outcomes in the level-2 model

$$\pi_{0jk} = \beta_{00k} + \beta_{01k}(mean\ books)_{jk} + \beta_{02k}(class\ size)_{jk}$$
$$+ \beta_{03k}(school\ size)_{jk} + \beta_{04k}(urban)_{jk} + u_{0jk}$$

$$\pi_{1jk} = \beta_{10k} + u_{1jk},$$

$$\pi_{2jk} = \beta_{20k} + u_{2jk}$$

(13)

where

β_{00k}	is the mean outcome for country k (all class-level predictors are expressed as deviations from their country means);
$(mean\ books)_{jk}$	is the mean of log-books in the homes of students in class jk; so that
β_{01k}	is the compositional effect of log-books in the home within country k;
$(class\ size)_{jk}$,	$(school\ size)_{jk}$, and $(urban)_{jk}$ are, respectively, the enrollment of the class, the enrollment of the school, and an indicator for urban location, each deviated around their country means; so that
β_{02k}, β_{03k}, and β_{04k}	are the associated regression coefficients within country k;
β_{10k} and β_{20k},	are the means of π_{1jk} and π_{2jk} respectively, across classrooms within country k; and
u_{0jk}, u_{1jk}, and u_{2jk}	are random effects defined on classrooms within country k and are assumed trivariate normal in distribution, that is

$$\begin{pmatrix} u_{0jk} \\ u_{1jk} \\ u_{2jk} \end{pmatrix} \sim N \left[\begin{pmatrix} 0 \\ 0 \\ 0 \end{pmatrix}, \begin{pmatrix} \tau_{\pi 00k} & \tau_{\pi 01k} & \tau_{\pi 02k} \\ \tau_{\pi 10k} & \tau_{\pi 11k} & \tau_{12k} \\ \tau_{\pi 20k} & \tau_{\pi 21k} & \tau_{\pi 22k} \end{pmatrix} \right].$$

(14)

Restricted Maximum Likelihood Estimation Within Countries. Sufficient data were available to permit estimation of all country level parameters in separate, within-country analyses. Specifically, the computer package HLM3.0 of Bryk, Raudenbush, and Congdon (1992) was used to produce restricted maximum likelihood (REML) estimates of the variance-covariance components (σ_k^2, $\tau_{\pi k}$), where $\tau_{\pi k}$ is the 3-by-3 covariance matrix described in Equation 14. As described in Raudenbush (1988), inferences about

22

the regression coefficients (the β_k's) are then based on their posterior means and variances given the REML variance-covariance components.[8]

We define b_k as the country-specific vector of estimates of the regression coefficients (the β_k's) and V_k as its covariance matrix. These summarize the results of estimation in country k and provide input into the third level of the model, the between-country level.

Three β's are of particular interest in the between-country analysis: β_{00k} (mean literacy); β_{01k} (the compositional effects of log-books); and β_{10k} (the within-class effect of log-books); and β_{20k} (the gender gap). These are the latent outcomes to be synthesized in the Bayesian between-country analysis.

5.5.   A Bayesian Synthesis of Results Across Countries

The two-level analyses based on each country's data produce the input for the between-country synthesis. A new computing algorithm was needed to compute the posterior distributions using Gibbs sampling, and this algorithm is described in detail by Raudenbush, Cheong, and Fotiu (1994). We summarize the estimation method briefly below.

The Likelihood. Conditional on the true value of the regression coefficients, the estimates b_k are assumed normal, i.e.,

$$b_k | \beta_k \sim N(\beta_k, V_k) \tag{15}$$

where b_k is a vector of estimates from country k, $\beta_k = (\beta_{00k}, \beta_{01k}, \beta_{10k})^T$ is the corresponding vector of parameters, and V_k is the variance-covariance matrix of the estimates b_k. The dimensions of b_k and V_k vary according to the analytic task at hand.

An Exchangeable Prior for β_k. Conditional on a set of known country-level predictors contained in the matrix W_k, the parameters β_k are assumed exchangeable. That is

$$\beta_k = W_k \gamma + u_k, \quad u_k \sim N(0, T). \tag{16}$$

Estimation via REML. It is possible to estimate T in Equation 16 via REML and then, conditioning on this point estimate, to base inferences about γ on its posterior mean vector and covariance matrix. The difficulty with this approach is that T will be estimated imprecisely based on only 22 countries, and inferences about γ may be highly sensitive to this imprecision. The Bayesian approach via Gibbs sampling, designed to overcome this problem, uses the REML estimates as starting values. We checked the new Bayes results against the REML results, and they behaved as expected in comparison.

Estimation via Bayes. We now formulate noninformative priors for β, γ, and T (Fotiu 1989) as described in detail in the Appendix. Then the joint posterior density of the parameters is

---

[8]A vague prior is specified for the regression coefficients so that their posterior means are equivalent to generalized least squares estimates given the REML variance-covariance estimates.

$$p(\beta, \gamma, T \mid b, V) = const. * L(b \mid V, \beta, \gamma, T) f(\beta \mid \gamma, T) p_1(\gamma) p_2(T) \qquad (17)$$

where $L(b \mid \beta, V, \gamma, T)$ is the likelihood of Equation 15, $f(\beta \mid \gamma, Y)$ is the exchangeable prior of Equation 16, and p_1 and p_2 are noninformative priors described in Raudenbush, Cheong, and Fotiu (1994). Inferences about the country-level regression coefficients, β, the between-country regression coefficients, γ, and the between-country variance-covariance matrix, T, are then based on their marginal posteriors:

$$g_1(\beta \mid b, V) = \iint p(\beta, \gamma, T \mid b, V) \, \partial\gamma \, \partial T$$

$$g_2(\gamma \mid b, V) = \iint p(\beta, \gamma, T \mid b, V) \, \partial\beta \, \partial T \qquad (18)$$

$$g_3(T \mid b, V) = \iint p(\beta, \gamma, T \mid b, V) \, \partial\beta \, \partial\gamma .$$

Gibbs Sampling. Unfortunately, the integrals in Equation 18 are difficult to evaluate numerically, as is the integral required to find the normalizing constant of Equation 17. Recently, Gibbs sampling (Gelfand and Smith 1990) has become a popular approach to approximate such integrals. We refer the interested reader to Fotiu (1989) for details; see Seltzer (1993) in the univariate case. We used the final 2,000 realizations from the Gibbs sampling process to approximate the marginal posteriors of the parameters (Equation 18).

6.   Results: Primary Analysis

Our interest focuses on a) comparing country means and b) studying country differences in the equity of distribution of literacy with respect to home environmental inequality. However, as mentioned in Section 3, all of the necessary information for these purposes was obtained by estimating within each country the two-level model described by Equations 12 and 13. The key output from each country's analysis is a vector of three estimates: of the parameters β_{00k} (mean literacy); β_{01k} (the compositional effect of log-books); and β_{10k} (the within-classroom effect of log-books).[9] The uncertainty associated with parameter estimates from each country is summarized by their variance-covariance matrices. These data provided input to the Bayesian between-country analysis. Table 8 summarizes the marginal posterior distributions of these three parameters (as defined in Equation 12) for each country.

6.1.   Comparing Country Means

The first column of Table 8 gives the name of the country, and the second gives that country's GNP. For convenience, the countries are listed in ascending rank order by GNP. Column three summarizes the posterior distribution of β_{00k}, that is, mean literacy, for each country, by listing the posterior mean and standard deviation of the country mean. A moderate tendency for these posterior means to increase with GNP is manifest.

---

[9] These effects are adjusted for school size, class size, urban versus rural location, and student gender. However, the results presented below are insensitive to this specification.

Table 8. **Posterior estimates for Population A students, by country: IEA Reading Literacy Study, 1991**

Country	GNP per capita	Mean literacy β_{00k}		School-level books β_{01k}		Student-level books β_{10k}		Gender effect β_{20k}	
		Mean	Standard deviation	Mean	Standard deviation	Mean	Standard deviation	Mean	Standard deviation
Hungary	2.46	501.85	2.62	24.26	5.82	14.49	1.26	-10.98	2.48
Portugal	3.65	481.71	2.98	14.08	3.66	9.02	1.17	-5.29	2.61
Greece	4.80	509.63	3.45	15.98	5.77	9.12	1.07	-2.32	2.35
Slovenia	6.50	499.54	2.33	15.84	5.53	14.23	1.17	-13.67	2.32
Spain	7.74	507.45	1.95	24.52	3.44	11.09	0.87	-6.67	1.86
Ireland	7.75	506.85	2.67	11.51	4.90	14.51	1.20	-14.33	2.73
Singapore	9.07	511.52	1.88	22.18	3.46	10.92	0.58	-9.61	1.43
Hong Kong	9.22	523.59	2.87	13.16	4.57	5.53	0.88	-5.81	2.54
New Zealand	10.00	529.71	2.32	24.90	3.97	16.24	1.42	-19.28	2.67
Germany East	11.30	501.58	3.50	14.50	6.20	13.46	1.86	-12.92	3.36
Italy	13.33	536.89	4.55	5.73	7.29	11.87	1.36	-10.16	2.92
Belgium	14.49	510.92	2.59	25.11	4.52	11.27	1.35	-11.30	2.55
Netherlands	14.52	487.13	3.31	18.53	6.56	11.39	1.74	-7.48	3.02
France	16.09	533.47	3.03	4.83	5.42	11.60	1.47	-7.75	2.92
Iceland	16.59	516.47	3.02	15.78	7.41	13.41	2.18	-17.05	3.65
Canada (B.C.)	16.96	503.71	2.60	14.65	5.39	11.57	1.47	-10.97	2.70
Germany West	18.48	510.57	3.41	23.85	7.04	14.32	1.50	-10.55	3.05
Finland	18.59	568.59	2.59	-0.43	8.41	10.57	1.94	-11.78	3.51
Sweden	19.30	538.41	2.82	18.77	7.50	12.72	1.88	-12.43	3.00
USA	19.84	546.69	2.56	36.86	4.81	7.93	1.05	-8.10	2.19
Norway	19.99	528.47	2.61	8.84	5.34	13.98	1.84	-13.66	2.97
Switzerland	27.50	506.96	2.50	-2.25	5.25	15.60	1.63	-7.40	2.94
Column Mean	13.10	516.45	2.83	15.96	5.56	12.04	1.40	-10.43	2.72

Assessing Heterogeneity. How much do countries vary in their means relative to the variation within countries (after controlling GNP)? For our data, the between-country residual variance in their means will tend to be estimated with uncertainty despite the fact that each country has a substantial amount of data. The precision of that variance estimate depends quite heavily on the number of countries providing data. Figure 3 is a histogram that approximates the posterior distribution of the variance of the means, that is, the posterior distribution of

$$Var(\beta_{00k}) = \tau_{\beta 00} \tag{19}$$

This histogram is based on 2,000 sampled values of $\tau_{\beta 00}$.

As the figure indicates, all plausible values of this variance are positive, implying clearly that the country means are heterogeneous. The posterior mean of this between-country variance is 452.2. Recall that the overall standard deviation of the outcome across all countries is 78.54 (Table 5). Thus, it appears that the proportion of variance in the outcome that lies between countries is about $452.2/(452.2+78.54^2) = .068$ so that about 6.8 percent of the variance is between countries. However, as Figure 3 implies, values of $\tau_{\beta 00}$ as small as 200 and as large as 850 are plausible, implying that the percentage of variance lying between countries could be as small as 3.1 percent or as large as 12.1 percent, giving some sense of the degree of uncertainty about the extent to which literacy means vary across countries. Although no more than a fraction of the variability in literacy lies between countries by any estimate, this does not imply that country differences are trivial. As Table 8 indicates, it is common to find pairs of countries with posterior means differing by more than half the overall standard deviation, a quite substantial effect size.

Figure 4 displays the posterior distribution of the regression coefficient γ_{001} relating GNP to mean literacy. Our belief about the magnitude of this relationship does depend upon our opinion about the variance between country means (see Equations 4 and 5 and the associated discussion). The posterior distribution displayed in Figure 3 fully takes into account the uncertainty about this variance.

As Figure 4 indicates, the posterior probability distribution of γ_{001} is concentrated on values greater than zero, implying the existence of a positive relationship between GNP and mean literacy. The posterior mean is 1.42. Given the standard deviation of GNP of 6.38, we see that the posterior mean of $\gamma_{001} = 1.42$ is equivalent to a standardized regression coefficient of $1.42*6.38/78.54 = .12$. However, values of γ_{001} quite near zero are plausible, and the posterior mean is twice the posterior standard deviation. Values as large as 3.0 are also plausible, implying that the standardized regression coefficient could be as small as 0 or as large as .24.

Figure 5 displays the posterior distributions of mean literacy as a function of GNP. Certain countries that had appeared quite different from each other (e.g., Hungary and Norway) are achieving about as expected given their GNP. However, the low performance of Portugal and the high performance of Finland are not completely attributable to their substantial GNP differences, and the performance of Switzerland, relative to its GNP, is notable.

6.2.   Modeling Differences Between Countries in Social Inequality

Degree of Inequality and Segregation. Recall from Figure 2 that it is possible to locate countries on a plot that indicates the degree of social inequality in a society and the extent to which that society's schools (or classrooms) are socially segregated. Figure 6 provides such a plot for our data. Because the measure of interest is access to books in the home (measured on a logarithmic metric), we refer to the vertical axis as "home environmental inequality," literally, the standard deviation of our measure of access

Figure 3: Posterior distribution of the variance of mean literacy

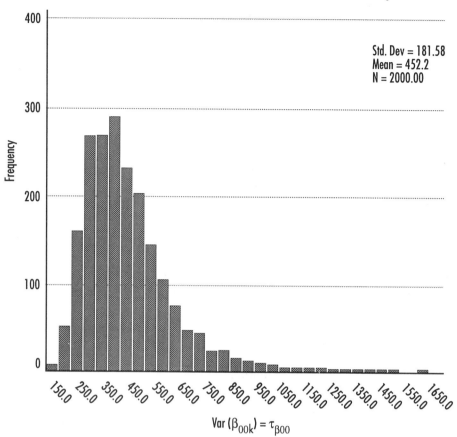

Std. Dev = 181.58
Mean = 452.2
N = 2000.00

$\mathrm{Var}\,(\beta_{00k}) = \tau_{\beta00}$

Figure 4:   Posterior distribution of the regression coefficients relating GNP with mean literacy

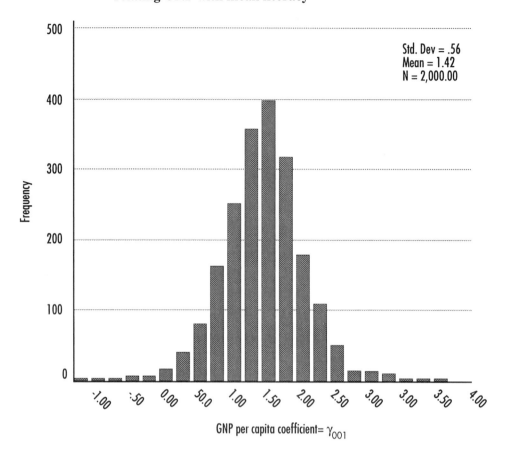

GNP per capita coefficient= γ_{001}

Figure 5: Posterior distribution of mean fourth grade literacy; 98% credibility intervals by country.

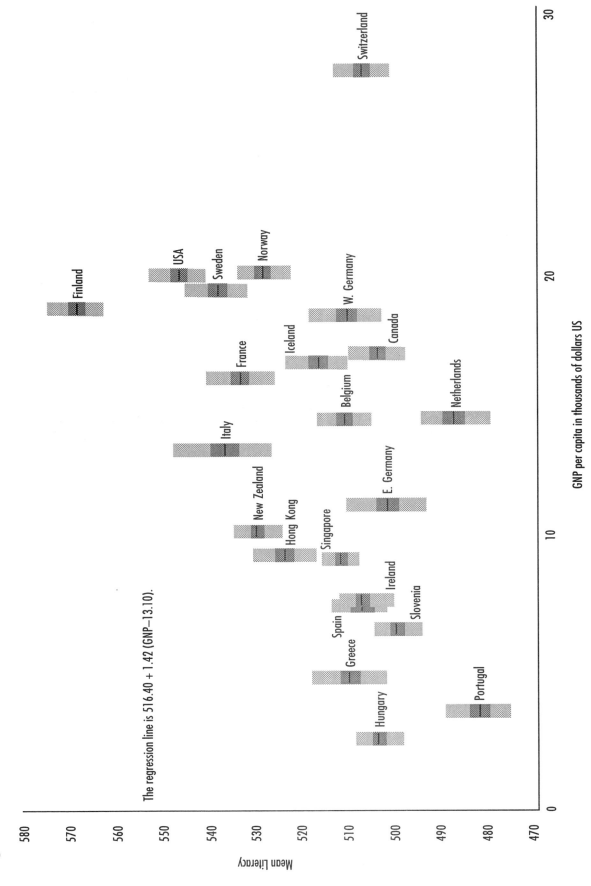

The regression line is 516.40 + 1.42 (GNP−13.10).

Figure 6: Home environmental inequality and classroom segregation; fourth graders by country

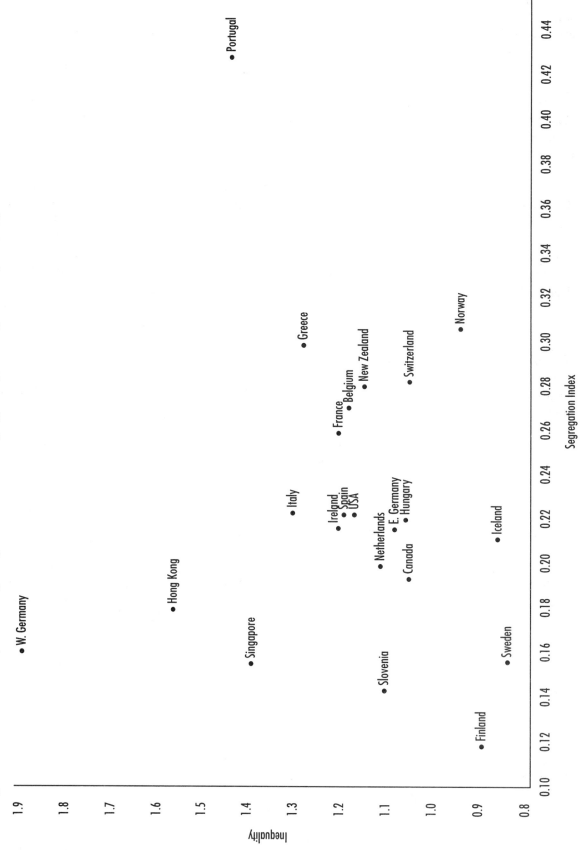

to books in each country. And because the sampling designs in most countries involved students nested within one classroom per school, we refer to the horizontal axis as the degree of segregation between classrooms, literally, the proportion of variation in log-books that lies between classrooms.

We see from the figure that the "egalitarian ideal" (low inequality, low segregation) is most closely approximated by those countries in the lower left quadrant, especially Finland and Sweden, and, to lesser degrees, Iceland, Canada, Netherlands, and the former socialist countries Slovenia, East Germany, and Hungary. West Germany is unusual in having a high degree of inequality but rather low segregation. Portugal is moderately high on inequality and very high on segregation. A cluster of countries, including the United States, is near the average on both dimensions.

An unfortunate feature of Figure 6 is its failure to represent uncertainty in the estimates, especially the estimate of the segregation index. Figure 7 gives the posterior distributions of the segregation index for each country.[10] The countries are listed in order of GNP. Note that the 98 percent credibility interval for the United States overlaps that of all other countries except Portugal (which has far higher segregation), Slovenia, and Finland (both of which have lower segregation). Thus, the data do not support the hypothesis that local funding and control of schooling lead to unusually high segregation. Rather, the degree of segregation in the United States is very nearly typical for the countries at hand.

Magnitude of Within-School and Compositional Effects of Log-books. Figures 8 and 9 display the posterior distributions of the student-level effect and compositional effect of log-books in 22 countries. Note that the United States exhibits a relatively large posterior mean for the compositional effect and a comparatively modest individual effect. This result provides some evidence to support the hypothesis that local control and funding of schools in the United States gives rise to especially large compositional effects.

Clearly, both the student-level and compositional effects, on average, are significantly positive across countries as indicated by their posterior distributions (see summary Table 9), with the student level effect having a posterior mean of 12.02 (posterior standard deviation = 0.81) and the compositional effect having a posterior mean of 15.90 (standard deviation = 2.99). Moreover, these effects do vary significantly from country to country as indicated by the posterior distributions of their variance components (Figures 10 and 11). The compositional effects are particularly highly variable.

Relationship Between Mean Literacy and Inequality in Literacy. An important policy question is whether countries approximating an equal distribution of literacy are able to produce high mean literacy. Figure 12 addresses this question, and a moderate negative relationship is manifest between inequality and mean literacy (r = -.36); that is, countries with comparative equality tend also to have high mean literacy. The clearest example is Finland, which exhibits the lowest degree of inequality and by far the highest mean literacy. The negative relationship must be interpreted with care, because countries with low inequality tend also to have high GNP (r = -.23 between inequality and GNP). However, the data suggest that reducing inequality in literacy need not work against producing high mean literacy.

---

[10]The sampling variance for each country's segregation index was computed via "parametric bootstrap" resampling (see Willms and Paterson 1993). If log-books were normally distributed within a country, the segregation index would be distributed as

$$\eta_x^2 \sim \frac{(\bar{n}\tau_x + \sigma_x^2)\,\chi_{J-1}^2}{(\bar{n}\tau_x + \sigma_x^2)\,\chi_{J-1}^2 + \sigma_x^2\chi_{J(\bar{n}-1)}^2}$$

where n is the harmonic mean sample size. Two thousand replicates of this statistic were generated by substituting maximum likelihood estimates of σ^2 and τ into the above formula and generating the necessary chi-squared variates. The standard deviation of the resulting sampling distribution was then treated as the standard error of the segregation index.

31

Figure 7: Posterior distribution of books segregation index effect; 98% credibility intervals for fourth graders by country

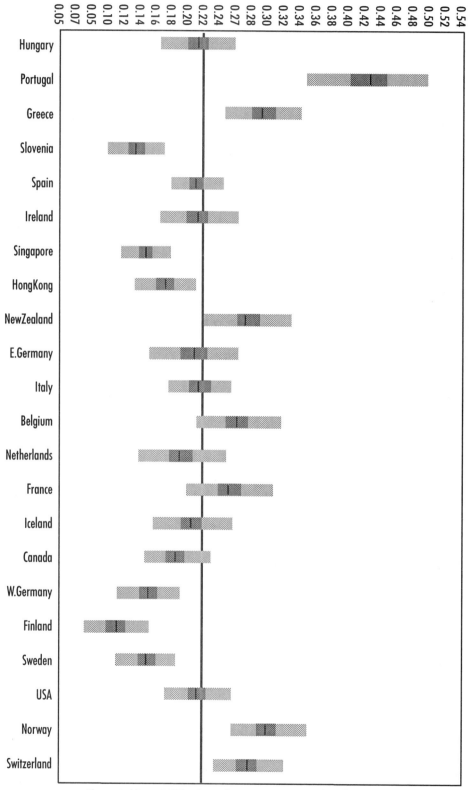

The vertical line at 0.222 indicates the mean segregation index effect across countries

Figure 8: Posterior distribution of fourth grade student-level books effect; 98% credibility intervals by country

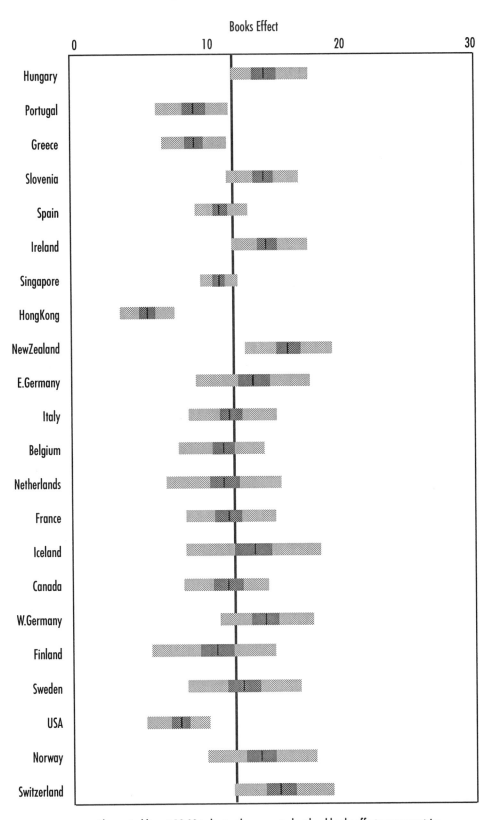

The vertical line at 12.02 indicates the mean student-level books effect across countries

Figure 9: Posterior distribution of fourth grade school-level books effect; 98% credibility intervals by country

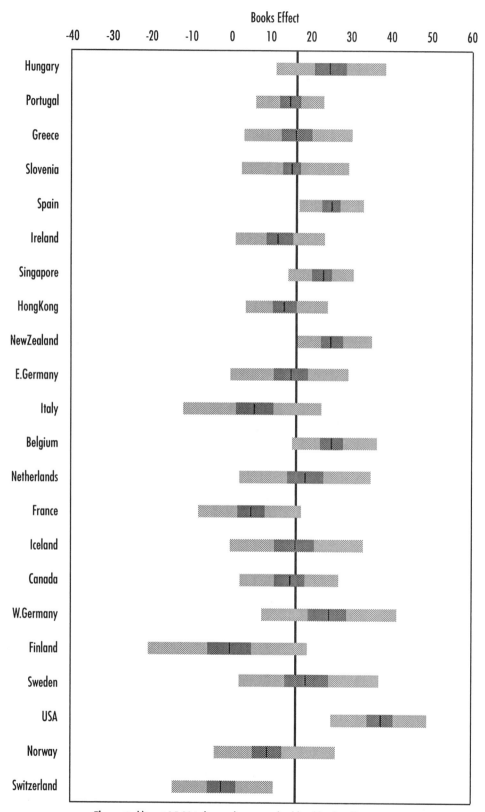

The vertical line at 15.90 indicates the mean school-level books effect across countries

34

Table 9. Between-country summaries: IEA Reading Literacy Study, 1991

Population A: Model 1 effects	Gamma	Standard error	Tau				Tau as correlations			
			GNP	School-books	Student-books	Gender	GNP	School-books	Student-books	Gender
Intercept	516.40	4.40								
GNP	1.42	0.56	452.24				1.000			
School-level books	15.90	2.99	-6.51	153.12			-0.025	1.000		
Student-level books	12.02	0.81	-16.06	-7.07	11.68		-0.221	-0.167	1.000	
Gender	-10.39	1.37	-15.32	-2.70	-10.33	30.24	-0.131	-0.040	-0.550	1.000

Population B: Model 1 effects	Gamma	Standard error	Tau				Tau as correlations			
			GNP	School-books	Student-books	Gender	GNP	School-books	Student-books	Gender
Intercept	517.24	7.82								
GNP	0.85	0.53	349.47				1.000			
School-level books	35.67	5.45	-25.38	584.35			-0.056	1.000		
Student-level books	13.76	1.72	34.78	-119.31	63.32		0.234	-0.620	1.000	
Gender	-2.99	1.38	-32.12	62.94	-34.32	32.50	-0.301	0.457	-0.757	1.000

Population B: Model 2 effects	Gamma	Standard error	Tau				Tau as correlations			
			GNP	School-mother's education	Student-books	Mother's education	GNP	School-mother's education	Student-books	Mother's education
Intercept	522.16	7.51								
GNP	0.64	0.48	290.23				1.000			
School-level mother's education	10.60	2.30	-8.55	110.51			-0.048	1.000		
Student-level books	12.22	1.42	31.83	-30.08	40.49		0.294	-0.450	1.000	
Mother's education	2.52	0.44	13.23	-7.85	9.66	3.82	0.397	-0.382	0.777	1.000

Population B: Model 3 effects	Gamma	Standard error	Tau				Tau as correlations			
			GNP	School-books	Student-books	Mother's education	GNP	School-books	Student-books	Mother's education
Intercept	522.28	7.46								
GNP	0.63	0.47	293.58				1.000			
School-level books	34.20	5.71	-62.50	667.31			-0.141	1.000		
Student-level books	11.56	1.44	34.20	-96.94	40.95		0.312	-0.586	1.000	
Mother's education	2.70	0.45	13.46	-37.26	10.76	4.11	0.387	-0.711	0.829	1.000

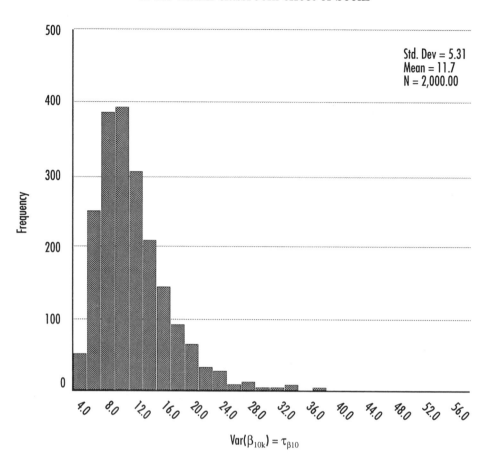

$$\mathrm{Var}(\beta_{10k}) = \tau_{\beta10}$$

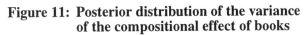

Figure 11: Posterior distribution of the variance of the compositional effect of books

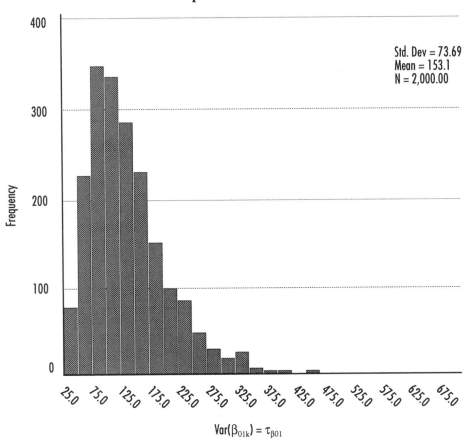

Std. Dev = 73.69
Mean = 153.1
N = 2,000.00

$Var(\beta_{01k}) = \tau_{\beta01}$

Figure 12: Mean literacy and inequality in literacy; fourth graders by country

The relationship between home environmental inequality and literacy can alternatively be viewed by comparing expected literacy levels for students who are comparatively advantaged or disadvantaged relative to their compatriots. Figure 13 plots the expected literacy level for a student "high" in log-books (vertical axis) and "low" in log-books (horizontal axis). The "high" student is one standard deviation above the country mean, and the "low" student is one standard deviation below the country mean on log-books. The diagonal line indicates the "egalitarian ideal" of equal expected values for these two students. We see, for example, that Finland is comparatively close to the diagonal line. The United States is about average in its distance from the diagonal but has the second highest expected scores for both advantaged and disadvantaged students. Thus, local control and funding of schools do not make the United States unusually inegalitarian, and, in fact, disadvantaged students fare reasonably well in the United States, though not nearly as well as advantaged students. The disadvantaged students in Finland appear to fare better than even the advantaged students in any other country.

6.3.   Conclusions from the Primary Analysis Based on the Population A Sample

The Population A data indicated quite substantial variation across countries in mean literacy with a tendency for countries of higher GNP to have higher literacy. An analysis of the home environmental inequality and classroom segregation based on such inequality revealed a set of countries that most closely approximated the egalitarian ideal of low inequality and low segregation. These included several Northern European countries and countries of the former socialist block. The United States was found to be quite typical in terms of its level of inequality and segregation. However, inequality and segregation with respect to a home environmental indicator may or may not translate into inequality in literacy. This depends on the magnitude of the effect of variation within classrooms and the magnitude of the between-classroom compositional effect.

We therefore computed a "literacy inequality index" that depends on a) the degree of inequality in the home environmental measure of interest; b) the extent of classroom (or school) segregation based on home environment; c) the magnitude of the within-classroom effect of home environment; and d) the magnitude of the between-classroom compositional effect. The data provided some evidence for a negative relationship between this index of variation and mean literacy.

Although the United States was found to have a relatively large compositional effect (meaning that the classroom or school composition is highly related to a child's literacy outcomes), the United States did not manifest an unusually high degree of overall literacy inequality. There are three reasons for this seeming paradox. First, the United States exhibits a comparatively low degree of variation in home environment. Second, the United States exhibits a low degree of segregation based on home environment. Third, the within-school effect of home environment is comparatively small in the United States. In fact, in the context of its overall high level of literacy, students who are disadvantaged in home literacy resources, as indicated by log-books, score comparatively high on literacy as compared to similarly disadvantaged students in other countries. Finally, the ideal of excellence (high mean literacy) and equality appears best approximated by Finland, which has both the highest literacy level and the lowest degree of inequality of any country in the sample.

All of these inferences are based on the Population A sample using only one indicator of home environmental advantage: log of the number of books at home. Yet, it is known that compositional effects can be amplified by underspecification of the student-level model (Hauser 1970; Hutchinson 1992). Moreover, other dimensions of home environmental advantage may not behave as does log-books; and the findings may vary if other grade levels are studied. For these reasons we turn to the Population B data, which include maternal education as well as books at home.

Figure 13: Expected literacy for advantaged and disadvantaged students; fourth graders by country

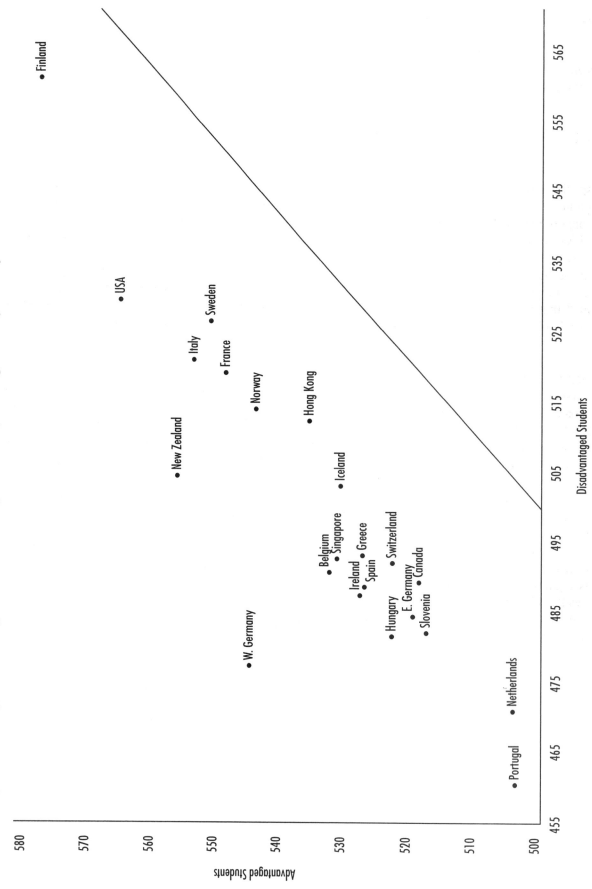

7.   Sensitivity Analyses

Our analyses of Population B data are based on 58,559 students attending 3,167 schools in the same 22 countries. These analyses were designed to respond to a series of questions arising from the "primary" analyses.

7.1.   Is the U.S. Compositional Effect an "Outlier"?

Hauser (1970) cautioned that compositional effects can arise as artifacts of poor measurement and specification of what we call the level-1 model. Suppose that the within-group effect, β_w, and the between-group effect, β_b, (Equation 1) were equal, meaning that the compositional effect was null. However, suppose that the home background indicator, X_{ij}, was unreliable. The aggregated variable (the group mean of X) would become increasingly reliable as the group sample size increases. This difference in reliabilities would then lead to estimates of β_w and β_b having different degrees of bias, producing the basis for an artifactual "compositional effect." Hutchinson (1992) conducted a simulation study showing exactly how this process works depending on the reliability of X, the group sample size, and the proportion of variance in X that lies between groups. Thus, a large compositional effect in a given country could arise because of reliability differences at level 1 and level 2 on X that are peculiar to that country.

However, it could also be that the Population A results were simply idiosyncratic. Therefore, our first analysis simply replicated the analysis of the data for this group. The posterior distributions of the compositional effects for the 22 countries are displayed in Figure 14. Once again, the point estimate (posterior mean) of the compositional effect in the United States exceeded that of other countries (though the United States' 98 percent credibility interval overlaps with those of a number of other countries). The point estimates of these effects across all countries correlated at $r = .51$ with those computed on the basis of the analysis of grade 4 data. There is, then, some modest evidence of continuity across grade levels.

It could also be that the compositional effects are specific to the home environmental measure. Here the Population B data are useful in providing a measure of years of maternal education in addition to log-books at home. We specified a level-1 model in which both maternal education and log-books were controlled, and the compositional effect of maternal education was estimated. Because both maternal education and log-books contributed independently to prediction of literacy in most countries, this model is arguably better specified than the model that controls only one home environmental indicator. The results (Figure 15) again show the United States as having a large compositional effect, though its point estimate is now exceeded by that of Singapore. These point estimates of compositional effects were quite highly related ($r = .79$) to those displayed in Figure 14, which were based on log-books at level 2, indicating that this effect is reasonably insensitive to choice of home environmental measure.

To get a more fine-grained sense of the effect of adding a second home environmental indicator at level 1, a model was then estimated in which maternal education and log-books were specified at level 1, but now the mean of log-books was specified at level 2. Compositional effect estimates were very similar to those displayed in Figure 14 ($r = .99$) with the average effect reduced by about one point. Thus, improved specification of the level-1 model had little impact on the estimate of the compositional effect.

41

Figure 14: Posterior distribution of ninth grade school-level books effect; 98% credibility intervals by country

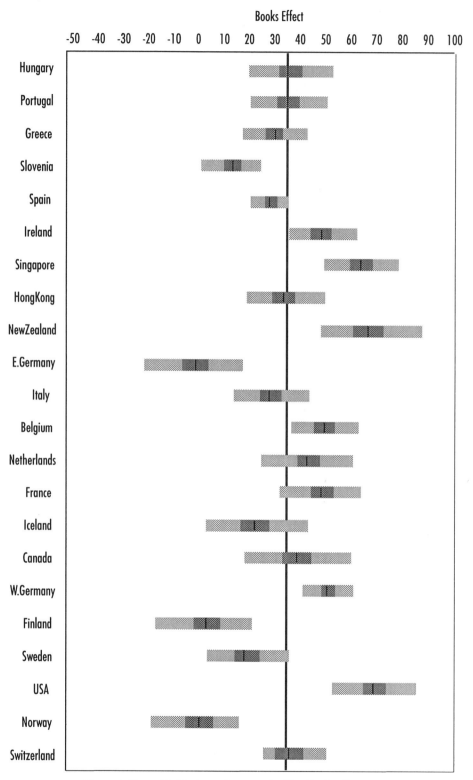

The vertical line at 35.67 indicates the mean school-level books effect across countries

Figure 15: Posterior distribution of ninth grade school-level mother's education effect; 98% credibility intervals by country

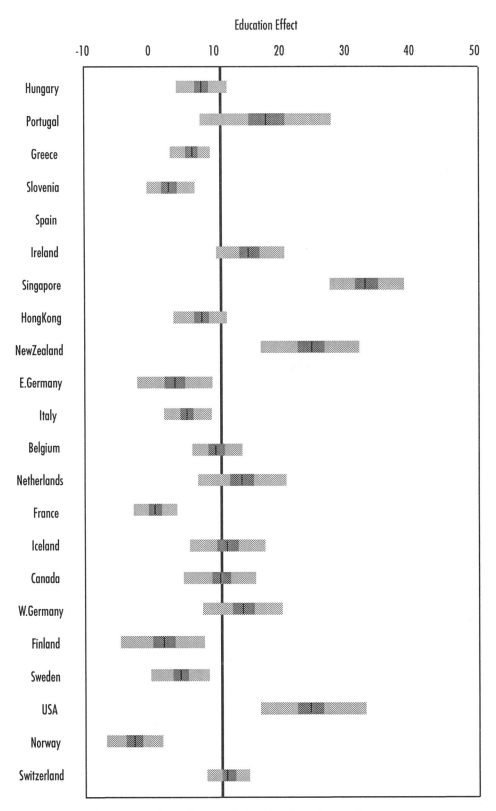

The vertical line at 10.60 indicates the mean school-level mother's education effect across countries

Even with two indicators of home environment at level 1, however, the compositional effects could be entirely artifactual. Suppose that the true compositional effect were null. Then the estimates

$$\beta_w = \frac{\sum_{j=1}^{J} \sum_{i=1}^{n_j} (X_{ij} - \overline{X}_j)(Y_{ij} - \overline{Y}_j)}{\sum_{j=1}^{J} \sum_{i=1}^{n_j} (X_{ij} - \overline{X}_j)^2} \tag{20}$$

and

$$\beta_b = \frac{\sum_{j=1}^{J} n_j (\overline{X}_j - \overline{X})(\overline{Y}_j - \overline{Y})}{\sum_{j=1}^{J} n_j (\overline{X}_j - \overline{X})^2} \tag{21}$$

would be independent, unbiased estimators of β_w. Now suppose that the reliabilities of the two measures differed, that is

$$reliablity(X_{ij}) = \rho_w \neq reliability(\overline{X}_j) = \rho_b. \tag{22}$$

Then the expected value of the estimated compositional effect would be

$$E(\beta_c) = E(\beta_b) - E(\beta_w) = \beta_w(\rho_b - \rho_w). \tag{23}$$

Now the level-2 reliability can be estimated via REML for each classroom as

$$\hat{\rho}_{bj} = \frac{\hat{\tau}_x}{\hat{\tau}_x + \hat{\sigma}_x^2/n_j} \tag{24}$$

where τ_x is the variance between classrooms on X, σ_x^2 is the variance within classrooms, and n_j is the classroom sample size. The average of these within a country represents the level-2 reliability for that country. We estimated the reliability of log-books as its level-1 correlation with maternal education. The two reliabilities are plotted in Figure 16, with the United States point highlighted.

Indeed, we found the difference between the two reliabilities to be highly correlated to the compositional effect estimates displayed in Figure 14, $r = .70$. This finding is consistent with the reasoning that compositional effects arise at least in part as a function of errors in variables at level 1. Nevertheless, this result cannot account for the especially large effect in the United States. First, as Figure 14 reveals, the United States is not unusual with respect to the difference between its two reliabilities, and therefore its unusually large compositional effect cannot be attributed entirely to this difference. Second, we estimate that in order for the U.S compositional effect estimate to be null, the level-1 reliability for log-books in the United States would have be very small at .09. This is implausible given the correlation of $r = .33$ within the United States between log-books and maternal education.

Figure 16: Reliability of the books measure at level 1 and level 2; ninth graders by country

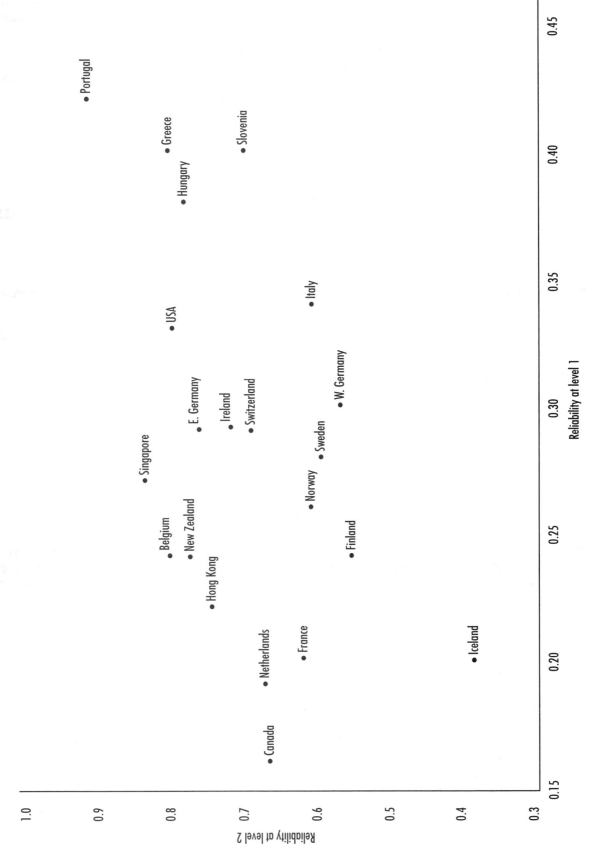

Although the unusually large compositional effect within the United States cannot be explained away as an artifact of errors in variables at level 1, the results of the sensitivity analysis do suggest extreme caution in interpreting these estimates. The magnitudes of these estimates do appear significantly inflated by level-1 underspecification.

7.2. Are Cross-National Inferences About Home Environmental Inequality Sensitive to Grade Level?

Recall that the overall inequality in literacy resulting from inequality in the home environment was specified as resulting from four sources: the degree of inequality in home environmental resources, the degree of segregation of classrooms by home environment, the effect within schools of home environment, and the compositional effect. This achievement inequality index was plotted for the fourth grade data in Figure 12. The same index was computed for grade 9, again using log-books at home as the indicator of home environmental resources. This grade 9 index was found reasonably highly correlated with the grade 4 index, r = .64. Paralleling Figure 13 for fourth grade, Figure 17 plots expected literacy levels for students advantaged and disadvantaged in home environmental resources as compared to their compatriots. Again, a student classified as advantaged is one standard deviation above average, and a student classified as disadvantaged is one standard deviation below average relative to other students in that country. A comparison of plots for Population A and Population B shows obvious similarities (note the position of Finland) and differences (see Portugal). The position of the United States appears somewhat less favorable at ninth than at fourth grade.

8. Final Conclusions

In this paper we have developed a conceptual framework and statistical methodology for studying cross-national differences in mean literacy and social inequality in literacy. Overall social inequality in literacy is viewed as arising from children's social inequalities of origin, social segregation, within-school effects of inequality, and between-school effects of social composition. We applied this idea not to a generic measure of social status, but rather to a measure of the educational resources available to children in 22 countries, specifically, the availability of books at home. This analysis was performed on large representative samples of fourth and ninth graders supplemented by sensitivity analyses involving years of maternal education at the ninth grade level. Conclusions involve the United States, the larger sample, and methodology for cross-national research generally.

8.1. Conclusions Regarding the United States

1. It was hypothesized that because of its policies of local control and funding of schools and the resulting residential social segregation, U.S. classrooms would be relatively highly segregated on the basis of children's home educational environments. This hypothesis was not supported: the United States was quite typical of the countries in regard to the degree of segregation, with a few countries, especially Finland (with low segregation) and Portugal (with high segregation) proving exceptional in this regard, for Population A.

2. For the same reasons, it was hypothesized that the United States would exhibit unusually large compositional effects. This hypothesis found support for both grade levels. Although the magnitude of the effect is quite uncertain given the artifactual inflation of the estimates, the United States does appear exceptional in the salience of a classroom's social composition for the literacy learning of its students.

Figure 17: Expected literacy for advantaged and disadvantaged students; ninth graders by country

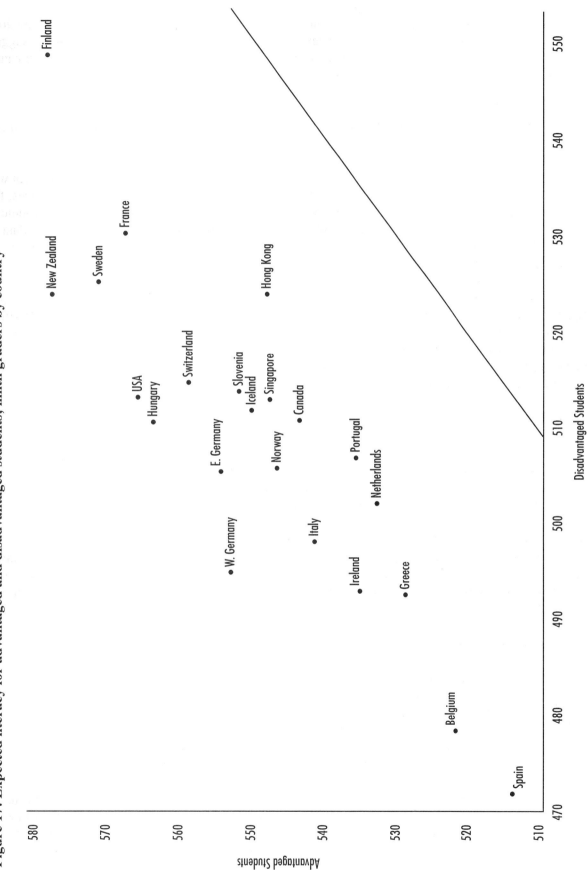

47

3.   Nevertheless, inequalities in literacy arising from variations in home educational environment do not appear exceptionally pronounced in the United States. The inequality index for the United States was near the middle of the distribution, and, given the high mean literacy of U.S. fourth graders, disadvantaged U.S. students fared comparatively better than disadvantaged students from most other countries. The seeming paradox—of large compositional effects in the United States without high inequality—can be explained by three factors: the comparatively moderate variation in home resources in the United States, the comparatively moderate degree of classroom segregation, and the comparatively moderate effect of home environment operating within classrooms.

8.2.   Conclusions Regarding the Larger Sample

1.   To label inequality "comparatively moderate" in the United States is not to endorse such inequality. Countries vary significantly in the inequality index, and the data from some countries clearly demonstrate the coexistence of high mean literacy and low inequality. Finland is the most prominent example at both grade levels. There was no evidence at either level that goals of excellence (high mean literacy) and equity (low inequality) are in conflict.

2.   Coefficients of stability across grade levels were moderately high for point estimates of mean literacy ($r = .59$), inequality in literacy arising from home environment ($r = .64$), compositional effects ($r = .79$), and within-school effects of log-books ($r = .49$). The segregation index was less stable ($r = .20$).

3.   Coefficients of stability across measures (using log-books versus using maternal education with ninth grade data) were also moderately high: $r = .79$ for compositional effects, and $r = .68$ for the segregation index.

8.3.   Conclusions for Cross-National Research on Literacy

1.   We recommend a concerted effort to construct, test, and administer a core of common measures of home environment, socioeconomic status, and community and school context across countries. Without this effort, it will be difficult to obtain meaningful estimates of social segregation and social composition effects, undermining also our ability to study social inequality in literacy cross-nationally. Moreover, estimates of other policy-relevant effects, including effects of school and classroom resources, policies, and processes, will be in question unless adequate control for social background and context are constructed.

2.   Because of limited data, the current study made no attempt to assess effects of ethnicity and linguistic background. The needed indicators will be country-specific because particular ethnic and linguistic minorities exist only in single countries or small sets of countries. Nevertheless, these effects can be studied using the methodology we have presented here (see Mason et al. 1991 in the context of restricted maximum likelihood (REML) using an approach that extends readily to our Bayesian approach).

3.   We recommend that multiple classrooms per school be sampled whenever possible in future cross-national surveys so that classroom and school variance, classroom and school segregation, and composition effects may be estimated separately.

4.   The Bayesian methodology for synthesizing results across countries, combined with REML estimation within countries appears promising in a) accounting for uncertainty within countries when there is a multistage cluster design, and b) accounting for uncertainty arising from between-country heterogeneity.

5.   It appears feasible and useful to compare countries not only with respect to mean literacy levels but also with respect to social inequality in literacy levels. Each country's index of social inequality in literacy can be further "unpacked" into components reflecting within-school social inequality in literacy and between-school social inequality in literacy, arising from between-school social segregation.

6.   It is then possible to compare the literacy levels of socially advantaged and disadvantaged students across societies.

References

Bosker, R.J., and Guldemond, H. (1991). Interdependency of performance indicators: An empirical study of a categorical school system. In S.W. Raudenbush and J.D. Willms (eds.), *Schools, pupils and classrooms: International studies of schooling from a multilevel perspective.* San Diego: Academic Press.

Bowles, S., and Gintis, H. (1976). *Schooling in capitalist America.* New York: Basic Books.

Bryk, A.S., and Raudenbush, S.W. (1988). Toward a more appropriate conceptualization of research on school effects: A three-level hierarchical linear model. *American Journal of Education*, 97(1), 65-108.

Bryk, A.S., and Raudenbush, S.W. (1992). *Hierarchical linear models in social and behavioral research: Applications and data analysis methods.* Beverly Hills: Sage Publications.

Bryk, A.S., Raudenbush, S.W., and Congdon, R.T. (1992). *An introduction to HLM: Computer program and users' guide. Version 3.0.* Chicago: Scientific Software, Inc.

Bryk, A.S., and Thum, Y.M. (1989). The effects of high school organization on dropping out: an exploratory investigation. *American Educational Research Journal*, 26(3), 353-383.

Burstein, L. (1980). The analysis of multi-level data in educational research and evaluation. *Review of Research in Education, 8,* 158-233.

Coleman, J., Campbell, E., Hobson, C., McPartland, J., Mood, A., Weinfield, F., and York, R. (1966). *Equality of educational opportunity.* Washington, DC: U.S. Government Printing Office.

de Lone, R. (1979). *Small futures: Children, inequality, and the limits of liberal reform.* New York: Harcourt, Brace, Jovanovich.

Edmonds, R.R. (1979). Effective schools for the urban poor. *Educational Leadership*, 37, 15-27.

Firebaugh, G. (1978). A rule for inferring individual-level relationships from aggregate data. *American Sociological Review*, 43, 557-572.

Fitz-Gibbon, C. (1991). Multilevel modeling in an indicator system. In S.W. Raudenbush and J.D. Willms (eds.), *Schools, pupils and classrooms: International studies of schooling from a multilevel perspective.* San Diego: Academic Press.

Fotiu, R.P. (1989). *A comparison of the EM and data augmentation algorithms on simulated small sample hierarchical data from research on education.* Unpublished Ph.D. diss. Michigan State University, East Lansing.

Fraser, E. (1959). *Home environment and the school.* London: University of London Press.

Gelfand, A.E., and Smith, A.F.M. (1990). Sampling-based approaches to calculating marginal densities. *Journal of the American Statistical Association*, 85, 398-409.

Gelfand, A.E., Hills, S.E., Racine-Poon, A., and Smith, A.F.M. (1990). Illustration of Bayesian inference in normal data models using Gibbs sampling. *Journal of the American Statistical Association*, 85, 972-985.

Goldstein, H. (1987). *Multilevel models in educational and social research.* London: Oxford University Press.

Grubb, W.N., and Lazerson, M. (1982). *Broken promises: How Americans fail their children.* New York: Basic Books.

Hauser, R. (1970). Context and consex: A cautionary tale. *American Journal of Sociology*, 75(4), 645-664.

Heyneman, S.P., and Loxley, W.A. (1983). The effect of primary school quality on academic achievement across twenty-nine high and low-income countries. *American Journal of Sociology*, 88, 1162-1194.

Hutchinson, D. (1992). Do compositional effects exist, really? Unpublished manuscript. London: National Foundation for Educational Research in England and Wales.

Huttenlocher, J.E., Haight, W., Bryk, A.S., and Seltzer, M. (1991). Early vocabulary growth: Relation to language input and gender. *Developmental Psychology,* 27(2), 236-249.

Jencks, C., et al. (1972). *Inequality: A reassessment of the effects of family and schooling in America.* New York: Basic Books.

Kenniston, K. (1977). *All our children: The American family under pressure.* New York: Harcourt, Brace, Jovanovich.

Kerckhoff, A.C. (1993). *Diverging pathways: Social structure and career reflections.* Cambridge, England: Cambridge University Press.

McPherson, A.F., and Willms, J.D. (1986). Certification, class conflict, religion and community: A psych-historical explanation of the effectiveness of contemporary schools. In A.C. Kerckhoff (ed.), *Research in sociology of education and socialization*, vol. 6, 227-302. Greenwich, CT: JAI Press.

Peaker, G.F. (1971). *The Plowden children four years later.* London: National Foundation for Education in England and Wales.

Raudenbush, S.W. (1988). Educational applications of hierarchical linear models: A review. *Journal of Educational Statistics*, 13(2), 85-116.

Raudenbush, S.W. (1992). Hierarchical linear models and experimental design. In L. Edwards (ed.), *Applied analysis of variance in behavioral science.* New York: Marcell-Decker.

Raudenbush, S.W., and Bryk, A.S. (1986). A hierarchical model for studying school effects. *Sociology of Education,* 59, 1-17.

Raudenbush, S.W., Cheong, Y.F., and Fotiu, R.P. (1994). Synthesizing cross-national classroom effects data: Alternative models and methods. In M. Binkley, K. Rust, and M. Winglee (eds.), *Methodological issues in comparative international studies: The case of the IEA Reading Literacy Study*. Washington, DC: U.S. Government Printing Office.

Ryan, W. (1971). *Blaming the victim*. New York: Pantheon Books.

Rutter, M., Maughan, B., Mortimore, P., Ousten, J., and Smith, M. (1979). *Fifteen thousand hours: Secondary schools and their effects on children*.

Rutter, M., and Rutter, M. (1993). *Developing minds: Challenge and continuity across the lifespan*. New York: Basic Books.

Seber, G.A.F. (1978). *Linear regression analysis*. New York: Wiley.

Seltzer, M.H. (1993). Sensitivity analysis for fixed effects in the hierarchical model: A Gibbs sampling approach. *Journal of Educational Statistics*, 18(3), 207-235.

Wheeler, C.W., Raudenbush, S.W., and Pasigna, A. (1992). Policy initiatives to produce teacher productivity in Thailand: An essay on implementation, constraints, and opportunities for educational reform. *International Journal of Educational Research*, 17, 2.

Willms, J.D. (1986). Social class segregation and its relationship to pupils' examination results in Scotland. *American Sociological Review*, 51, 224-241.

Willms, J.D. (1992). *Monitoring school performance: A guide for educators*. Lewes: Falmer.

Willms, J.D., and Paterson, L. (1996). *A multilevel model for community segregation*. Centre for Educational Sociology, University of Edinburgh (under review).

Wolf, R. (1968). The measurement of environments, in A. Anastasi (ed.), *Testing problems in perspective*. Washington, DC: American Council on Education.

Appendix
Empirical Bayes and Bayes Estimation Theory
for Two-Level Models with Normal Errors

1.   Introduction

Historically, the hierarchical linear model (HLM) has been developed and promoted from a Bayesian perspective.[1] More generally, Bayesian approaches to statistical problems have been studied since Thomas R. Bayes's (1763) famous paper,[2] but only recently have practical estimation techniques been available to implement Bayesian statistical methods for many current applications. One difficulty encountered with traditional implementation of Bayesian methods is the required integration over one or more parameter spaces. Many applications of scientific interest have complicated, multidimensional parameter spaces. Some of these integration problems can be solved with sophisticated numerical analytic techniques, while others have been resistant to analytic solution.

Two estimation techniques, the EM algorithm developed by Dempster, Laird, and Rubin[3] and the Gibbs sampler introduced by Geman and Geman[4] have been instrumental in making the Bayesian approach to the HLM a practical alternative. The EM approach to HLM as first described by Dempster, Rubin, and Tsutakawa[5] can be viewed either as a strictly classical procedure or as providing an approximation to the Bayesian posterior distribution. This approximation is known as an empirical Bayes approach because the parameters of certain prior distributions are estimated from the data rather than specified a priori. The empirical Bayes strategy we have adopted for within-country analysis is described briefly in the next section. In Section 3, we discuss the Gibbs sampler as an improved Bayes solution in the context HLM. The Gibbs sampler is a sampling-based algorithm for calculating finite approximations to posterior distributions enabling one to incorporate more information into the calculation of a posterior distribution and provide a better account of the uncertainty associated with parameter estimation than is possible using EM. Fotiu,[6] Gelfand and Smith,[7] and Seltzer[8] provide more detailed treatments.

We note that the stage-1 analysis employs the empirical Bayes approach within each country. The stage-2 analysis employs the Gibbs sampler to synthesize results from the several countries.

---

[1] D.V. Lindley, and A.F.M. Smith. Bayes Estimates for the Linear Model (with discussion). *Journal of the Royal Society*, Series B, 34, 1-41, 1972.

[2] T.R. Bayes. An Essay Towards Solving a Problem in the Doctrine of Chances. *Philosophical Transactions of the Royal Society*, 53, 370, 1763 (reprinted in *Biometrika*, 45, 293-315, 1958).

[3] A.P. Dempster, N.M. Laird, and D.B. Rubin. Maximum Likelihood from Incomplete Data Via the EM Algorithm (with discussion). *Journal of the Royal Statistical Society*, Series B, 39, 1-38, 1977.

[4] S. Geman, and D. Geman. Stochastic Relaxation, Gibbs Distributions and the Bayesian Restoration of Images. *IEEE Transactions on Pattern Analysis and Machine Intelligence*, 6, 721-741, 1984.

[5] A.P. Dempster, D.B. Rubin, and R.K. Tsutakawa. Estimation in Covariance Components Models. *Journal of the American Statistical Association*, 76, 341-353, 1981.

[6] R.P. Fotiu. *A Comparison of the EM and Data Augmentation Algorithms on Simulated Small Sample Hierarchical Data from Research on Education.* Unpublished doctoral dissertation, East Lansing, MI: Michigan State University, 1989.

[7] A.E. Gelfand, and A.F.M. Smith. Sampling-Based Approaches to Calculating Marginal Densities. *Journal of the American Statistical Association*, 85, 398-409, 1990.

[8] M.H. Seltzer. Sensitivity Analysis for Fixed Effects in the Hierarchical Model: A Gibbs Sampling Approach. *Journal of Educational Statistics*, 18(3), 207-235, 1993.

2.   Empirical Bayes Estimation with the EM Algorithm

2.1   The Model

We now consider the two-level HLM and its assumptions for the empirical Bayes estimation approach.[9] The model is formulated in submodels: a level-1 model that describes variation within clusters and a level-2 model that describes variation between clusters.

Level-1 Model. Within clusters such as classrooms, the outcome Y is viewed as depending on characteristics of level-1 units according to the model

$$Y = X\beta + r, \quad r \sim N(0, \Sigma) \tag{1}$$

where Y is a vector of outcomes, X is a matrix of known predictors, β is a vector of unknown level-1 regression coefficients describing the relationship between X and Y within the clusters, r is a vector of level-1 random effects, and Σ is a positive-definite level-1 covariance matrix. Assuming X to be of full rank and β known, one might estimate β via generalized least squares, i.e.,

$$\hat{\beta} = \left(X^T \Sigma^{-1} X\right)^{-1} X^T \Sigma^{-1} Y \tag{2}$$

$$V = Var(\hat{\beta}) = \left(X^T \Sigma^{-1} X\right)^{-1} \tag{3}$$

Typically, it is assumed that $\Sigma = \sigma^2 I$ in which case equation (2) reduces to ordinary least squares with $V = \sigma^2 (X^T X)^{-1}$.

Level-2 Model. Between clusters, the coefficients β are viewed depending upon cluster characteristics and random error according to the model

$$\beta = W\gamma + u, \quad u \sim N(0, T) \tag{4}$$

where W is a matrix of known cluster characteristics, γ is a vector of unknown level-2 regression coefficients describing the relationship between W and β between clusters, u is a vector of level-2 random effects, and T is a positive definite level-2 covariance matrix, having block diagonal structure with J identical submatrices τ along the main diagonal, one submatrix for every cluster $j = 1, 2, ..., J$, i.e., $T = \text{subdiag}(\tau)$.

Combined Model. Substituting equation (4) into equation (1) gives the combined model

$$Y = XW\gamma + Xu + r. \tag{5}$$

---

[9]We present the model in its "hierarchical form" as opposed to the more general mixed model form. Raudenbush (S.W. Raudenbush. *Educational Applications of Hierarchical Linear Models: A Review. Journal of Educational Statistics*, 13,2,85-116, 1988) discusses the two forms of the model. This clarifies the parallels with our application of Gibbs sampling, although the mixed model form is actually more general and will be employed in the stage-1 analysis.

Premultiplying equation (5) by $VX^T\Sigma^{-1}$ yields the equivalent model

$$\hat{\beta} = W\gamma + u + VX^T \Sigma^{-1} r \qquad (6)$$

showing that the marginal distribution of $\hat{\beta}$ is $N(W\gamma, \Delta)$ with $\Delta = V + T$. Thus, the generalized least squares estimator of γ and its covariance matrix are given by

$$\gamma^* = (W^T\Delta^{-1}W)^{-1}W^T\Delta^{-1}\hat{\beta} \qquad (7)$$

and

$$Var(\hat{\gamma}) = D_\gamma = (W^T\Delta^{-1}W)^{-1}. \qquad (8)$$

Empirical Bayes Estimation. Following Dempster, Rubin, and Tsutakawa,[10] we now formulate a noninformative prior distribution for γ such that, a priori,

$$\gamma \sim N(0,\Gamma), \ \Gamma^{-1} \rightarrow 0 \qquad (9)$$

Equation (9) assumes that the prior precision, Γ^{-1}, of our knowledge about the value of γ approaches 0. As a result, the specific value of the location parameter is inconsequential, and we have chosen 0 for convenience. Then the conditional posterior density of $\gamma \,|\, Y,\Sigma,T$ is $N(\gamma^*, D_\gamma)$ and the conditional density of $\beta \,|\, Y,\Sigma,T$ is $N(\beta^*, D_\beta)$ where γ^* is given by equation (7), D_γ is given by equation (8), and we have

$$\beta^* = \Lambda\hat{\beta} + (I-\Lambda)W\gamma* \qquad (10)$$

and

$$D_\beta = L^{-1} + (I-\Lambda)WD_\gamma W^T(I-\Lambda)^T, \qquad (11)$$

where

$$L = V^{-1} + T^{-1}, \qquad (12)$$

$$\Lambda = L^{-1}V^{-1}.$$

We note that the conditional covariance between β and γ, is

$$Cov(\beta,\gamma \,|\, Y,\Sigma,T) = -L^{-1}X^T \Sigma^{-1}XWD_\gamma. \qquad (13)$$

Empirical Bayes inferences about β and γ are typically made by substituting maximum likelihood (ML) estimates of Σ and T in equations (7), (8), (10) and (11). Such inferences do not take into account the uncertainty of the ML estimates.

---

[10]See footnote 5.

55

2.2 Covariance Estimation via EM

Suppose that, in addition to the data Y, the level-1 random effects r and the level-2 random effects u were also observed. Then, with $T =$ subdiag (τ) and $\Sigma = \sigma^2 I$, ML estimators of the covariance components τ and σ^2 could be computed simply as

$$\hat{\tau} = \frac{1}{J} \sum u_j u_j^T \tag{14}$$

$$\hat{\sigma}^2 = \frac{1}{N} r^T r$$

where J is the number of clusters, N is the number of level-1 units, u_j is the jth subvector of u, and r_j is the jth subvector of r. Of course, the quantities u and r are not observed. However, given current estimates of the covariance parameters, the sufficient statistics defined by equation (14) (termed "complete-data sufficient statistics")[11] can be *estimated* by their conditional expectations given the data and these current parameter estimates. Thus, based on equations 10 to 13, and denoting current estimates with the superscript $"p"$, we have

$$E\left(\sum u_j u_j^T \mid Y, \tau^p, \sigma^{2p}\right) = \sum \left(\beta_j^{*p} - W_j \gamma^{*p}\right) \left(\beta_j^{*p} - W_j \gamma^{*p}\right)^T$$

$$+ \sum Var\left(u_j \mid Y, \tau^p, \sigma^{2p}\right)$$

$$\tag{15}$$

$$E\left(r^T r \mid Y, \tau^p, \sigma^{2p}\right) = \left(Y - X\beta^{*p}\right)^T \left(Y - X\beta^{*p}\right)$$

$$+ Trace\left(X^T X D_\beta^p\right)$$

where

$$Var\left(u_j \mid Y, \tau, \sigma^2\right) = L_j^{-1} + L_j^{-1} W D_\gamma W^T L_j^{-1}. \tag{16}$$

Given an initial estimate of τ and σ^2, and therefore of the posterior distribution of γ (from equations (7) and (8) and ß (from equations 10 to 13), the EM algorithm iteratively computes the complete-data sufficient statistics (equation 15) and then uses these to compute new complete-data ML estimators using equation (14). Equation (15) is called the "E" or "Expectation" step and Equation (14) is called the "M" or "Maximization" step. Under quite mild conditions, each E-M cycle increases the observed data likelihood

$$L\left(Y \mid \tau, \sigma^2\right) = \frac{f\left(Y \mid \beta, \tau, \sigma^2\right) g\left(\beta \mid \tau, \sigma^2\right)}{h\left(\beta \mid Y, \tau, \sigma^2\right)} \tag{17}$$

until convergence to a maximum.

---

[11]See footnote 5.

At convergence, empirical Bayes estimates are based on

$$p(\beta,\gamma\,|\,Y,\sigma^2=\hat{\sigma}^2,\tau=\hat{\tau})=\text{const.}\times f(Y\,|\,\beta,\hat{\sigma}^2)g(\beta\,|\,\gamma,\hat{\tau})p(\gamma).\tag{18}$$

As mentioned, the empirical Bayes approach does not take into consideration the uncertainty of our knowledge of the unknown variance-covariance components σ^2 and τ.

3.   Bayesian Estimation with the Gibbs Sampler

Bayes (Via Gibbs) Versus Empirical Bayes (Via EM). The Gibbs sampler is a special case of the data-augmentation algorithm described by Tanner and Wong.[12] These two approaches are compared by Gelfand and Smith.[13] A number of methodologies that offer solutions on a continuum between the Gibbs sampler and the EM algorithm are discussed by Tanner.[14] The essential difference between empirical Bayes estimation via the EM algorithm and Bayesian estimation via the Gibbs sampler applied to the HLM is that the Bayesian approach using the Gibbs sampler computes a posterior distribution for the variance-covariance components in the model, rather than summarizing this information into a point estimate as illustrated in equation 18. Hence, Bayesian inferences about β, γ are based on

$$p(\beta,\gamma\,|\,Y)=\text{const.}\times\!\int\!\!\int f(y\,|\,\beta,\sigma^2)g(\beta\,|\,\gamma,\tau)p(\gamma)p(\tau)p(\sigma^2)\partial\tau\,\partial\sigma^2.\tag{19}$$

This Bayesian approach provides more information about the posterior distribution of a model's parameters than is available with empirical Bayes because more elements of uncertainty are accounted for explicitly.

The following assumptions for the Bayesian formulation are the same as those specified earlier for the empirical Bayes approach, except that we now add prior distributions for the parameters σ^2 and τ. The variance parameter, σ^2, is assumed a priori to have an inverse chi-square distribution given by

$$\sigma^2 \sim \nu_0\sigma_0^2\chi^{-2}(\nu_0)\tag{20}$$

with the degrees of freedom parameter ν_0 and noncentrality parameter σ_0^2. This prior distribution for σ^2 is considered noninformative in its contribution to the posterior distribution of σ^2 as ν_0 approaches 0. In addition, the variance-covariance matrix, τ, is assumed a priori to have an inverse Wishart prior distribution given by

$$\tau \sim W^{-1}(\Psi,\nu)\tag{21}$$

where Ψ is the precision matrix of the inverse Wishart distribution and ν is the degrees of freedom parameter. This prior distribution for ν is assumed to be noninformative in its contribution to the posterior distribution of τ as the degrees of freedom parameter, ν, approaches 0, and Ψ approaches 0.

---

[12]M.A. Tanner. *Tools for Statistical Inference* (New York: Springer-Verlag, 1992).

[13]See footnote 7.

[14]See footnote 12.

It is the assumptions concerning the model in conjunction with the data that determine the joint distribution of all unknowns given by

$$p(Y,\beta,\sigma^2,\gamma,\tau)=f(Y|\beta,\sigma^2)g(\beta|\gamma,\tau)p(\sigma^2,\gamma,\tau).$$ (22)

Two alternative expressions for this joint density[15] are

$$p(Y,\beta,\sigma^2,\gamma,\tau)=q_1(Y)q_2(\beta,\sigma^2|Y)q_3(\gamma,\tau|\beta,\sigma^2)$$

$$=r_1(Y)r_2(\beta,\sigma^2|Y,\gamma,\tau)r_3(\gamma,\tau|Y)$$ (23)

with $q_1 = r_1$. Gibbs sampling exploits the fact that, although this joint density is not tractable, both q_3 and r_2 are readily accessible (as shown below) so that it is simple to sample from those. Starting from rough guesses at the values of γ and τ, Gibbs works by sampling from r_2 to obtain new values of β and σ^2. Knowing those values, it is easy to sample from q_3, yielding new values of γ and τ. This process iterates as described in more detail in the next section. The goal is to obtain the joint posterior densities of all unknowns, i.e.,

$$p(\beta,\sigma^2,\gamma,\tau|y)=\frac{p(Y,\beta,\sigma^2,\gamma,\tau)}{q_1(y)}$$ (24)

The marginal posteriors are readily derived from this joint posterior.

The Gibbs Sampler. The Gibbs sampler uses the data and distribution assumptions to generate approximate posterior distributions by Monte Carlo sampling. Successive iterations move closer to the true posterior distribution until stochastic convergence is achieved. After convergence, we can collect a sufficiently large set of generated parameters from subsequent iterations as a finite approximation to the true posterior distribution.

There are two basic steps to this algorithm. The first step is to calculate a current approximation of a required posterior distribution. The second step is to sample from this distribution.

Initially, suppose the parameters γ and τ from q_3 in (23) and σ^2 were observed. Then β^* and D_β could be calculated, where the asterisk (*) indicates an estimated posterior mean. Next, given β^* and D_β just calculated, β can be sampled by Monte Carlo methods from the posterior distribution of $\beta|Y,\gamma,\tau,\sigma^2$. With the knowledge of β, an estimate of the central tendency of the conditional distribution of σ^2 (given β) can be calculated and then σ^2 is sampled from its conditional distribution given Y and β (see below). The resulting parameter pair of β and σ^2 approximates a sample from r_2 in (23).

In a similar manner, a sample of γ and τ can be obtained. Given parameters β and σ^2 from r_2 just realized along with τ from the previous iteration, the posterior mean and variance of γ can be calculated from the distribution of γ given β,σ^2, and τ. Next, the location parameter for the conditional density of γ (given β and this new γ) can be calculated and then τ can be sampled from its conditional

---

[15]C.N. Morris. Comment on article by Tanner and Wong. *Journal of American Statistician*, 82, 542-543, 1987.

density given β and γ. This results in the parameter pair of γ and τ approximating a sample from q_3 in (23).

To improve the approximations, the resulting sample from q_3 is considered an intermediate approximation of q_3 and recycled back to calculate estimated conditional distributions and generate a new sample to update r_2. The new sample from r_2 is used in the same manner to calculate estimated conditional distributions and obtain a sample from q_3. This iteration scheme is repeated until convergence. Afterwards, m more iterations are completed and the parameter values from each iteration are collected. If m is large, the mixture of the densities can be considered a finite approximation to the joint posterior distribution given in (24).

One advantage of this algorithm is that not only are point estimates generated, but the results also include finite approximations to the true joint posterior distribution. For example, the sampled values for a parameter of interest can be sorted in order and then the $\alpha/2$ percent tails of the distribution can be easily determined. As a consequence, highest posterior densities can be easily determined for both symmetric and nonsymmetric distributions.

Initial Values. It does not matter at what level parameter estimation begins. In the example detailed next, we shall begin at the first level in the hierarchy to obtain values for β and σ^2. Initial values for γ, τ, and σ^2 are required for the start of this algorithm, in addition to the ordinary least squares (OLS) estimate of β. Initial parameter estimates may be calculated by a variety of techniques. Of course, better initial estimates will result in faster convergence. One strategy is to use the empirical Bayes modal estimates of the posterior distributions as a starting point.

Calculating and Sampling the First-Level Parameters β and σ^2. The sampling of the first-level parameters β requires the knowledge of γ, τ and σ^2. The data Y are summarized in the OLS estimator, $\hat{\beta}$ and its sampling variance, V. The first iteration of the algorithm uses the initial values, while subsequent iterations use the previous iteration's generated values.

The desired posterior density r_2 can be rewritten as

$$r_2(\beta,\sigma^2,|Y,\gamma,\tau)=r_2'(\beta|Y,\gamma,\sigma^2,\tau)r_2''(\sigma^2). \tag{25}$$

Let $\sigma^{2(i-1)}$, $\gamma^{(i-1)}$, and $\tau^{(i-1)}$ indicate the previous iteration's sample. New values for the $\beta_j^{*(i)}$'s can be calculated as

$$\beta_j^{*(i)} = \Lambda^{(i-1)}\hat{\beta}+\left(I-\Lambda^{(i-1)}\right)W_j\gamma^{(i-1)}. \tag{26}$$

A new set of βj's can be sampled from the density of β given γ, τ, σ^2, which is $N\{\beta_j^{*(i)},D(\beta_j^{(i-1)})\}$, where

$$D\left(\beta_j^{(i-1)}\right) = \mathrm{Var}\left(\beta_j|\sigma^{2(i-1)},\gamma^{(i-1)},\tau^{(i-1)}\right) = L_j^{(i-1)-1}. \tag{27}$$

59

First, the matrix $D\left(\beta_j^{(i-1)}\right)$ is factored by the Cholesky method such that $D\left(\beta_j^{(i-1)}\right) = M_j^{(i)}M_j^{(i)T}$, where $M_j^{(i)}$ is a lower triangular matrix. Next, the $\beta_j^{(i)}$'s are sampled with the following equation:

$$\beta_j^{(i)} = \beta^{*(i)} + M_j^{(i)}x_j^{(i)} \tag{28}$$

where $x_j^{(i)}$ is a vector containing independent and identically distributed elements sampled from $N(0, 1)$.

After generating new $\beta_j^{(i)}$'s from (28), $\sigma^{2*(i)}$ can be calculated as follows:

$$\sigma^{2*(i)} = \sum \left(Y_j - X_j\beta_j^{(i)}\right)^T\left(Y_j - X_j\beta_j^{(i)}\right)/N, \tag{29}$$

where $N = \Sigma n_j$. Alternatively, equation (29) can be expressed as

$$\sigma^{2*(i)} = \left[\sum \left(Y_j - X_j\hat{\beta}_j\right)^T\left(Y_j - X_j\hat{\beta}_j\right) + \sum \left(\hat{\beta}_j - \beta_j^{(i)}\right)^T X_j^T X_j\left(\hat{\beta}_j - \beta^{(i)}\right)\right]/N, \tag{30}$$

to minimize computation and illustrate the partitioning of the sources of variation. The first part of the expression enclosed in brackets computes the sum of the squared deviations of the ordinary least squares prediction from the observed data vector Y. This expression can be computed once because its value is constant across iterations of the algorithm. The second part of the expression adds the variance as a function of the deviation of $\hat{\beta}_j$ from the ith iteration's realization of the parameter $\beta_j^{(i)}$. It has been assumed that σ^2 has an inverse chi-square prior distribution with υ_0 degrees of freedom. The posterior distribution of σ^2 given the data and $\beta^{(i)}$ is

$$\sigma^2 \sim \left(\upsilon_0\sigma_0^2 + N\sigma^{2*(i)}\right)|\chi^{-2}(\upsilon_0 + N). \tag{31}$$

For a noninformative prior, we can let υ_0 approach 0 in its contribution to the posterior distribution and (31) becomes

$$\sigma^2 \sim N\sigma^{2*(i)}|\chi^{-2}(N). \tag{32}$$

To sample σ^2, we generate a chi-square variate with N degrees of freedom, invert it, and substitute it in (32) to obtain $\sigma^{2(i)}$.

Now we have a sample from r_2 of the parameter pair $\left(\beta^{(i)},\sigma^{2(i)}\right)$.. These are passed on to calculate and sample the second-level parameters in the HLM.

Calculating and Sampling the Second-Level Parameters γ and τ. Given a pair of $\left(\beta,\sigma^2\right)$ drawn from $r_2 \left(\beta,\sigma^2|Y,\gamma,\tau\right)$ we can calculate the posterior mean, γ^* and with $\tau^{(i-1)}$ from the previous iteration a sample is drawn from the posterior distribution of γ. In a similar manner, we can then use our sampled γ to calculate a conditional distribution for τ and then sample from it. The goal is to achieve a realization of the parameter pair (γ, τ) from q_3. The distribution of q_3 may be expressed in the following form:

$$q_3(\gamma,\tau \mid \beta,\sigma^2) = q_3'(\gamma \mid \tau,\beta,\sigma^2)q_3''(\tau). \tag{33}$$

We note in passing that the calculation and sampling of γ and τ does not directly depend on σ^2.

A posterior sample of $\gamma^{(i)}$ given β and τ is drawn from the normal distribution

$$\gamma^i \sim N\left(\gamma^{*(i)}, \left[\sum W_j^T \tau^{-1^{(i-1)}} W_j\right]^{-1}\right). \tag{34}$$

The posterior mean value for γ^* can be calculated as:

$$\gamma^{*(i)} = \left(\sum W_j^T W_j\right)^{-1} \sum W_j^T \beta_j^{(i)}. \tag{35}$$

A sample is drawn from equations 34 and 35 given $\beta^{(i)}$ and $\tau^{(i-1)}$ as follows. Let

$$A^{(i)} = \left(\sum W_j^T \tau^{(i-1)} W_j\right)^{-1}. \tag{36}$$

The matrix $A^{(i)}$ is then factored such that

$$A^{(i)} = B^{(i)}B^{(i)T}, \tag{37}$$

where $B^{(i)}$ is a lower triangular Cholesky factor of $A^{(i)}$. The matrix equation used to generate a new $\gamma^{(i)}$ is

$$\gamma^{(i)} = \gamma^{*(i)} + B^{(i)}x^{(i)}. \tag{38}$$

The column vector $x^{(i)}$ contains elements that are independently and identically distributed $N(0, 1)$.

The new $\gamma^{(i)}$ vector is used to update the posterior distribution of τ. Let

$$C^{(i)} = J^{-1}\sum\left(\beta_j^{(i)} - W_j\gamma^{(i)}\right)\left(\beta_j^{(i)} - W_j\gamma^{(i)}\right)^T. \tag{39}$$

Based on the noninformative inverse Wishart prior distribution with parameters Ψ and υ, the posterior distribution of τ given β and γ is given by

$$\tau \sim W^I(C^{(I)} + \Psi, \; J + \nu) \tag{40}$$

If we assume that the prior precision matrix Ψ approaches 0 and that the prior degrees of freedom parameter υ approaches 0, we can sample τ from

$$\tau \sim W^{-1}(C^{(i)}, \; J). \tag{41}$$

61

To sample τ from equation (41), we find the Cholesky factor of the $C^{(i)}$ such that $C^{(i)} = D^{(i)}D^{(i)}T$, where $D^{(i)}$ is a lower triangular matrix. For $E^{(i)}$, a lower triangular matrix, define

$$F^{(i)} = J^{-1}D^{(i)}E^{(i)}E^{(i)T}D^{(i)T} = J^{-1}(D^{(i)}E^{(i)})(D^{(i)}E^{(i)})^T. \qquad (42)$$

If e_{ij} is an element of E where each e^2_{jj} element on the main diagonal is an independent chi-square variable with J degrees of freedom and the elements below the diagonal are independently distributed $N(0, 1)$, then $F^{(i)}$ will have an inverted Wishart distribution with J degrees of freedom.[16]

This concludes one complete iteration of the Gibbs sampler. To improve the approximation to the posterior distribution of interest the new values for $\gamma^{(i)}$ and $\tau^{(i)}$ are passed to the next iteration to generate new updated values for β and σ^2. This process of calculation and sampling is continued until convergence. After the algorithm has converged, a sequence of m further iterations are performed. The parameter samples resulting from each iteration are collected. This sample of size m of the model's parameters is considered a finite approximation to the true joint posterior distribution.

3.1   The *V*-Known Modification

There are some situations when the dispersion matrix V can be estimated with enough precision to be considered known. This may be a reasonable assumption when the sample size used to compute V is sufficiently large, as in the case of the IEA Reading Literacy Study data from each country. An advantage resulting when the V-known simplifying assumption is tenable is a reduction in the algorithm's computational burden. In this situation, computing an estimate of V and sampling from its posterior distribution every iteration is not required. Another advantage occurs frequently in meta-analysis situations. Typically, access to the raw data is impossible and one is forced to work with summary statistics. For the case where V is considered known, the only modification required of the Gibbs sampler developed above is to skip the estimation and sampling of elements of V such as σ^2. Otherwise the algorithm is the same.

---

[16]M.S. Bartlett. On the Theory of Statistical Regression. *Proceedings of the Royal Statistical Society of Edinburgh*, 53, 260-283, 1933.

A Nine-Country Study: What Were the Differences Between the Low- and High-Performing Students in the IEA Reading Literacy Study?

Karin Taube
University of Umea, Sweden

Jan Mejding
Danish Institute for Educational Research

While it is clear that differences in students' reading ability can be found between countries (Elley 1992, 1994; Ross and Postlethwaite 1992; Linnakylä and Lundberg 1993), differences in reading ability also exist within countries. The goal of the study described in this paper was to investigate whether within-country differences in reading between low- and high-performing students share common traits across countries. The traits in question are those that may originate either from the student, the home background, the teaching and the resources at school, or the resources and reading behavior in the society.

The data analyzed here came from nine countries: Denmark, Finland, France, Germany, Italy, Spain, Sweden, Switzerland, and the United States. The questions addressed are of the following kind: To what extent were the factors of significant importance identical in relation to the students' reading performances in these countries? Was the pattern of important variables the same no matter the country?

1. Method

1.1 Students

Two populations in each country were included in the reading literacy study: Population A, the 9-year-olds, and Population B, the 14-year-olds. The samples were picked to be representative of the populations at these ages in the particular country.

1.2 Instruments

The students' reading abilities were measured by a reading test that included three different types of written material: narrative passages, expository passages, and documents (maps, tables, charts, etc.) (Elley 1992). The tests were scored on an international scale with 500 as the international mean and 100 as one standard deviation. In the current study, the total score based on the results in the three types of passages has been used. Each student also answered a background questionnaire covering such areas as student attitudes, reading behavior, and family circumstances.

1.3 Procedure

Three groups of students—high, medium, and low performing—were identified as a first step. The medium group was designated as a reference group, and the three were characterized as follows:

- *High-performing students:* Those with a reading score > 1.3 standard deviations above the mean;

- *Middle-performing students:* Those with a reading score ±0.13 standard deviations around the mean; and

- *Low-performing students:* Those with a reading score >1.3 standard deviations below the mean.

Given a normal distribution, these cutoff points would assign approximately the top 10 percent, the middle 10 percent, and the lowest 10 percent to the three respective performance groups.

Tables 1 and 2 show for each country the number of students at the two age levels, the grade level tested, and the mean age of the students. The students in Denmark, Finland, Sweden, and Switzerland start school at age 7, while students in France, Germany, Italy, Spain, and the United States start at age 6. This is one of the reasons that different countries test students at different grade levels.

Table 1. **Number of students participating in the IEA Reading Literacy Study, by country, performance group, grade level, and total sample mean age: Population A**

Sample characteristic	Denmark	Finland	France	Germany	Italy	Spain	Sweden	Switzerland	USA	Total
IEA sample size............	3,148	1,462	1,817	2,753	2,216	8,192	4,190	3,306	6,461	33,545
Selected student group	891	419	543	831	657	2,440	1,280	985	1,931	9,977
Grade level tested.........	3	3	4	3	4	4	3	3	4	-
Mean age...	9.8	9.7	10.1	9.4	9.9	10.0	9.8	9.7	10.0	-

- Not applicable.

Table 2. **Number of students participating in the IEA Reading Literacy Study, by country, performance group, grade level, and total sample mean age: Population B**

Sample characteristic	Denmark	Finland	France	Germany	Italy	Spain	Sweden	Switzerland	USA	Total
IEA sample size............	3,582	1,209	2,425	4,062	3,059	8,426	3,361	6,282	3,217	35,623
Selected student group	1,049	361	693	1,223	918	2,509	1,024	1,852	943	10,572
Grade level tested.........	8	8	9	8	8	8	8	8	9	-
Mean age...	14.8	14.7	15.4	14.6	14.1	14.2	14.8	14.9	15.0	-

- Not applicable.

1.4   Variables

A number of background variables from the student questionnaire, assumed to be of importance in relation to reading ability, were studied in both populations (Table 3).

The investigated variables in Population A were as follows:

Student characteristics:
>   age, gender, reading self-image, frequency reading books, frequency reading comics, frequency reading magazines, frequency reading newspapers, frequency borrowing library books.

Home characteristics:
>   number of books at home, a daily newspaper at home, number of meals per week, frequency speaking the language of the reading test at home, hours watching TV, frequency people at home read to student, frequency student reads to someone at home, frequency student reads aloud at home.

The investigated variables in Population B were as follows:

Student characteristics:
>   age, gender, reading self-image, expected further education, frequency borrowing library books.

Home characteristics:
>   parental education, number of books at home, a daily newspaper, number of meals per week, frequency speaking the language of the reading test at home, hours watching TV, job or duties, time spent on job.

School characteristics:
>   frequency reading at school

The Student Characteristics. Age is a somewhat complicated variable. For very young children it is certainly important in relation to reading. For one, before a certain age, children cannot be expected to be able to read at all. However, for teenagers differences in terms of reading performances connected to differences in age tell another story. Students older than their classmates may be in those classes for various reasons: Some may have started school very late. The biological maturation rate differs from individual to individual, and in some countries it is possible to postpone starting school if the child is still considered immature. Others may have been retained in grade because of long periods of absence or because of their failure to meet the educational demands expected by the school system. In some cases, students simply have their birthday in the very first part of the school year and, therefore, are older than their classmates. The first mentioned situations could be expected to be connected to low reading performances, while the latter probably is not.

Table 3. Variables used in the discriminant analyses: Populations A and B

Type of variables	Var. names, Pop A	Var. names, Pop B	Variable labels	Variable definitions
Student characteristics	AGEY	AGEY	Very "young"	student is at least 1.3 standard deviations below the country mean =1; else=0
	AGEO	AGEO	Very "old"	student is at least 1.3 standard deviations above the country mean =1; else=0
	GENDER	GENDER	Boy or girl	boy=0, girl=1
	ASSRATE	BSSRATE	Reading self-image	not very good=1, average=2, good=3, very good=4
		BSEDUCAR	Expected further education	0 year=1, 1 or 2 years=2, etc. more than 10 years=7
	ASBOOKF		Freq reading books	almost never=1, about once a month=2, about once per week=3; almost every day=4
	ASCOMIF		Freq read comics	almost never=1, about once a month=2, about once per week=3; almost every day=4
	ASMAGAF		Freq read magazines	almost never=1, about once a month=2, about once per week=3; almost every day=4
	ASNEWSF		Freq read newspapers	almost never=1, about once a month=2, about once per week=3; almost every day=4
	ASBORBO	BSBORBO	Freq borrow library books	never=1, almost never=2, once a month=3, once per week=4 etc.
Home characteristics		PAREDQ	Parental education	number of years of education for parent with the longest education=PARED 25% lowest PARED=1, 50% middle PARED=2, 25% highest PARED=3
	ASBOOKS	BSBOOKS	Number of books at home	none=0, 1-10=2, 11-50=3, 51-100=4, 101-200=5, >200=6
	NEWS	NEWS	Newspaper at home or not	daily newspaper=1, else=0
	MEALS	MEALS	Meals per week	3 meals 7 days per week=1, else=0
	ASUSLANR	BSUSLANR	Freq speak lang of the reading test at home	never=1, almost never=2, sometimes=3, almost always=4, always=5
	ASTVR	BSTVR	Hours watching TV at home	none=0, up to one hour=0.5, 1-2 = 1.5 ...etc >5 hours=5.5
	TVSQ*	TVSQ*	Hours watching TV at home	ASTVR x ASTVR BSTVR x BSVTVR
	ASPRHTL		People read to student at home	never=1, 1 or 2 times a week=2, 3 or 4 times a week=3, almost every day=4
	ASREATL		Student read to someone at home	never=1, 1 or 2 times a week=2, 3 or 4 times a week=3, almost every day=4
	ASALOUF		Read aloud at home	never=1, <1 hour a week=2, 1-3 times a week=3, nearly every day=4
		JOBNONE	Job or duties	job=1, else=0
		JOB	Time with job	>1 hour per day=1, else=0
School characteristics		BSSREADD	Frequency reading at school	total time spent on school reading per week

*This variable was created because in some countries the relation between TV watching and the test score was not linear.

SOURCE: IEA Reading Literacy Study, 1991.

Students who are younger than their classmates may have parents who started them in school sooner than they were meant to, and these students are likely to be good at reading. Young students may also be those born in the last part of the school year. This may be a disadvantage during their first grades, but it seems reasonable to assume that after 8 or 9 years in school this disadvantage has disappeared.

In this analysis we have focused on the two extreme age groups: AGEO is the older students more than 1.3 standard deviations older than the country mean for that population; AGEY is the younger students more than 1.3 standard deviations below the country mean.

Gender differences have given rise to some concern in the reading research literature. In most cases girls outperform boys (Thorndike 1973; Downing 1972), but there are also examples of the opposite being true (Preston 1962). Two explanations have mainly been brought up in connection with gender differences and reading. One is based on the biological fact that some boys are less mature at school start than girls of the same age, and as a result, these boys face difficulties when trying to learn how to read. The other is of more social/psychological nature, focusing on role modeling: most primary school teachers are females, which makes it easier for girls to identify positively with their teachers and accordingly to learn better.

Though age and gender are important student characteristics, we also have information on student-related variables that give us a more diversified picture. Low-performing students can be distinguished from high-performing students in several ways. One of them is self-esteem (Taube 1988). Low-performing students often have lost faith in their own abilities, and consequently they give up more easily when confronted with demands on performance. Hence, if they perceive reading as difficult, they tend to read less than their peers of same age and instead prefer other activities. The variables ASSRATE and BSSRATE: how good are you at reading? and BSEDUCAR: how much further education do you expect to have in the future? are indicators of the students' perception of their own abilities in reading. The variables ASBORBO and BSBORBO: how often do you borrow a book at the library? BSSREADD: how often do you read at school? and ASBOOKF, ASCOMIF, ASMAGAF, and ASNEWSF: how frequently do you read books, comics, magazines, and newspapers? tell us something about their reading activities, while ASTVR and BSTVR: how much do you watch TV outside school? and TVSQ: the squared function of (A/B)STVR, used because of a nonlinear relationship found in some countries, tell us about another activity strongly competes with reading.

Although the frequency with which the student reads at school can also be thought of as a student-related variable, we have chosen to classify it as related more to the school level. The school, as an organization, can leave more or less room for the students to read on their own during the school hours. However, given the time to read at school, it is expected that the better students will engage more frequently in this activity than the less able students.

The Home Characteristics. Finally, students' home background is often seen to influence school performance: the stronger the educational tradition in the family, the more readily reading material is available in the home. The more often the language in which students receive education is also the language spoken in their homes, the more likely it is that they will perform well at school in reading. A number of variables in this study depict different aspects of home environmental support. PAREDQ: number of years of education for the parent with the most education, ASBOOKS and BSBOOKS: amount of books at home, NEWS: whether a daily newspaper is available at home or not, and ASUSLANR and BSUSLANR: frequency with which the language taught in school is also spoken at home, are all examples of such conditions that are believed either to promote or to obstruct school performance. The same goes for the following three variables: MEALS: whether the student is used to having three regular daily meals or not, JOBNONE: whether the student has a job or other family responsibilities, and JOB: if so, how much time is then spent at that job.

The interesting point is to see whether the power of these variables that are generally accepted as influential remains constant across the nine countries, or if different countries will show different patterns within the functions that separate the high-performing student and the low-performing student from the ordinary student.

1.5   Analysis Procedures

The discriminant analysis used in the current study consisted of both an *interpretation* and a *classification phase*. The interpretation phase was a canonical discriminant analysis. It involved

- Deriving canonical discriminant functions;

- Establishing how many canonical discriminant functions to use;

- Examining the importance of the remaining functions; and

- Interpreting the meaning of the remaining functions for explaining differences between low-, middle-, and high-performing 9- and 14-year-old students.

Canonical Discriminant Analyses. Canonical discriminant function analysis was used to study the characteristic differences among the three performing groups. A canonical discriminant function is a linear combination of discriminating variables and has the following mathematical form (Klecka 1980):

$$f_{km} = u_0 + u_1 X_{1km} + u_2 X_{2km} + \dots + u_p X_{pkm}'$$

where

$f_{km}=$ the value (score) on the canonical discriminant function for the case m in group k;

$X_{ikm}=$ the value on discriminating variable X_i for case m in group k; and

$u_i=$ coefficients to be estimated.

The coefficients for the first function are derived so that the group means on the function differ as much as possible. The coefficients for the second function are derived in the same way. However, the values on the second function are constrained not to be correlated with the values of the first function. The largest number of functions it is possible to derive in this way equals to number of groups minus one. Each dimension can be tested for statistical significance. Functions found to be insignificant can then be ignored.

Selection of Variables. In a first set of runs all the variables described above were used, resulting in the so-called full model. To reduce the number of variables, we ran a stepwise discriminant analysis with backward elimination. This works in much the same way as backward elimination in multiple regression. The analysis starts by using all variables. At each step the least important variable will be excluded until only those of significant importance for the discrimination between the groups are left—the so-called reduced model.

When interpreting the results, levels of significance, percentage of correctly classified, etc., it should be remembered that they pertain only to the chosen subsample of approximately 10 percent low-, medium-, and high-performing students, respectively.

2.   Results

2.1   Between-Country Analysis

To get an impression of how the three performance groups scored on the reading test within and among countries, we plotted the mean results from the three groups according to their reading accuracy and their reading speed. In this case reading accuracy was based on a scale that took into consideration only the attempted items, and reading speed was the percentage of items attempted within the given time limit.

Figure 1 shows the results for the 9-year-old population. There are clear differences between the performance groups within each country, and within the middle- and low-performing group, there are differences among countries. It is noteworthy that in the low-performing group the mean completion rate for the United States was as high as 95 percent, while in Denmark it was only 52 percent.

Figure 2 shows the results for the 14-year-old population. Again, we find clear within-country differences, and, in the low-performing group, between-country differences as well.

2.2   Interpretation Phase

Stepwise canonical discriminant analysis was used to get a total model and a reduced model for each country. Only the reduced models will be discussed here.

Using One or Two Functions. The order of importance of the functions is known since the functions are derived in descending order of importance with the first function providing the greatest discrimination. The second function contributes with the greatest power after the power of the first function has been removed. In our case, the maximum number of unique functions would be two since we used three groups of students. But are both the derived functions statistically and substantively significant? Even a statistically significant function may be considered of less importance if it does not discriminate among the three groups well enough. Although the first function always is the relatively most powerful one, it may only show a weak relationship with the groups (Klecka 1980). The canonical correlation coefficients summarize the relationship between the discriminant function and the groups. A high canonical correlation coefficient, close to 1.0, shows a strong such relation. A comparison of how much of the total discriminating power each of the functions contributes is also valuable in terms of evaluating their importance.

Figure 1. Reading performance, by group and country: Population A

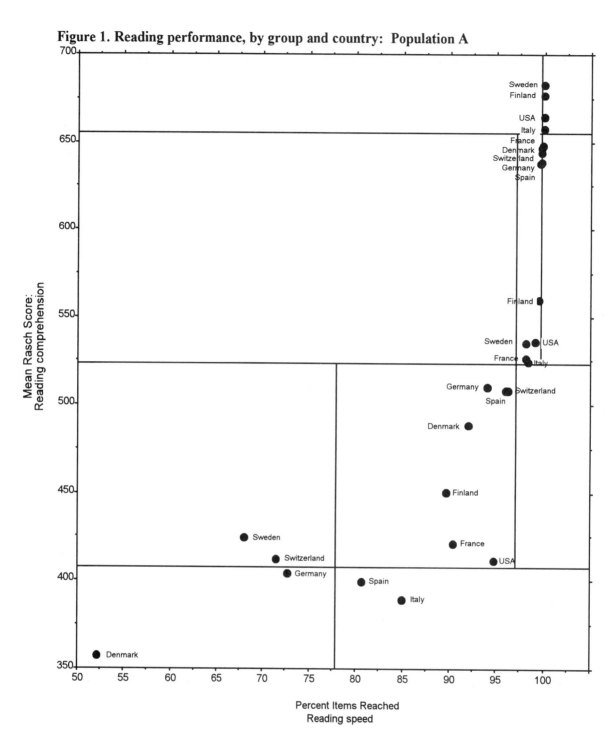

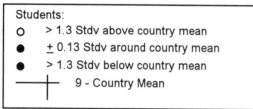

Students:

○   > 1.3 Stdv above country mean

●   ± 0.13 Stdv around country mean

●   > 1.3 Stdv below country mean

┼   9 - Country Mean

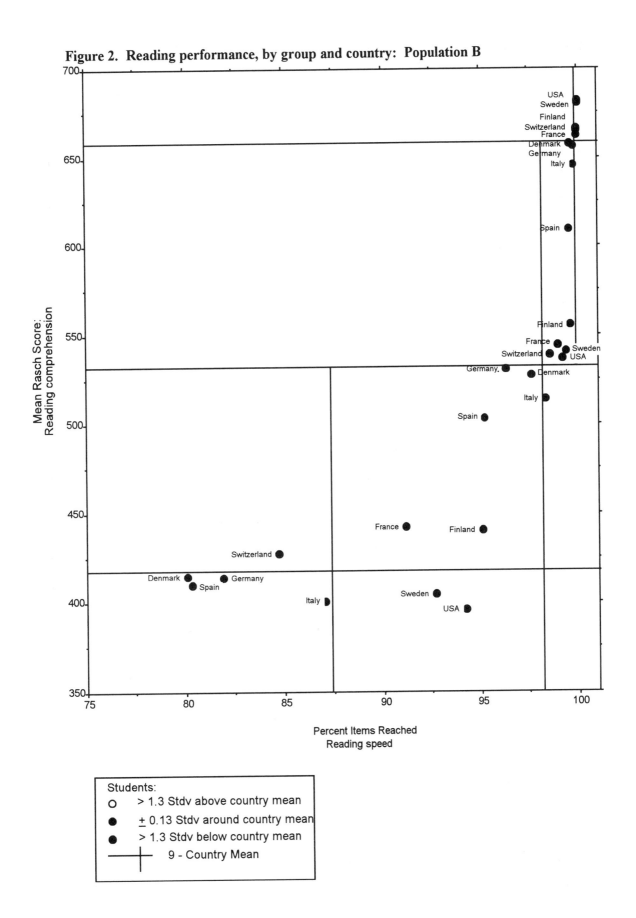

Figure 2. Reading performance, by group and country: Population B

Mean Rasch Score: Reading comprehension

Percent Items Reached
Reading speed

Students:
○ > 1.3 Stdv above country mean
● ± 0.13 Stdv around country mean
● > 1.3 Stdv below country mean
┼ 9 - Country Mean

Klecka (1980) recommends an examination of both the canonical correlation coefficients and the relative percentage of the discriminating power. Tables 4 and 5 show the canonical correlation coefficients, the percentage of the total discriminating power, and the statistical significance for the two functions in the reduced models for Populations A and B in each of the nine countries.

Table 4. **Canonical correlation coefficients, percentage of the total discriminating power, and significance for the two canonical discriminant functions in the reduced models for the nine countries: Population A**

Country	Canonical discriminant function number	Canonical correlation coefficient	Percent of the total discriminant power	Pr>F
Denmark..	1	0.71	97.8	0.0001
	2	0.51	2.2	0.0171
Finland	1	0.62	90.7	0.0001
	2	0.24	9.3	0.0196
France...	1	0.60	96.3	0.0001
	2	0.14	3.7	0.0277
Germany..	1	0.64	93.2	0.0001
	2	0.22	6.8	0.0130
Italy..	1	0.50	83.2	0.0001
	2	0.25	16.9	0.0001
Spain	1	0.63	95.8	0.0001
	2	0.13	4.3	0.0001
Sweden..	1	0.66	97.4	0.0001
	2	0.14	2.6	0.0095
Switzerland....................................	1	0.71	94.0	0.0001
	2	0.24	6.0	0.0001
USA...	1	0.55	97.6	0.0001
	2	0.10	2.4	0.0383

SOURCE: IEA Reading Literacy Study, 1991.

As Table 4 shows, the canonical correlation for the first functions in Population A varied between 0.50 and 0.71. The relationship between the discriminant function and the groups seemed to be highest in Denmark (0.71) and Switzerland (0.71) and lowest in Italy (0.50) and the United States (0.55).

The percentage of the total discriminating power for the first function in the nine countries varied between 83.2 percent and 97.8 percent. Denmark (97.8 percent) and the United States (97.6 percent) had the first function with the highest percentage and Italy (83.2 percent) the first function with the lowest percentage of the total discriminating power. All the first functions were highly statistically significant.

In all cases, the second function showed a much lower canonical correlation with the groups (0.10-0.25) and percentage of the total discriminating power (2.2 percent-16.9 percent). In relation to the other countries, Italy seemed to be the one with a second function of most importance, while the second discriminant functions for Denmark and the United States were of minor importance.

Table 5. Canonical correlation coefficients, percentage of the total discriminating power, and significance for the two canonical discriminant functions in the reduced models for the nine countries: Population B

Country	Canonical discriminant function number	Canonical correlation coefficient	Percent of the total discriminant power	Pr>F
Denmark	1	0.74	97.1	0.0001
	2	0.19	2.9	0.0002
Finland	1	0.66	99.3	0.0001
	2	0.07	0.7	0.8829
France	1	0.70	98.9	0.0001
	2	0.10	1.1	0.3444
Germany	1	0.73	95.1	0.0001
	2	0.23	4.9	0.0001
Italy	1	0.67	98.2	0.0001
	2	0.12	1.8	0.1312
Spain	1	0.68	96.5	0.0001
	2	0.18	3.5	0.0001
Sweden	1	0.68	96.6	0.0001
	2	0.17	3.4	0.0010
Switzerland	1	0.64	94.9	0.0001
	2	0.19	5.1	0.0001
USA	1	0.70	91.7	0.0001
	2	0.28	8.2	0.0001

SOURCE: IEA Reading Literacy Study, 1991.

As is shown in Table 5, the canonical correlation for the first functions in Population B varied between 0.64 and 0.74. The relationship between the discriminant function and the groups seemed to be highest in Denmark (0.74) and Germany (0.73) and lowest in Switzerland (0.64).

The percentage of the total discriminating power for the functions varied between 91.7 percent and 99.3 percent, with Finland having the first function with the highest percentage of the total discriminating power (99.3 percent) and the United States having the lowest (91.7 percent). All the first functions were statistically significant. There seemed to be strong evidence for considering the first functions in all countries as substantively meaningful with a fairly high level of utility in explaining group differences.

As expected the second functions showed much lower canonical correlation with the groups (0.07 to 0.28) and much lower percentages of total discriminating power (0.7 percent to 8.2 percent). In relation to the other countries, the United States and Germany seemed to be the ones with the most important second function, while the second discriminant functions for Finland, France, and Italy were not even significant. For the latter countries, only the first functions will be used for further analyses.

2.3   The Most Important Structure Coefficients

A step towards understanding the meaning of the derived functions involves examination of the relations between the individual background variables and the functions. This can be done using two kinds of information: the standardized discriminant coefficients and the total structure coefficients.

The standardized discriminant coefficient tell us the relative importance of the individual background variables in terms of contribution to the discriminant score. The total structure coefficients show the correlation between each individual variable and the discriminant function. Klecka (1980) suggests that the function in question should be "named" after including variables having the highest structure coefficients, since these identify what kind of information in the function gives us most discrimination between groups.

The use of standardized coefficients to evaluate the importance of a certain variable has a serious limitation, and the total structure coefficients may be a better guide to the meaning of the canonical discriminant functions (Klecka 1980). The limitation brought up by Klecka concerns the fact that two highly correlated variables sharing almost the same discriminating information have to share their contribution to the score. As a result, it may happen that their standardized coefficients are smaller than would be the case if only one of the two variables was used.

Table 6 shows the most important structure coefficients for the first functions in Population A in all the countries.

Table 6. The most important structure coefficients for the first functions: Population A

Country	Var. 1	Coeff	Var. 2	Coeff	Var. 3	Coeff	Var. 4	Coeff
Denmark......	ASSRATE	0.88	ASNEWSF	0.49	ASCOMIF	0.44	ASBOOKF	0.38
Finland	ASSRATE	0.76	ASBOOKF	0.41	AGEO	-0.39	GENDER	0.29
France..........	ASSRATE	0.87	AGEO	-0.53	ASUSLANR	0.35	MEALS	0.26
Germany......	ASSRATE	0.84	ASBOOKS	0.63	ASBOOKF	0.47	NEWS	0.39
Italy	ASSRATE	0.74	AGEO	-0.49	ASBOOKS	0.47	ASCOMIF	0.46
Spain	ASSRATE	0.75	AGEO	-0.55	ASBOOKS	0.55	ASBOOKF	0.40
Sweden........	ASSRATE	0.74	ASNEWSF	0.51	ASBOOKF	0.37	ASREATL	-0.35
Switzerland..	ASSRATE	0.86	ASBOOKF	0.49	ASBOOKS	0.43	ASUSLANR	0.36
USA.............	ASSRATE	0.74	TVSQ	-0.42	ASCOMIF	-0.37	MEALS	0.34

KEY:
ASSRATE	=	reading self-image
NEWS	=	newspaper at home
ASBOOKF	=	freq. reading books;
AGEO	=	very "old";
ASBOOKS	=	number of books at home;
ASNEWSF	=	freq. reading newspapers;
TVSQ	=	hours watching TV at home;
ASCOMIF	=	freq. reading comics;
ASUSLANR	=	freq. speaking the language of the test at home;
ASREATL	=	student read to someone at home
MEALS	=	meals per week
GENDER	=	student gender

SOURCE: IEA Reading Literacy Study, 1991.

74

To summarize Population A:

- In all countries, **reading self-image** was the strongest discriminating variable.

- In Finland, France, Italy, and Spain being **overaged** was an important discriminating factor.

- The United States was the only country in which **watching TV** was a factor with strong discriminating power.

- **Number of books at home** had substantial discriminating power in Germany, Spain, Italy, and Switzerland.

- **Frequency of book reading** showed discriminating power in Switzerland, Finland, Germany, Sweden, Denmark, and Spain.

- **Frequency of reading comics** was important in the United States, Denmark, and Italy. However, in the United States, it was the low-performing students who most often read comics, while in Denmark and Italy, this activity was done most often by the high-performing students.

- Denmark and Sweden were the only countries where **frequency of reading newspapers** showed strong discriminating influence.

- Meals showed discriminating power in the United States and France.

Table 7 shows the most important structure coefficients for the first functions in Population B in all the countries.

Table 7. The most important structure coefficients for the first function: Population B

Country	Var. 1	Coeff	Var. 2	Coeff	Var. 3	Coeff	Var. 4	Coeff
Denmark......	BSSRATE	0.82	BSEDUCAR	0.62	BSBOOKS	0.61	PAREDQ	0.54
Finland	BSSRATE	0.70	BSEDUCAR	0.61	BSBORBO	0.52	JOBNONE	0.43
France..........	BSEDUCAR	0.81	BSBOOKS	0.68	BSSRATE	0.64	AGEO	-0.47
Germany......	BSBOOKS	0.84	BSEDUCAR	0.68	BSSRATE	0.53	BSTVR	0.30
Italy	BSEDUCAR	0.82	BSSRATE	0.75	BSBOOKS	0.61	PAREDQ	0.61
Spain	BSEDUCAR	0.85	BSSRATE	0.70	BSBOOKS	0.69	AGEO	-0.52
Sweden	BSSRATE	0.78	BSEDUCAR	0.67	BSBOOKS	0.61	BSSREADD	0.43
Switzerland..	BSSRATE	0.67	BSBOOKS	0.67	PAREDQ	0.61	BSEDUCAR	0.49
USA.............	BSSRATE	0.73	BSEDUCAR	0.60	BSBOOKS	0.59	AGEO	-0.52

KEY: BSSRATE   = reading self-image
           BSEDUCAR   = expected further education
           BSBOOKS   = number of books at home
           BSBORBO   = freq. borrowing library books
           PAREDQ   = parental education
           JOBNONE   = having a job or duties
           AGEO   = very "old";
           BSTVR   = hours watching TV at home
           BSSREADD   = freq. reading at school
SOURCE: IEA Reading Literacy Study, 1991.

To summarize Population B:

- Although the rank order of the variables varied between the countries, **reading self-image, expected further education,** and **number of books at home** were the three most discriminating variables in seven of the nine countries.

- In Denmark, Sweden, and the United States **reading self-image, expected further education,** and **number of books at home** were the most significant discriminant variables.

- In Italy and Spain **expected further education, reading self-image,** and **number of books at home** were most important variables, and in the order shown.

- Germany and France were similar since **expected further education, number of books at home,** and **reading self-image** were their most discriminating variables. However, in Germany the most discriminating variable was number of books at home, while in France it was expected further education.

- In Finland **reading self-image, expected further education,** and **frequency borrowing books** were the most important discriminant variables.

- In Switzerland **reading self-image** and **number of books** showed equal discriminant power followed by **parental education** and **expected further education.**

3.   **Conclusion**

As the term "reading self-image" suggests, the high- and low-performing students during the first years of schooling soon become aware how well they are doing compared to other children. The developed reading self-image probably will influence the students' evaluation of their ability to succeed in further education. Home background clearly is an important factor in this respect. The availability of reading material at home (ASBOOKS, NEWS), the language of the home (ASUSLANR), and the regularity of meals (MEALS) play a role in six of the nine Population A countries. In Population B, books in the home (BSBOOKS) and parental education (PAREDQ) play a role in eight of the nine countries examined. Student activities also differentiate between the high- and low-performing students: generally, the more often the students are engaged in reading books, newspapers, and comics, the better they are at reading. But some student activities may also count in the opposite direction, as the results from the United States show: here extensive television viewing and comic reading are correlates of lower reading ability. Finally, if the country allows for grade repetition for students that do not meet the academic requirements, then age becomes a factor for the low-performing students—indicating that grade repetition in itself does not eliminate reading problems.

As the students grow older, the influence of the home background factors seems to become even stronger. Parental education, the availability of books at home, reading self-image, and the length of the expected future education fit perfectly to our stereotypes of high- and low-performing students. However, such student activities as borrowing books at the library and reading on one's own at school may also indicate high-performing students in some countries.

3.1   Classification Phase

The classification phase involves classifying the students into the low, medium, and high groups according to the discriminant function. In this phase, each individual was classified into the group with the highest score on a discriminant function. This function is determined by a measure of generalized squared distance from the individual to the respective group centroids, so that the individual is classified into the closest group. (Distance is measured in an n-dimensional space for n variables, and the group centroid is the position of the group means of the variables in this space.)

The discriminant function used here is built directly on the discriminating variables. Classification can also be based on the canonical discriminant functions from the canonical discriminant analysis. However, "the final classifications will generally be identical" (Klecka 1980, 47).

The measure of interest in this phase is the percentage of correctly classified students. As the same students were used both for derivation of the discriminant function and for classification, this is a biased estimate of the probability of correct classification. It will tend to overestimate the power of the classification procedure.

Table 8 shows the percentage of correctly classified students in Population A in each of the performance groups and in total for each country with the countries ordered by the percent correctly classified overall. Table 9 show the corresponding data for Population B.

Table 8. Percentage of correctly classified students, by country: Population A

Country	Percent correctly classified as low-performing students	Percent correctly classified as middle-performing students	Percent correctly classified as high-performing students	Percent correctly classified
Denmark..............	75.77	40.30	77.91	64.66
Sweden...............	67.67	38.57	78.35	61.53
Finland	63.54	47.47	72.41	61.14
Switzerland..........	62.03	39.15	81.06	60.74
Germany..............	24.66	27.66	86.67	59.05
Spain	53.18	36.72	80.79	56.90
USA....................	58.21	39.25	73.17	56.87
Italy	21.98	40.55	76.33	55.52
France.................	52.08	15.63	92.51	53.41
Mean	53.24	36.14	79.91	58.87

SOURCE: IEA Reading Literacy Study, 1991.

Table 9. Percentage of correctly classified students, by country: Population B

Country	Percent correctly classified as low-performing students	Percent correctly classified as middle-performing students	Percent correctly classified as high-performing students	Percent correctly classified
Finland	71.57	50.40	72.41	64.79
Denmark	62.69	50.27	80.50	64.49
Italy	65.64	49.85	74.02	63.17
Germany	61.06	47.69	80.24	62.99
USA......................	48.03	57.05	81.75	62.28
Spain	58.91	37.60	85.73	60.75
France..................	63.21	33.75	83.89	60.28
Sweden	46.46	51.47	80.80	59.58
Switzerland...........	65.17	31.56	75.88	57.54
Mean	60.30	45.52	79.47	61.76

SOURCE: IEA Reading Literacy Study, 1991.

As shown in Tables 8 and 9, in all countries and both populations, the highest performance group had the highest percentage of correctly classified students. With a few exceptions (i.e., Italy and Germany in Population A; the United States and Sweden in Population B), it was most difficult to classify students correctly to the middle performance group. A comparison of the two populations revealed that it was somewhat easier to classify students in Population B than in Population A, mainly because of a better ability to classify the low- and middle-performing students in the former than the latter.   The highest percentage of correctly classified students in Population A were in the three Nordic countries, and in Population B, in Finland, Denmark, and Italy. The lowest percentage of correctly classified students in Population A were in France, and in Population B, in Switzerland.

3.2   Within-Country Analysis

Relations between the variables and the function. As mentioned earlier, an examination of the relations between the individual background variables and the functions can be done using the standardized discriminant coefficients and the total structure coefficients. Both coefficients will be listed in the tables that follow: the standardized discriminant coefficient shows the relative importance of the individual background variables in terms of contribution to the discriminant score, and the total structure coefficients shows the correlation between each variable and the discriminant function.

Plotting centroids to understand the meaning. With only two discriminant functions the location of the data cases can easily be plotted. However, if the number of cases is large, as in the current study, the result will become a blur. One way of avoiding that outcome is to compute "centroids," which serve to summarize the position of groups. The centroids of each group can then be plotted. In the following figures the centroids for each performance group within each country and for both populations have been plotted to illustrate the extent to which the functions discriminate between the groups.

3.2.1 Denmark

Population A

Relations between the variables and the function. Table 10 presents standardized discriminant functions and the structure coefficients for the first and second functions in Denmark. As shown, nine variables were kept in the reduced model for Denmark. The reading self-image (ASSRATE) and frequency of reading different reading materials seem to be most important for the first function and gender for the second function.

Table 10. **Standardized discriminant and structure coefficients for the first and second functions in Denmark: Population A**

| \multicolumn{4}{c}{Function 1 "Self, Newsp. & Comics"} | | | | \multicolumn{4}{c}{Function 2 "Gender"} | | | |
Variable	Stand coeff	Variable	Struct coeff	Variable	Stand coeff	Variable	Struct coeff
ASSRATE	0.99	ASSRATE	0.88	ASMAGAF	0.72	GENDER	0.65
ASREATL	-0.40	ASNEWSF	0.49	GENDER	0.56	ASMAGAF	0.57
ASNEWSF	0.27	ASCOMIF	0.44	ASCOMIF	-0.34	ASREATL	0.29
AGEO	-0.25	ASBOOKF	0.38	ASNEWSF	-0.28	ASCOMIF	-0.25
ASCOMIF	0.20	ASREATL	-0.34	ASREATL	0.25	AGEO	-0.17
ASBOOKF	0.17	ASMAGAF	0.30	AGEO	-0.08	ASNEWSF	-0.17
GENDER	0.15	ASBOOKS	0.24	ASSRATE	0.08	ASBOOKS	-0.15
ASBOOKS	0.12	AGEO	-0.22	ASBOOKS	-0.06	ASBOOKF	0.14
ASMAGAF	0.07	GENDER	0.15	ASBOOKF	-0.00	ASSRATE	0.03

SOURCE: IEA Reading Literacy Study, 1991.

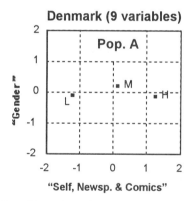

Denmark (9 variables)

Figure 3. Two-function plot of group centroids for low- (L), middle- (M) and high- (H) performing students in Denmark for Population A

Using centroids to understand the meaning. Figure 3 shows three very different groups for the first function. The students in the high-performing group have a better reading self-image and more often read newspapers, comics, and books. For the second function, the low- and high-performance groups were fairly close and the middle group was apart. Gender was the critical factor for the second function. There was a higher percentage of females in the middle group than in the other two. In the low-performing group, there was a higher percentage of males as compared to the other groups.

Population B

Relations between the variables and the function. Table 11 presents the standardized discriminant coefficients and the structure coefficients for the first and second functions for Population B in Denmark. As shown, as many as 11 variables could offer significant contributions to the reduced model for Denmark. The three variables in the top for the first function were reading self-image (BSSRATE), expected further education (BSEDUCAR), and number of books at home (BSBOOKS) and the function was labeled "Self,

Further Ed & Books." The second function was more difficult to interpret. Obviously, gender, home language, job outside school, and TV viewing were involved. However, gender dominated, and thus the function was named after that variable.

Table 11. **Standardized discriminant and structure coefficients for the first and second functions in Denmark: Population B**

Function 1 "Self, Further Ed. & Books"				Function 2 "Gender"			
Variable	Stand coeff	Variable	Struct coeff	Variable	Stand coeff	Variable	Struct coeff
BSSRATE	0.84	BSSRATE	0.82	TVSQ	1.78	GENDER	-0.45
TVSQ	-0.45	BSEDUCAR	0.62	BSTVR	-1.53	BSUSLANR	-0.37
BSEDUCAR	0.39	BSBOOKS	0.61	GENDER	-0.52	JOB	-0.35
BSBOOKS	0.33	PAREDQ	0.54	BSBORBO	0.42	TVSQ	0.34
PAREDQ	0.22	TVSQ	-0.37	JOB	-0.31	BSBORBO	0.34
BSUSLANR	0.19	BSTVR	-0.35	BSEDUCAR	0.30	BSEDUCAR	0.27
JOB	-0.16	BSBORBO	0.28	BSUSLANR	-0.27	AGEO	0.24
BSTVR	0.16	BSUSLANR	0.26	AGEO	0.18	BSTVR	0.23
AGEO	-0.14	AGEO	-0.24	PAREDQ	0.14	PAREDQ	0.18
GENDER	-0.08	JOB	-0.21	BSSRATE	-0.14	BSBOOKS	-0.08
BSBORBO	0.07	GENDER	0.08	BSBOOKS	0.10	BSSRATE	-0.01

SOURCE: IEA Reading Literacy Study, 1991.

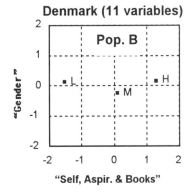

Denmark (11 variables)

Figure 4. Two-function plot of group centroids for low- (L), middle- (M) and high- (H) performing students in Denmark for Population B

Using the centroids to understand the meaning. Figure 4 shows the group centroids for the two functions. The three performance groups are very different on the first function. According to the standardized group means for the most important variables, the better readers have a better reading self-image, expect more further education, and have more books at home than the other two groups of students. On the second function the group differences are much smaller. However, gender stands out as the most important variable for the function. The group means for gender revealed that the highest percentage of females can be found in the middle- performing group.

The highest percentage of males can be found in the low-performing group, while there is an almost similar percentage of males and females in the high-performing group.

To summarize the data for Denmark:

- The three performance groups could be distinguished on the basis of 9 variables in Population A and 11 variables in Population B.

- The most important discriminating variables in Population A were reading self-image, frequency reading newspapers, and frequency reading comics; in Population B, reading self-image, expected further education, and number of books at home.

- The canonical correlation for the first function was a little higher in Population B than in Population A, while the percentage of the total discriminant power for the first function was almost the same in the two populations.

- Denmark had the highest canonical correlation of all nine countries for the first discriminant function in both populations, though sharing this status with Switzerland in Population A.

3.2.2 Finland

Population A

Relations between the variables and the function. Table 12 shows the standardized discriminant coefficients and the structure coefficients for the first and second functions for Population A in Finland. As shown, only 8 of 18 variables remained in the reduced models for Finland. Reading self-image (ASSRATE) was the most important discriminant factor for the first function, and it was called "Self, Bookreading & Age" after its most important structure coefficients. The most important variable for the second function was frequency people read to the student at home (ASPRHTL), and the second function got its name from that variable.

Table 12. Standardized discriminant and structure coefficients for the first and second functions in Finland: Population A

Function 1 "Self, Bookreading & Age"				Function 2 "People at home read"			
Variable	Stand coeff	Variable	Struct coeff	Variable	Stand coeff	Variable	Struct coeff
ASSRATE	0.87	ASSRATE	0.76	ASPRHTL	0.76	ASPRHTL	0.80
GENDER	0.38	ASBOOKF	0.41	ASCOMIF	0.55	ASCOMIF	0.64
AGEO	-0.38	AGEO	-0.39	AGEO	-0.23	AGEO	-0.18
ASCOMIF	0.37	GENDER	0.29	ASSRATE	-0.15	ASALOUF	0.12
ASBOOKF	0.33	ASCOMIF	0.28	AGEY	0.10	AGEY	0.11
ASALOUF	-0.26	ASALOUF	-0.23	GENDER	-0.08	GENDER	-0.05
ASPRHTL	-0.24	ASPRHTL	-0.12	ASALOUF	0.05	ASSRATE	-0.04
AGEY	-0.23	AGEY	-0.05	ASBOOKF	-0.00	ASBOOKF	0.00

SOURCE: IEA Reading Literacy Study, 1991.

Finland (8 variables)

"Self, Book reading & Age"

Figure 5. Two-function plot of group centroids for low- (L), middle- (M) and high- (H) performing students in Finland for Population A

Using centroids to understand the meaning. In Figure 5, the centroids for the low- (L), middle- (M) and high- (H) performing groups on the two functions for Population A in Finland are presented. As shown, the group means for the three groups are clearly distinguishable for the first function. The middle- and high-performing students are somewhat closer to each other in comparison with the low- performing group on the first function. On the second function, the middle-performing students seem to have a more positive value than both the other groups. Thus, the first and most important function discriminated among the low-, middle- and high-performing groups on the basis of eight variables, of which reading self-image, frequency reading books, and age were the most important.

An inspection of the total-sample standardized group means for these three important discriminating variables showed that the students in the low-performing group had the lowest reading self-image, seldom read books, and were older to a higher extent than students in the other groups. Furthermore, the high-performing 9-year-old students in Finland are quite the opposite. They have a better reading self-image, read books more often, and are seldom overaged in comparison with the students in the low-performing group. From the second function and the group means, it is obvious that people at home read most often to the middle-performing students, seldom to the low-performing, and very seldom to the high-performing students.

Population B

Relations between the variables and the function. Table 13 shows the standardized discriminant coefficients and the structure coefficients for the first function for Population B in Finland. As a closer look at the two types of coefficients in the table revealed, only two of the six variables left in the reduced model—job and frequency watching TV (JOBNONE and TVSQ)—had lower rank when compared among the structure coefficients than among the standardized coefficients. These two variables also had very weak correlation both with each other and with the other variables in the table. Thus, the standardized discriminant coefficients for these variables could not have yielded a higher rank than they "deserved" because the variables were highly correlated with each other or with any of the other variables.

Among the remaining four variables in the reduced model, there were some moderate correlations, as between frequency reading at school (BSSREADD) and frequency borrowing library books (BSBORBO) (corr=.31) and between reading self-image (BSSRATE) and BSBORBO (corr=.30), which could have been the reason for the lower positions of these variables among the standardized discriminant coefficients than among the structure coefficients (Klecka 1980). A comparison of the latter coefficients showed that BSSRATE, expected further education (BSEDUCAR), and BSBORBO had the highest correlation with the discriminant function. Reading self-image and expected further education are conceptually connected. A high self-image will often involve higher expectations and higher aspirations. Furthermore, since a good reading ability is of crucial importance in connection with success in education, it seems reasonable to assume that a student with a good reading ability expects many years of further education. This function is labeled "Self, Aspir. and Borrow" after its three most important structure coefficients: reading self-image, expected further education, and frequency borrowing books.

Table 13. **Standardized discriminant and structure coefficients for the first function in Finland: Population B**

Function 1		Function 1 "Self, Aspir. & Borrow"	
Variable	Standard Coefficients	Variable	Structure Coefficients
BSSRATE	0.62	BSSRATE	0.70
JOBNONE	0.59	BSEDUCAR	0.61
BSEDUCAR	0.45	BSBORBO	0.52
BSBORBO	0.37	JOBNONE	0.43
TVSQ	-0.32	BSSREADD	0.42
BSSREADD	0.21	TVSQ	-0.27

SOURCE: IEA Reading Literacy Study, 1991.

Using centroids to understand the meaning. Only the first function was significant in Finland. The class means on the canonical variables for the high- (H), middle- (M) and low- (L) performing groups were 0.99, 0.08 and -1.21, respectively. Thus, the groups were clearly distinguishable, with the distance between the high- and middle-performing groups somewhat smaller than between the middle- and the low-performing groups. The high-performing group could be distinguished from the middle- and low-performing students from their better reading self-image, longer expected further education, and a higher frequency of borrowing books.

To summarize the data for Finland:

- The canonical correlation and the percentage of the total discriminant power for   the first function was higher in Population B than in Population A.

- In Population B, only the first function was significant.

- The three performing groups could be distinguished on the basis of eight variables in Population A and six variables in Population B.

- The most important discriminating variables in Population A were reading self-image, frequency of book reading, and age; and in Population B, reading self-image, expected further education, and frequency borrowing books.

3.2.3 France

Population A

Relations between the variables and the function. Table 14 presents the standardized discriminant coefficients and the structure coefficients for the first and the second functions in France. As shown, only 5 of the 18 variables were left in the reduced model. The first function was dominated by reading self-image (ASSRATE) and age (AGEO), while the dominating variable for the second function was language at home (ASUSLANR). The first function was named "Self & Age," and the second, "Language."

The second function concentrated on language at home. The high-performing students spoke the language of the reading test more often and had a better reading self-image than the other groups. The low-performing group consisted to a higher extent of students who were overaged.

Table 14. **Standardized discriminant and structure coefficients for the first and second functions in France: Population A**

Function 1 "Self & Age"				Function 2 "Language"			
Variable	Stand coeff	Variable	Struct coeff	Variable	Stand coeff	Variable	Struct coeff
ASSRATE	1.01	ASSRATE	0.87	ASUSLANR	-0.71	ASUSLANR	-0.68
AGEO	-0.37	AGEO	-0.53	AGEO	0.48	AGEO	0.46
ASUSLANR	0.30	ASUSLANR	0.35	MEALS	0.42	MEALS	0.32
ASREATL	-0.27	MEALS	0.26	ASSRATE	0.38	ASSRATE	0.31
MEALS	0.05	ASREATL	-0.23	ASREATL	-0.27	ASREATL	-0.17

SOURCE: IEA Reading Literacy Study, 1991.

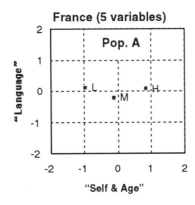

France (5 variables)

Using centroids to understand the meaning. Figure 6 shows the centroids of the group means on the canonical variables for low-, middle-, and high-performing students in France. For the first function the three group means are clearly distinguishable. For the second function the class means for the low- and the high-performing groups are very close, while the middle group seems to deviate from the others. Thus, the three performance groups can be discriminated in terms of reading self-image and age. The high-performing students have a much better reading self-image than the low-performing group. The low-performing students are older than the students in the other groups.

Figure 6. **Two-function plot of group centroids for low- (L), middle- (M), and high-(H) performing students in France for Population A**

Population B

Relations between the variables and the function. Table 15 presents the standardized discriminant coefficients and the structure coefficients for the first function for Population B in France. As shown, the rank order for the seven remaining variables in the reduced model was much the same for the standardized coefficients and the structure coefficients. The variables BSEDUCAR, BSBOOKS, and BSSRATE were relatively highly correlated (.34 to .37) and thus had higher total structure coefficients than standardized discriminant coefficients. A possible name for this function would be "Aspir., Books & Self," indicating the high importance of expected further education, number of books at home, and reading self-concept in discriminating between different performing groups in France. Although not as important as the three most important variables, age (AGEO) seemed to be of certain significance too. This fact may reflect the relatively high retention rate in France, and consequently, the older students may not be the best readers.

Table 15. **Standardized discriminant and structure coefficients for the first function in France: Population B**

Function 1		Function 1 "Aspir., Books and Self"	
Variable	Standard Coefficients	Variable	Structure Coefficients
BSEDUCAR	0.70	BSEDUCAR	0.81
BSBOOKS	0.42	BSBOOKS	0.68
BSSRATE	0.41	BSSRATE	0.64
AGEO	-0.25	AGEO	-0.47
JOB	-0.20	BSUSLANR	0.31
BSUSLANR	0.18	JOB	-0.31
BSTVR	-0.15	BSTVR	-0.26

SOURCE: IEA Reading Literacy Study, 1991.

Using centroids to understand the meaning. The group means on the canonical variables for the high-, middle-, and low-performing groups in France on the first and only significant discriminant function were 1.04, 0.02, and -1.34, respectively, and, thus, they were highly discriminating.

To summarize the data for France:

- The canonical correlation and the percentage of the total discriminant power for the first function in France was slightly higher in Population B than in Population A.

- Only the first function was significant in Population B.

- The three performance groups could be distinguished on the basis of five variables in Population A and seven variables in Population B.

- The most important discriminating variables in Population A were reading self-image and age; and in Population B, expected further education, number of books at home, and reading self-image.

3.2.4 Germany

Population A

Relations between the variables and the function. Table 16 presents the standardized discriminant coefficients and the structure coefficients for the first and second functions for Population A in Germany. As shown, eight variables contributed significantly to the reduced model for Population A in Germany.

Reading self-image, number of books at home, and frequency of reading books were the variables with the highest correlation with the first function. For the second function, number of books at home was the most significant variable.

Table 16. **Standardized discriminant and structure coefficients for the first and second functions in Germany: Population A**

Function 1 "Self & Books"				Function 2 "Books"			
Variable	Stand coeff	Variable	Struct coeff	Variable	Stand coeff	Variable	Struct coeff
ASSRATE	0.79	ASSRATE	0.84	ASBOOKS	0.79	ASBOOKS	0.55
ASBOOKS	0.43	ASBOOKS	0.63	ASBOOKF	-0.71	ASBOOKF	-0.46
ASALOUF	-0.26	ASBOOKF	0.47	TVSQ	-0.39	TVSQ	-0.26
AGEO	-0.24	NEWS	0.39	AGEO	0.35	AGEO	0.24
ASBOOKF	0.23	AGEO	0.35	ASSRATE	-0.17	AGEY	0.20
AGEY	-0.22	AGEY	-0.24	NEWS	0.14	ASALOUF	-0.17
NEWS	0.20	TVSQ	-0.19	AGEY	0.13	ASSRATE	-0.13
TVSQ	-0.04	ASALOUF	-0.14	ASALOUF	-0.07	NEWS	0.09

SOURCE: IEA Reading Literacy Study, 1991.

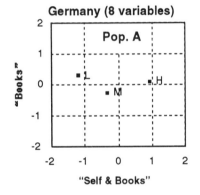

Figure 7. Two-function plot of group centroids for low- (L), middle- (M), and high- (H) performing students in Germany for Population A

Using centroids to understand the meaning. Figure 7 shows the centroids for the three performance groups on the two functions. As expected, the group centroids are well separated for the first function and close for the second function. An inspection of the standardized group means shows a picture of the high-performing students as students who have many books at home, good reading self-image, read books frequently, and watch TV less often than the students in the other groups.

Population B

Relations between the variables and the function. Table 17 presents the standardized discriminant coefficients and the structure coefficients for the first and second functions for Population B in Germany. As shown, 11 variables were able to contribute significantly to the reduced model for Germany. The most important variables for the first function were number of books at home, expected further education and reading self-image. The first function was labeled "Books & Aspir." The most important variable for the second function was language at home.

Table 17. Standardized discriminant and structure coefficients for the first and second functions in Germany: Population B

Function 1 "Books & Aspir."				Function 2 "Language"			
Variable	Stand coeff	Variable	Struct coeff	Variable	Stand coeff	Variable	Struct coeff
BSBOOKS	0.70	BSBOOKS	0.84	BSTVR	-0.68	BSUSLANR	-0.56
BSEDUCAR	0.53	BSEDUCAR	0.68	BSEDUCAR	0.61	BSEDUCAR	0.53
BSSRATE	0.32	BSSRATE	0.53	TVSQ	0.58	AGEO	0.35
BSTVR	0.30	BSUSLANR	0.48	BSUSLANR	-0.49	MEALS	0.35
TVSQ	-0.30	AGEO	-0.43	BSBOOKS	-0.37	BSSRATE	0.21
BSUSLANR	0.29	NEWS	0.41	MEALS	0.36	BSBOOKS	-0.17
AGEO	-0.21	MEAL	0.25	BSSRATE	0.24	BSTVR	-0.14
NEWS	0.16	TVSQ	-0.22	AGEO	0.24	GENDER	-0.13
JOB	-0.12	BSTVR	-0.19	JOB	-0.13	NEWS	-0.12
GENDER	-0.11	JOB	-0.19	GENDER	-0.12	JOB	-0.11
MEALS	0.08	GENDER	-0.05	NEWS	-0.02	TVSQ	-0.04

SOURCE: IEA Reading Literacy Study, 1991.

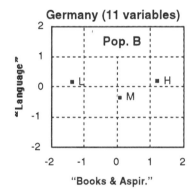

Germany (11 variables)

Figure 8. Two-function plot of group centroids for low- (L), middle- (M), and high- (H) performing students in Germany for Population B

Using centroids to understand the meaning. Figure 8 shows the centroids for the three performance groups on the two functions. The groups were quite distinct on the first function. For the second function the middle group deviated somewhat, while the low- and high-performing groups hold nearly the same positions. According to the group means for the variables, the group of high-performing students have many books at home, expect longer further education, have a better self-image, and speak the language of the reading test more often at home in comparison with the two other groups.

To summarize the data for Germany:

- The canonical correlation and the percentage of the total discriminant power for the first function was higher in Population B than in Population A.

- The three performing groups could be distinguished on the basis of 8 variables in Population A and 11 variables in Population B.

- The most important discriminating variables in Population A were reading self-image, number of books at home, and frequency of bookreading; and in Population B, number of books at home, expected further education, and reading self-image.

3.2.5   Italy

Population A

Relations between the variables and the function. Table 18 shows the standardized discriminant coefficients and the structure coefficients for the first and the second functions for Population A in Italy. As shown, there were eight variables in the reduced model for Italy in Population A. For the first function, reading self-image, age, and number of books at home were the most important discriminant variables, and these were used as the name for the function. Italy was the country with the most important second function in Population A—people at home read to student (ASPRHTL)—and the table shows it as one of the two most powerful of the variables included in the second function.

Table 18.   **Standardized discriminant and structure coefficients for the first and second functions in Italy: Population A**

Function 1 "Self, Age & Books"				Function 2 "People at home read"			
Variable	Stand coeff	Variable	Struct coeff	Variable	Stand coeff	Variable	Struct coeff
ASSRATE	0.62	ASSRATE	0.74	ASPRHTL	-0.69	ASPRHTL	-0.59
AGEO	-0.45	AGEO	-0.49	ASNEWSF	0.64	ASNEWSF	0.57
ASBOOKS	0.36	ASBOOKS	0.47	ASMAGAF	0.36	ASMAGAF	0.29
ASNEWSF	0.34	ASCOMIF	0.46	ASCOMIF	-0.35	ASCOMIF	-0.27
TVSQ	-0.32	ASNEWSF	0.37	ASBOOKS	-0.17	AGEO	0.20
ASCOMIF	0.24	TVSQ	-0.31	AGEO	0.14	ASBOOKS	-0.20
ASMAGAF	-0.12	ASMAGAF	0.14	ASSRATE	0.11	TVSQ	-0.03
ASPRHTL	-.09	ASPRHTL	0.09	TVSQ	0.00	ASSRATE	0.01

SOURCE: IEA Reading Literacy Study, 1991.

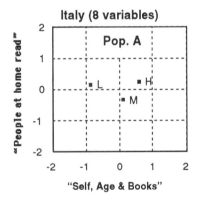

Figure 9.   **Two-function plot of group centroids for low- (L), middle- (M), and high- (H) performing students in Italy for Population A**

Using centroids to understand the meaning. Figure 9 shows the centroids for the high-, middle-, and low-performing groups. For the first function, the three group means are clearly distinguishable. For the second function, the group means for the low- and the high-performing groups are very close, while the middle group shows a slightly more negative value. Thus, the three performance groups can be discriminated in terms of differing reading self-image, age, and number of books at home. As compared with the other groups, the high-performing students had a better reading self-image, had more books at home, and were seldom overaged. The low-performing students were overaged to a higher extent than the students in the other groups.

The second discriminant function showed that the variable, people at home read to student, had a certain importance. The group means for the latter variable tells that people at home rarely read to low- and high-performing students as opposed to the behavior of families of the middle-performing group.

Population B

Relations between the variables and the function. Table 19 presents the standardized discriminant coefficients and the structure coefficients for the first function for Population B in Italy. As shown, 10 variables were kept in the reduced model. The four first variables, expected further education (BSEDUCAR), reading self-image (BSSRATE), number of books at home (BSBOOKS), and parental education (PAREDQ) had the same position in both rank orders of coefficients. They were also highly correlated, and their importance became much more obvious when comparing the structure coefficients than when comparing the standardized discriminant coefficients. To have responsibilities or work beside the school work (JOB) showed a moderate importance. However, the discriminating power of expected further education and reading self-image was much stronger. This function is labeled "Aspir. & Self."

Table 19. Standardized discriminant and structure coefficients for the first function in Italy: Population B

Function 1 "Aspir. & Self"		Function 1 "Aspir & Self"	
Variable	Standard Coefficients	Variable	Structure Coefficients
BSEDUCAR	0.59	BSEDUCAR	0.82
BSSRATE	0.59	BSSRATE	0.75
BSBOOKS	0.25	BSBOOKS	0.61
PAREDQ	0.25	PAREDQ	0.61
BSBORBO	0.19	JOB	-0.34
AGEY	-0.17	BSBORBO	0.29
JOB	-0.17	MEALS	0.16
NEWS	-0.14	NEWS	0.14
JOBNONE	-0.11	JOBNONE	0.12
MEALS	0.11	AGEY	-0.09

SOURCE: IEA Reading Literacy Study, 1991.

Using centroids to understand the meaning. The class means on the canonical variables for the high-, middle-, and low-performing groups were 1.09, -0.06, and -1.18, respectively, and thus are clearly distinguishable.

> To summarize the data for Italy:
> - The canonical correlation and the percentage of the total discriminant power for the first function was higher in Population B than in Population A.
>
> - In Population B only the first function was significant.
>
> - The three performance groups could be distinguished on the basis of 8 variables in Population A and 10 variables in Population B.
>
> - The most important discriminating variables in Population A were reading self-image, age, and number of books at home; and in Population B, expected further education, reading self-image, number of books at home, and parental education.

3.2.6 Spain

Population A

Relations between the variables and the function. Table 20 shows the standardized discriminant coefficients and the structure coefficients for the first and second functions in Population A in Spain. As shown, 11 variables contributed significantly to the reduced model for Population A in Spain. Reading self-image, age, and number of books at home were the variables with the highest correlation with the first function, and age was the most important variable for the second function.

Table 20. **Standardized discriminant and structure coefficients for the first and second functions in Spain: Population A**

Function 1 "Self, Age & Books"				Function 2 "Age"			
Variable	Stand coeff	Variable	Struct coeff	Variable	Stand coeff	Variable	Struct coeff
ASSRATE	0.69	ASSRATE	0.75	AGEO	0.72	AGEO	0.64
TVSQ	-0.68	AGEO	-0.55	ASNEWSF	0.41	ASNEWSF	0.42
ASTVR	0.63	ASBOOKS	0.55	ASBOOKF	0.38	ASSRATE	0.34
AGEO	-0.46	ASBOOKF	0.40	ASSRATE	0.38	ASBOOKF	0.31
ASBOOKS	0.38	ASPRHTL	-0.39	ASCOMIF	-0.29	GENDER	-0.22
ASPRHTL	-0.36	ASCOMIF	0.29	ASPRHTL	-0.27	ASPRHTL	-0.21
ASBOOKF	0.22	ASMAGAF	0.08	TVSQ	-0.23	ASBOOKS	-0.11
ASCOMIF	0.16	GENDER	0.07	GENDER	-0.21	ASCOMIF	-0.03
GENDER	0.09	ASNEWSF	0.07	ASTVR	0.16	TVSQ	-0.02
ASNEWSF	-0.05	TVSQ	-0.06	ASBOOKS	-0.13	ASMAGAF	0.02
ASMAGAF	-0.04	ASTVR	-0.01	ASMAGAF	-0.09	ASTVR	-0.01

SOURCE: IEA Reading Literacy Study, 1991.

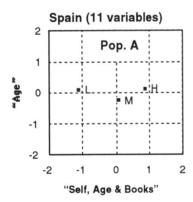

Spain (11 variables)

Figure 10. **Two-function plot of group centroids for low- (L), middle- (M), and high- (H) performing students in Spain for Population A**

Using centroids to understand the meaning. Figure 10 shows the centroids for the three performance groups on the two functions. The group centroids are well separated for the first function and little separated for the second function. The group means for the most important variables show that the low-performing students in relation to the other students are more often overaged. Furthermore, the high-performing students had a more positive reading self-image and more books at home than the low- and middle-performing students.

90

Population B

Relations between the variables and the function. Table 21 shows the standardized discriminant coefficients and the structure coefficients for the first and second functions for Population B in Spain. As shown, expected further education (BSEDUCAR), reading self-image (BSSRATE), and number of books at home (BSBOOKS) dominate the first function, while age (AGEO) seems to be most important for the second function in Spain. The first function was labeled "Aspir., Self & Books," and the second, "Age."

Table 21. Standardized discriminant and structure coefficients for the first and second functions in Spain: Population B

| Function 1 "Aspir., Self & Books""				Function 2 "Age"			
Variable	Stand coeff	Variable	Struct coeff	Variable	Stand coeff	Variable	Struct coeff
BSEDUCAR	0.68	BSEDUCAR	0.85	BSTVR	-0.93	AGEO	0.56
BSSRATE	0.52	BSSRATE	0.70	TVSQ	0.69	BSBORBO	0.45
BSBOOKS	0.43	BSBOOKS	0.69	AGEO	0.62	GENDER	-0.37
BSTVR	0.30	AGEO	-0.52	BSBORBO	0.47	BSTVR	-0.27
TVSQ	-0.24	JOBNONE	0.16	GENDER	-0.35	BSSRATE	0.26
AGEO	-0.21	BSSREAD	0.12	BSSRATE	0.32	BSSREADD	-0.23
JOBNONE	0.15	BSBORBO	0.09	BSSREAD	-0.29	TVSQ	-0.19
GENDER	0.05	GENDER	0.08	BSBOOKS	0.27	BSBOOKS	0.19
BSSREADD	-0.04	TVSQ	-0.05	JOBNONE	-0.07	BSEDUCAR	-0.08
BSBORBO	0.01	BSTVR	-0.03	BSEDUCAR	-0.05	JOBNONE	-0.05

SOURCE: IEA Reading Literacy Study, 1991.

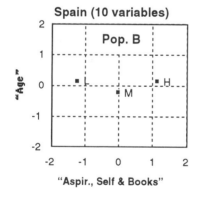

Spain (10 variables)

Pop. B

"Age"

"Aspir., Self & Books"

Figure 11. Two-function plot of group centroids for low- (L), middle- (M), and high- (H) performing students in Spain for Population A

Using centroids to understand the meaning. The same pattern that has been shown for the other countries is repeated here: obvious differences among the three performance groups on the first function and very small differences for the second function. The standardized group means for the most important variables showed the high-performing group to be expecting longer further education, having a more positive reading self-image and more books at home, and not being overaged. For the low-performing group the opposite was true, while the middle- performing group had values in between the other two groups.

To summarize the data for Spain:

- The canonical correlation and the percentage of the total discriminant power for the first function were higher in Population B than in Population A.

- The three performance groups could be distinguished on the basis of 11 variables in Population A and 10 variables in Population B.

- The most important discriminating variables in Population A were reading self-image, age, and number of books at home; and in Population B, expected further education, reading self-image, and number of books in the home.

3.2.7 Sweden

Population A

Relations between the variables and the function. Table 22 presents the standardized discriminant coefficients and the structure coefficients for the first and second functions in Population A. As shown, 12 variables remained in the reduced model. Reading self-image (ASSRATE), frequency reading newspapers (ASNEWSF), and frequency reading books (ASBOOKF) were the variables with the highest correlation with the first function, which was called "Self & Newspaper reading." The second function, "Books," was dominated by the variables number of books at home (ASBOOKS), gender (GENDER), and frequency borrowing books (ASBORBO).

Table 22. **Standardized discriminant and structure coefficients for the first and second functions in Sweden: Population A**

Function 1 "Self & Newspaper reading"				Function 2 "Books"			
Variable	Stand coeff	Variable	Struct coeff	Variable	Stand coeff	Variable	Struct coeff
ASSRATE	0.75	ASSRATE	0.74	ASTVR	1.06	ASBOOKS	-0.53
TVSQ	-0.62	ASNEWSF	0.51	TVSQ	-1.01	GENDER	0.41
ASTVR	0.43	ASBOOKF	0.37	ASBOOKS	-0.57	ASBORBO	0.36
ASREATL	-0.42	ASREATL	-0.35	GENDER	0.50	ASREATL	0.26
ASNEWSF	0.39	ASCOMIF	0.34	ASBORBO	0.41	ASNEWSF	-0.19
ASUSLANR	0.28	ASUSLANR	0.31	ASBOOKF	-0.35	ASCOMIF	0.18
GENDER	0.26	ASBOOKS	0.28	ASREATL	0.35	ASBOOKF	-0.14
ASCOMIF	0.25	ASPRHTL	-0.23	ASCOMIF	0.28	ASUSLANR	0.13
ASBOOKF	0.18	GENDER	0.22	ASNEWSF	-0.26	TVSQ	-0.11
ASPRHTL	-0.15	TVSQ	-0.17	ASSRATE	0.21	ASSRATE	0.08
ASBOOKS	0.12	ASBORBO	0.10	ASUSLANR	0.20	ASPRHTL	0.06
ASBORBO	-0.05	ASTVR	-0.10	ASPRHTL	-0.06	ASTVR	-0.04

SOURCE: IEA Reading Literacy Study, 1991.

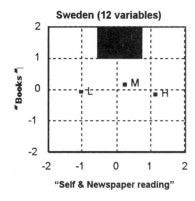

Figure 12. Two-function plot of group centroids for low- (L), middle- (M), and high- (H) performing students in Sweden for Population A

Using the group centroids to understand the meaning. Figure 12 shows the three group centroids were, as expected, well separated on the first function and rather close to each other on the second function. The total-sample standardized group means indicate that the high-performing students had a more positive reading self-image, read the newspaper and books more often, and had more books at home in comparison with the other two groups. The low-performing students seldom borrowed books but read more often to someone at home in comparison with the students in the other two groups. Furthermore, there were relatively more females than males in the high- and middle- performing groups, while the low-performing group had a higher percentage of males.

Population B

Relations between the variables and the function. Table 23 shows the standardized discriminant coefficients for the first and second functions in Population B in Sweden. As shown, 10 variables remained in the reduced model for Population B. Reading self-image, expected further education, and number of books at home were the most important variables for the first function, which was called "Self, Aspir. & Books." The second function was dominated by the three factors age (AGEO), job (JOB), and TV watching (TVSQ).

Table 23. Standardized discriminant and structure coefficients for the first and second functions in Sweden: Population B

Function 1 "Self & Aspir. & Books"				Function 2 "Age"			
Variable	**Stand coeff**	**Variable**	**Struct coeff**	**Variable**	**Stand coeff**	**Variable**	**Struct coeff**
BSSRATE	0.67	BSSRATE	0.78	AGEO	0.49	AGEO	0.56
BSEDUCAR	0.43	BSEDUCAR	0.67	TVSQ	-0.41	JOB	0.41
BSBOOKS	0.33	BSBOOKS	0.61	MEALS	0.39	TVSQ	-0.39
TVSQ	-0.27	BSSREADD	0.43	BSBORBO	0.37	MEALS	0.37
JOB	-0.18	TVSQ	-0.37	BSBOOKS	-0.37	BSBORBO	0.37
BSUSLANR	0.18	BSBORBO	0.35	JOB	0.37	BSBOOKS	-0.27
BSSREADD	0.16	MEALS	0.27	BSEDUCAR	0.10	BSUSLANR	-0.19
AGEO	-0.15	AGEO	-0.25	BSSREADD	0.10	BSSREADD	0.17
MEALS	0.11	BSUSLANR	0.22	BSSRATE	-0.09	BSEDUCAR	0.15
BSBORBO	0.10	JOB	-0.18	BSUSLANR	-0.07	BSSRATE	0.01

SOURCE: IEA Reading Literacy Study, 1991.

93

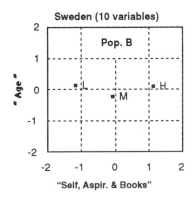

Figure 13. **Two-function plot of group centroids for low- (L), middle- (M), and high- (H) performing students in Sweden for Population B**

Using the centroids to understand the meaning. Figure 13 shows the group centroids for the first and second functions. The standardized class means for the dominating variables reveals that the high-performing students had a more positive reading self-image, expected longer further education, and had more books at home than the other students.

The low-performing students had a less positive reading self-image, expected the least further education, had the smallest number of books at home, and watched TV for more hours than the students in the other groups.

Furthermore, the high- and middle-performing groups were at about the same level in terms of age and having a job outside school, while the low-performing students to a higher extent than the others were overaged and had a job or duties outside school.

To summarize the data for Sweden:

- The canonical correlation for the first function were essentially the same in Populations A and B.

- The percentage of the total discriminant power for the first function was almost the same in Populations A and B.

- The three performance groups could be distinguished on the basis of 12 variables in Population A and 10 variables in Population B.

- The most important discriminating variables in Population A were reading self-image, frequency reading newspapers, and frequency reading books; and in Population B, reading self-image, expected further education, and number of books at home.

3.2.8 Switzerland

Population A

Relations between the variables and the function. Table 24 presents the standardized discriminant coefficients and the structure coefficients for the first and second functions in Population A. As shown, reading self-image (ASSRATE), frequency reading books (ASBOOKF), and number of books at home (ASBOOKS) were the most important variables for the first function, whereas frequency reading comics (ASCOMIF) and age (AGEY) were the most significant for the second function.

Table 24. **Standardized discriminant and structure coefficients for the first and second functions in Switzerland: Population A**

Function 1 "Self & Book reading"				Function 2 "Comic reading"			
Variable	Stand coeff	Variable	Struct coeff	Variable	Stand coeff	Variable	Struct coeff
ASSRATE	0.98	ASSRATE	0.86	ASCOMIF	0.61	ASCOMIF	0.40
AGEO	-0.32	ASBOOKF	0.49	ASMAGAF	-0.59	AGEY	0.37
ASBOOKF	0.30	ASBOOKS	0.43	ASSRATE	0.44	ASALOUF	0.36
ASBOOKS	0.28	ASUSLANR	0.36	ASALOUF	0.41	ASMAGAF	-0.33
ASALOUF	-0.24	AGEO	-0.33	ASBOOKF	-0.33	ASSRATE	0.25
TVSQ	-0.20	TVSQ	-0.31	AGEY	0.32	TVSQ	0.22
ASUSLANR	0.19	ASCOMIF	0.30	TVSQ	0.29	ASREATL	0.20
ASREATL	-0.17	ASMAGAF	0.28	ASUSLANR	0.23	AGEO	0.19
ASCOMIF	0.15	ASALOUF	-0.11	ASBOOKS	-0.23	ASBOOKF	-0.16
AGEY	-0.10	AGEY	-0.04	AGEO	0.21	ASUSLANR	0.10
ASMAGAF	-0.05	ASREATL	0.00	ASREATL	0.06	ASBOOKS	-0.10

SOURCE: IEA Reading Literacy Study, 1991.

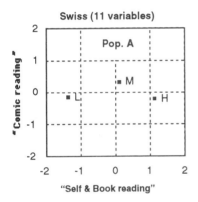

Figure 14. **Two-function plot of group centroids for low- (L), middle- (M), and high- (H) performing students in Switzerland for Population A**

Using the centroids to understand the meaning. Figure 14 shows the group centroids for the first and second functions in Population A. The figure shows a big difference between the group means for the first function and very small ones for the second function. The standardized group means for the dominating variables for the first function revealed that the good readers have a more positive reading self-image, more often read books, and have more books at home than the students in the other two groups. The poor readers have the lowest reading self-image, seldom read books, and have the smallest number of books at home.

The standardized group means for the dominating variables for the second function revealed that the low-performing students read comics very seldom in comparison with the middle- and high-performing students, who were very similar to each other in terms of comic reading.

Population B

Relations between the variables and the function. Table 25 presents the standardized discriminant coefficients and the structure coefficients for the first and second functions in Population B. As shown, reading self-image (BSSRATE) and number of books at home (BSBOOKS) are of similar importance for the first function, followed by parental education (PAREDQ). For the second function, frequency speaking the language of the test at home (BSUSLANR) and gender (GENDER) were the most significant variables.

Table 25. **Standardized discriminant and structure coefficients for the first and second functions in Switzerland: Population B**

Function 1 "Self & Books"				Function 2 "Language & Gender"			
Variable	Stand coeff	Variable	Struct coeff	Variable	Stand coeff	Variable	Struct coeff
BSSRATE	0.58	BSSRATE	0.67	GENDER	-0.60	BSUSLANR	-0.52
PAREDQ	0.36	BSBOOKS	0.67	BSUSLANR	-0.45	GENDER	-0.51
BSBOOKS	0.36	PAREDQ	0.61	BSBORBO	0.38	NEWS	-0.32
BSUSLANR	0.27	BSEDUCAR	0.48	BSEDUCAR	0.29	BSBORBO	0.31
BSEDUCAR	0.23	BSUSLANR	0.45	BSSRATE	0.27	AGEO	0.30
JOB	-0.21	TVSQ	-0.39	NEWS	-0.27	BSEDUCAR	0.27
TVSQ	-0.20	BSBORBO	0.35	AGEO	0.27	BSSRATE	0.20
NEWS	0.13	NEWS	0.32	JOB	0.24	JOB	0.14
GENDER	-0.10	AGEO	-0.28	TVSQ	-0.23	TVSQ	-0.09
AGEO	-0.09	JOB	-0.27	BSBOOKS	-0.11	BSBOOKS	-0.07
BSBORBO	0.07	GENDER	0.04	PAREDQ	-0.01	PAREDQ	-0.02

SOURCE: IEA Reading Literacy Study, 1991.

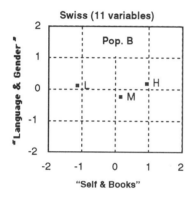

Figure 15. **Two-function plot of group centroids for low- (L), middle- (M), and high- (H) performing students in Switzerland for Population B**

Using the centroids to understand the meaning. Figure 15 shows big difference between the group means for the first function and very small ones for the second function. The standardized group means for the dominating variables for the first function revealed that the group of good readers have the most positive reading self-image, the highest number of books at home, and the parents with the most education. The low-performing students were very low on all these variables.

The standardized group means for the most important variables for the second function showed that students in the low-performing group spoke the language of the test at home less often than the students in the other two groups, who actually were fairly similar on that point. Furthermore, the low-performing and the high-performing students included a higher percentage of males than the middle-performing students.

To summarize the data for Switzerland:

- As opposed to what has been found out for all the other countries in the current study, the canonical correlation for the first function was somewhat higher in Population A than in Population B.

- The percentage of the total discriminant power for the first function was almost the same in Populations A and B.

- The three performance groups could be distinguished on the basis of 11 variables in Population A and 11 variables in Population B.

- The most important discriminating variables in Population A were reading self-image, frequency of reading books, and number of books at home; and in Population B, reading self-image, number of books at home, and parental education.

3.2.9 The United States

Population A

Relations between the variables and the function. Table 26 presents the standardized discriminant coefficients and the structure coefficients for the first and second functions in Population A. As shown, reading self-image (ASSRATE), frequency watching TV (TVSQ), and frequency reading comics (ASCOMIF) were the most important variables for the first function. In the second function, read to the students at home (ASPRHTI) and watching television (TVSQ) were the most significant variables.

Table 26. Standardized discriminant and structure coefficients for the first and second functions in the United States: Population A

Function 1 "Self, TV & Comics"				Function 2 "Read to students & TV"			
Variable	Stand coeff	Variable	Struct coeff	Variable	Stand coeff	Variable	Struct coeff
ASSRATE	0.78	ASSRATE	0.74	ASPRHTL	0.59	ASPRHTL	0.52
ASCOMIF	-0.38	TVSQ	-0.42	TVSQ	0.57	TVSQ	0.51
ASREATL	-0.33	ASCOMIF	-0.37	ASREATL	-0.38	NEWS	0.41
TVSQ	-0.32	MEAL	0.34	ASBORBO	0.37	ASBORBO	0.32
MEALS	0.23	NEWS	0.33	NEWS	0.37	MEALS	-0.21
NEWS	0.23	ASBORBO	0.27	MEALS	-0.25	ASREATL	-0.18
ASNEWSF	0.20	ASNEWSF	0.27	ASCOMIF	-0.14	ASNEWSF	-0.08
ASBORBO	0.19	ASREATL	-0.24	ASNEWSF	-0.06	ASCOMIF	-0.06
ASPRHTL	-0.10	ASPRHTL	-0.06	ASSRATE	0.02	ASSRATE	0.06

SOURCE: IEA Reading Literacy Study, 1991.

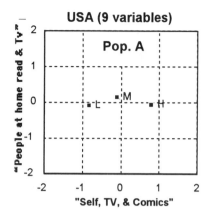

USA (9 variables)

Figure 16. Two-function plot of group centroids for low- (L), middle- (M), and high- (H) performing students in the United States for Population A

Using the centroids to understand the meaning. Figure 16 shows the group centroids for the first and second functions in Population A. The figure shows again significant difference between the group means for the first function, but very small differences for the second function. The standardized group means for the dominating variables for the first function show that the high-performance group have a more positive reading self-image, seldom read comics, and watch less TV at home than the students in the other two groups. The poor readers have the lowest reading self-image, often read comics, and spend more time in front of the TV at home.

Population B

Relations between the variables and the function. Table 27 presents the standardized discriminant coefficients and the structure coefficients for the first and second functions in Population B. As shown, 11 variables remained in the reduced model for Population B. Reading self-image, expected further education, and number of books at home were the most important variables for the first function, called "Self, Aspir. & Books." The second function was dominated by the factors age (AGEO) and meals per week.

Table 27. Standardized discriminant and structure coefficients for the first and second functions in the United States: Population B

Function 1 "Self, Aspir. & Books"				Function 2 "Age"			
Variable	Stand coeff	Variable	Struct coeff	Variable	Stand coeff	Variable	Struct coeff
BSSRATE	0.62	BSSRATE	0.73	BSTVR	-0.96	AGEO	0.51
TVSQ	-0.58	BSEDUCAR	0.60	AGEO	0.73	MEALS	0.42
BSTVR	0.35	BSBOOKS	0.59	TVSQ	0.68	BSSRATE	0.39
BSSREADD	0.32	AGEO	-0.52	BSSRATE	0.55	BSTVR	-0.37
AGEO	-0.32	BSSREADD	0.51	MEALS	0.34	BSUSLANR	-0.35
BSBOOKS	0.30	PAREDQ	0.48	BSUSLANR	-0.29	TVSQ	-0.31
BSUSLANR	0.27	BSUSLANR	0.31	BSBOOKS	-0.24	BSBOOKS	-0.13
PAREDQ	0.23	TVSQ	-0.30	BSEDUCAR	0.23	BSEDUCAR	0.10
JOB	-0.21	BSTVR	-0.29	PAREDQ	-0.13	BSSREADD	0.07
BSEDUCAR	0.20	JOB	-0.23	BSSREADD	0.05	JOB	0.06
MEALS	-0.03	MEALS	0.13	JOB	0.04	PAREDQ	-0.04

SOURCE: IEA Reading Literacy Study, 1991.

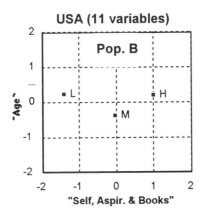

USA (11 variables)

Pop. B

L   H

M

"Self, Aspir. & Books"

"Age"

Figure 17. Two-function plot of group centroids for low- (L), middle- (M) and high- (H) performing students in USA for Population B

Using the centroids to understand the meaning. Figure 17 shows the group centroids for the United States for Population B. The figure shows large difference between the group means for the first function but very small differences between the high- and the low-performing group for the second function. The standardized group means for the most significant variables for the first function show that the high-performance group have a more positive reading self-image, expect more further education, have parents with more education, and have more books at home than the students in the other two groups. The poor readers have the lowest reading self-image, tend to be older than the rest, often watch TV, and often have job responsibilities.

To summarize the data for the United States:

- The canonical correlation for the first function was higher in Population B than in Population A.

- The percentage of the total discriminative power for the first function was somewhat higher in Population A than in Population B.

- The three performance groups could be distinguished on the basis of 9 variables in Population A and 11 variables in Population B.

- The most important discriminating variables in Population A were reading self-image, frequency of watching TV, and frequency of reading comics; and in Population B, reading self-image, expected further education, and number of books at home.

References

Downing, J. (1972). *Comparative reading.* New York: MacMillan.

Elley, W.B. (1992). *How in the world do students read?* Hamburg: The International Association for the Evaluation of Educational Achievement.

Elley, W.B. (ed.). (1994). *The IEA study of reading literacy: Achievement and instruction in thirty-two school systems.* Oxford: Pergamon/Elsevier.

Klecka, W.R. (1980). Discriminant analysis. *Quantitative Applications in the Social Sciences.* No. 19. Newbury Park, CA: Sage Publications.

Linnakylä, P., and Lundberg, I. (1993). *Teaching around the world.* The Hague: The International Association for the Evaluation of Educational Achievement.

Preston, R.C. (1962). Reading achievement of German and American children. *School and Society,* 90, 350-354.

Ross, K., and Postlethwaite, N. (1992). *Effective schools in reading.* The Hague: The International Association for the Evaluation of Educational Achievement.

Taube, K. (1988). *Reading acquisition and self-concept,* Ph.D. Diss. Department of Psychology, University of Umeå, Umeå, Sweden.

Thorndike, R.L. (1973). *Reading comprehension education in fifteen countries.* Uppsala, Sweden: Almqvist & Wiksell.

Reading Literacy Among Immigrant Students in the United States and the Former West Germany

Rainer Lehmann
Humboldt University, Germany

1. Introduction

Virtually all industrialized countries have immigrant students in their schools, even if those countries have not considered themselves open to permanent immigration. In general, under conditions of uninhibited mobility, economic and/or political disparities between regions and countries will result in migratory movements and, subsequently, in the establishment of sizable ethnic and language minorities in the areas that appear to offer more favorable conditions. It is a fairly regular pattern of migration that opportunity-seeking individuals, usually male, are soon followed by their families. Others find families after immigration, and they often prefer partners from their home country or at least home culture. Children from their marriages will then attend schools in the host country, for even if remigration ultimately may occur, the schooling age of the children coincides with the economically active phase of their parents' lives. It is typical of some minorities that intracultural marriage preferences are maintained in the second and subsequent generations, so that the size of the minority may grow substantially even if immigration policy is restricted. This is particularly true if birth rates within these groups are higher than what is average in the host country.

Thus, immigration groups become part of a nation's history. They become involved in—and in turn, actively influence—social institutions of all kinds, including schools. In spite of the general pattern just outlined, however, conditions and effects may vary considerably between countries and between immigrant groups within a given country. In attempting to compare and contrast the status of immigrant groups across countries, it is not easy to take the variation between countries and between immigrant groups within countries into account. In particular, the term "immigrant student" is not as clear as it might appear at first. Consequently, insufficient attention has been paid in the IEA Reading Literacy Study to deriving internationally comparable concepts. As a result, the present task of producing comparative analyses for the United States and the former West Germany has been hampered by more ambiguity than was anticipated. Nevertheless, we will attempt to reach as much comparability as possible in order to investigate the social position and reading achievement of immigrant students in these two educational systems to determine whether, and if so, why, disadvantages associated with an immigrant status vary between the two countries.

The United States has a long tradition of immigration and may well owe its very existence to such movements. Consequently, American schools can build upon a wealth of accumulated experience when faced with the need to integrate the children of immigrant groups. For a number of reasons, however, the flow of immigration has varied considerably, in terms of both origins and intensity. Obvious indications of this are local and regional concentrations of certain ethnic groups and their relative growth over time. For a discussion of the history of the education of language minority immigrant students in the United States, see, for example, Hakuta (1986) and Crawford (1991).

In contrast to the United States, Germany has not officially declared itself open to immigration. There has been, to be sure, a substantial influx of persons over the last three or four decades. Beginning in the late 1950s, recruitment campaigns have attracted unskilled labor, mainly from

101

Mediterranean countries, most notably Turkey, to provide the booming West German economy with a much-needed supplement to its work force. Although this practice was officially discontinued in 1973, a policy including the right of "family reunification" has kept this group approximately stable in size, in spite of other programs that awarded incentives to migrant workers returning to their home countries. A second group of immigrants is composed of persons from Eastern Europe who can claim German ancestry and who, for that reason, are awarded German citizenship immediately upon arrival. Some of these people come from territories that were part of Germany until 1945, others from regional or local minorities in Eastern and Southeastern Europe; in both groups, the use of standard German as a language has generally not been part of their experience. A third group is made up of immigrants who have entered the country under liberal procedures of reviewing requests for political asylum in Germany. Many of these persons, mainly from Third World countries and, more recently, from war-affected areas in the Balkans, will ultimately stay in the country, although in well over 90 percent of the cases the courts have decided that the request for asylum was unjustified. Given that due process of law has often extended over many years, repatriation is the exception, because concomitant social and economic hardships are pragmatically acknowledged. A final group that might be of interest here is difficult to define. Inspection of the IEA data revealed that there is a surprisingly large number of students who are German according to their teachers' records but who at least occasionally speak some foreign language in their homes. In most cases, these students will be from mixed marriages: they are German by virtue of the citizenship of at least one of their parents, yet they appear to live in a bilingual home environment.

2. Definitions of "Immigrant Students"

There are several ways to define operationally the groups to be investigated here. It is important to note that the adequacy of such definitions depends to a large degree on certain context factors, such that formally equivalent definitions could even lead to incomparable results. In order to make this clear, it may be instructive to mention some of the similarities and dissimilarities between immigrant groups in the United States and in Germany.

The United States considers itself open to immigration, at least in principle, and is prepared under certain conditions to award citizenship after a relatively short period of time. Since it cannot be assumed that the children of recently arrived citizens are soon integrated into the majority culture (which is least likely to happen in "closed" ethnic neighborhoods), nationality or citizenship are ruled out as defining elements, because too few presumably disadvantaged students would be captured by the respective operationalization. Self-ascribed ethnicity, in turn, would result in too broad a definition, considering, for example, many extremely well-adapted Asian students whose ethnic background has remained a socially relevant trait because of its visibility. Race, finally, is hardly a suitable criterion here, for even though it may be associated with educational disadvantages in some definable minorities, the respective distinctions have little to do with recent migratory movements.

In the specific American context, a language-based definition of the term "immigrant student" seems to be the most appropriate of the various options available, given the relatively scarce information on minority aspects in the IEA student questionnaires. In particular, *those students whose first language is not English are considered immigrant to the United States* for the present purpose. This definition assumes that potential disadvantages in educational biographies are primarily linked to differences between the child's first language and the English-dominated educational system. It assumes further that possible cultural biases against these students will be highly correlated with the language issue, and this also implies that, other factors being equal, possible disadvantages of students from culturally or ethnically definable subgroups tend to disappear once language assimilation has reached the parent generation. It should be noted that the language used in the home is ignored in the present definition. This is based on the observation that this variable has a much smaller effect on reading achievement than the child's first language. Table 1 presents these findings for the two populations in the United States, together with the percentages of students included in the above definition of immigrant students (9.2 percent of Population A students and 10.7 percent of Population B students).

Table 1. Students' immigrant status according to first language and language at home, and reading scores: United States

Immigrant status/child's first language and language in the home	Population A 9-year-olds (N=6,248)		Population B 14-year-olds (N=3,209)	
	Percent	Reading score*	Percent	Reading score*
Nonimmigrant				
English first language; use English at home	74.9	554	76.8	544
English first language; other language at home	15.9	538	12.5	534
Immigrant				
Other first language; use English at home	1.2	518	1.7	515
Other first language; other language at home	8.0	526	9.0	501

*Equally weighted average of international domain scores for narrative, expository texts, and documents (cf. Elley 1993, p. 45f; 57).
SOURCE: IEA Reading Literacy Study, U.S. National Study data, 1991.

Using the German IEA data to determine immigrant students requires an indirect approach. Fortunately, it is possible to do this in a way that closely parallels the approach taken with the U.S. data. As in the United States, German citizenship is ruled out as a defining element because of its ambiguous relationship with the immigrant status: the lack of German citizenship may or may not be related to a migration having occurred in the last two generations, and conversely, the criterion of having German citizenship would include many recent arrivals from Eastern Europe. In both cases, language—presumably a major factor in putting immigrant students at a disadvantage—would be captured only partially. There are, however, two variables in the German data set that provide the relevant information incorporated into the definition for the American sample: *teacher's indication of student nationality* and *student indication of his/her mother tongue*. These two variables coincide almost perfectly (99.7 percent in both samples). It was therefore determined to use the teacher variable that leads to the following definition: *Those students who are judged as being non-German by their teachers are considered immigrant to Germany.* It should be reiterated that this definition corresponds almost perfectly to the language-based definition used for the United States: only 0.3 percent of all students (or no more than 3 percent of the immigrant students) would be categorized differently if the student-identified mother tongue had been used in the definition.

It is also useful to consider the information pertaining to students from a mixed background, as opposed to immigrants as defined above and German monolinguals. As shown in Table 2, the additional use of a foreign language in the home does not put the students at a disadvantage if the mother tongue is recognized by the teacher (and indicated by the student) as being German. If, however, the foreign language in the home is truly the first language in the home and forms part of a syndrome often characterized by an unstable situation in the migratory process and unfavorable social conditions, a very noticeable achievement gap is observed. Some 13.6 percent of the Population A students and 11.7 percent of the Population B students in the former West Germany are affected by this situation.

Table 2.   Students' immigrant status according to teachers' judgments and the use of a foreign language in the home, and reading scores: former West Germany

Immigrant status/foreign language in the home	Population A 9-year-olds (N=2,813)		Population B 14-year-olds (N=4,208)	
	Percent	Reading Score*	Percent	Reading Score*
Nonimmigrants				
Only German in the home . .	76.0	511	79.8	532
Also foreign language	10.4	510	8.5	539
Immigrants	13.6	456	11.7	463

*Equally weighted average of international domain scores.

SOURCE: IEA Reading Literacy Study, West German National Study data, 1991.

3.   The Problem: Which Factors Affect the Achievement Gap Between Immigrant and Nonimmigrant Students?

The above discussion of the various options for defining immigrant status has already made reference to some contextual factors that are apparently related to student reading achievement: The use of language(s) in the home was demonstrated to be associated with differences in student performance on the IEA reading test, and quite clearly, language use has to be seen in the wider perspective of the migration process as a whole. Although Tables 1 and 2 present information on test performance in the various subgroups, it may be helpful to show these findings in terms of the dichotomous, country-specific definitions of immigrant student (Table 3).

Table 3. Mean reading achievement by immigrant status and population: United States and former West Germany*

Country	Population A	Population B
United States Nonimmigrant students . . . . Immigrant students	551 (2) 525 (7) (Standard deviation = 73.7)	543 (2) 503 (11) (Standard deviation = 84.4)
Former West Germany Nonimmigrant students . . . . Immigrant students	511 (3) 456 (7) (Standard deviation = 82.9)	532 (3) 463 (6) (Standard deviation = 77.4)

*Standard errors of the mean are given in parentheses. Standard errors were derived using estimated design effects of 5.5 (United States, both populations), 2.7 (West Germany, Population A), and 3.5 (West Germany, Population B). Design effects were calculated as given by Kish (1965).

SOURCE: IEA Reading Literacy Study, U.S. and West German National Study data, 1991.

The international scores were calibrated to achieve a population mean of 500 (averaged across all countries participating in the IEA study) and a corresponding standard deviation of 100. With these scales in mind, two important observations can be made from Table 3. First, the achievement gap between immigrant and nonimmigrant students in the United States is substantially smaller than it is in former West Germany. Second, the immigration gap appears to widen between populations in both educational systems (although this trend is not statistically significant), but in spite of its tracking system for secondary schools, the overall standard deviation of reading achievement decreases in West Germany. The problem is, then, to ascertain why it is that in these two countries with similar levels of "human development" (according to UNESCO), and with similar percentages of immigrant students in their educational systems, such differences occur.

Obviously, there are great difficulties in providing a well-justified answer to this question because, technically speaking, immigrant status is confounded with many other variables—few of which are available for the present analysis. Mere descriptions of the special economic, social, legal, cultural, and political context into which immigrant groups are embedded in each of the two countries would at best be suggestive, rather than constituting a convincing explanation. The strategy adopted here is, therefore, to use the available data to determine the relative impact of those factors actually measured in an attempt to find evidence related to the differences between the two countries regarding their successful integration of immigrant students.

This course of analysis is pursued in three broad steps. First, we will consider the extent to which the home backgrounds between immigrant and nonimmigrant students differ in the United States and in the former West Germany. It may well be that society as a whole, rather than the educational system, is the primary source of the observed achievement gaps in that pronounced social disadvantages impose higher demands on the schools' ability to compensate. Second, the results of these analyses are checked against insights that may arise from the aggregate scores for language-defined subgroups of immigrants. Finally, the educational systems' ability to compensate for specific immigration-related disadvantages can then be analyzed by contrasting the influence of the immigrant status variable with that of known social determinants of reading achievement.

4.   The Relative Social Position of Immigrant Students

As was suggested in the introductory remarks, the population of immigrant students is quite heterogeneous, both in the United States and in former West Germany, as far as their origins and migratory backgrounds are concerned. Thus, it is not unlikely that their relative social positions will also vary substantially, depending on the particular group to which they belong. Also, it will be useful for subsequent interpretations to begin with a brief characterization of the groups to be investigated here.

In the case of the United States, it appeared appropriate to distinguish groups of students whose mother tongue is not English: (1) the Spanish-speaking; (2) those with an Asian language as mother tongue; (3) those with a European language other than English as mother tongue; and (4) those with another language background. Table 4 contains the respective percentages for each group, as well as measures of their relative position on key social variables.

Table 4.   Indicators for the relative social position and the linguistic integration of four language groups of immigrant students in the United States: Standardized distance of group centroids from the total means (Population A)

Indicator	English (reference group)	Spanish	Asian	European	Other
Size of community	-.04	.38	.24	.21	.65
Socioeconomic status	.03	-.52	.09	.19	-.27
Wealth	.04	-.53	.16	-.04	-.47
Advanced-skill orientation	.03	-.47	.33	.05	-.49
Percent	90.8	5.3	0.7	1.6	1.6
Use of English in the home	-	-.11	.02	.32	.05
Percent	-	57.3	7.8	17.1	17.8

SOURCE: IEA Reading Literacy Study, U.S. National Study data, 1991.

These data reflect, in a quantitative way, some basic patterns of migratory movements into the United States. First of all, migration is a predominantly metropolitan phenomenon. There is a clear general overrepresentation of immigrant students in urban communities, most noticeably among members of the Spanish and the Other groups. Secondly, there is a divergent pattern in terms of socioeconomic status (parents' education, availability of books and encyclopedias, regularity of family meals), wealth (primarily the existence of long-lasting consumer goods), and advanced-skill orientation (availability of computers, calculators, typewriters, specialized literature in the home). In these terms, the Spanish and the Other groups are markedly below the general averages, whereas Europeans and, above all, Asians tend to rank higher than average. As far as the use of English in immigrant homes is concerned, the differences between the various immigrant groups appear to suggest a close relationship to the history of migratory waves. In the face of its generally precarious social position and its heavy concentration in certain areas, the Spanish group has made the least progress in the process of substituting English for the original mother tongue, whereas the European group is the most assimilated linguistically. A more complete investigation, quite beyond the present scope, could perhaps reveal to what extent this is due to the respective arrival times and to what extent it is related to opportunities for immigrants to establish (or reinforce) cultural and linguistic communities sufficiently large to counteract linguistic assimilation. If the latter is a significant factor and if the use of a non-English language in the home inhibits an easy integration into the monolingual schools, then one would expect the larger and regionally more concentrated groups to be associated with higher achievement gaps with respect to the majority-language reading comprehension.

Table 5 contains some comparative data for the former West Germany.

Table 5. Indicators for the relative social position and linguistic integration of five language groups of immigrants in the former West Germany: Standardized distance of group centroids from the total means (Population A)

Indicator	German (reference group)	Turkish	Eastern Europe	Mediterranean	English/ French	Other
Size of community	-.09	.53	.51	.58	.87	.60
Socioeconomic status	.07	-.73	-.38	-.30	-.08	-.44
Wealth	.06	-.40	-.61	-.32	.56	-.34
Advanced-skill orientation . .	.07	-.55	-.46	-.22	.42	-.42
Percent	86.4	4.5	3.7	2.8	0.4	2.2
Use of German in the home	-	-.07	.10	.09	-.50	-.08
Percent	-	33.6	27.4	21.0	2.7	15.3

SOURCE: IEA Reading Literacy Study, West German National Study data, University of Hamburg, 1991.

The German situation is similar to the American one in that the concentration of immigrants in urban areas in also apparent, albeit in a still more pronounced fashion. This in itself would suggest that there are less incentives for immigrant groups in Germany to actively seek social integration, since urban areas provide the opportunities to maintain familiar cultural environments similar to those from the original backgrounds. In addition, with the exception of the very small and clearly privileged Anglo-French group, the relative social position of immigrants in Germany is less favorable than it appears to be in the United States. Only the Turks (including the Kurds), as the single largest group, are in a situation more or less comparable to that of Spanish-speaking immigrants in the United States, but it is worth noting that their disadvantages are less economically accentuated and more pronounced in terms of socioeconomic status (as will be recalled, heavily related to educational background) and advanced-skill orientation.

These differences can be summarized by defining a multiple-regression equation evaluated so that differences between immigrant and nonimmigrant students are optimally predicted (equivalent to a discriminant analysis, since in each instance only two groups are being compared). Table 6 presents the standardized regression coefficients, the magnitudes of which indicate the unique relative import of each of the predictors considered. In order to take student characteristics more fully into account, some key student variables have been added to the model.

Table 6.   Beta coefficients[+] from multiple regression analyses with immigrant (i.e., low) versus nonimmigrant (i.e., high) status of students as dependent variable: Two populations from the United States and former West Germany

Predictor	United States		Former West Germany	
	Population A	Population B	Population A	Population B
Size of community	-.13 **	-.13 ***	-.20 ***	-.11 ***
Parents' SES	.08 ***	.15 ***	.10 **	.15 ***
Parents' advanced-skill orientation	.08 ***	.05 n.s.	.11 ***	.07 **
Type of school[++] (high = private)	.05 *	-.10 ***	-.07 ***	.02 n.s.
Student gender (high = female)	-.04 n.s.	-.01 n.s.	.00 n.s.	-.01 n.s.
Student age	-.00 n.s.	-.02 n.s.	-.17 ***	-.18 ***
Student voluntary reading	-.05 *	-.03 n.s.	.00 n.s.	-.01 n.s.
Student educational aspirations	-	-.01 n.s.	-	.11 ***
R^2	.04	.06	.13	.12

[+]Statistical significance levels are indicated, incorporating design effects as given in footnote of Table 3: not significant (n.s.); significant at 10 percent level (*); significant at 5 percent level (**); significant at 1 percent level (***).

[++]For West Germany, Population B secondary school track, high denotes Academic.

SOURCE: IEA Reading Literacy Study, U.S. and West Germany National Study data, 1991.

Earlier interpretations are confirmed by these figures. The fact that the model discriminates better between immigrants and nonimmigrants in both German samples (as indicated by R^2) establishes on a broader basis that background differences are greater there than in the United States. While one should resist the temptation to interpret small differences between the two countries, three observations stand out. First, the much greater influence of size of community in the German Population A as compared with Population B reflects recent migratory movements: More recent immigrant waves with younger families apparently have tended to arrive in urban centers, which can be substantiated by the disproportionately larger numbers of Eastern European and Other students in Population A (data not shown here). Second, the negative within-grade association between student age and nonimmigrant status, which is present in the German data only, is a result of attempts to facilitate immigrant students' entry into the educational system by special preparatory classes, compromises between educational attainment and (basically age-defined) grade membership, and—if other means fail—by grade repetition. Third, the mechanism of allocating students to various tracks in secondary school, depending on their perceived aptitude, appears to reinforce segregation tendencies that would, at this stage, be less visible if only subjective educational aspirations were taken into account.

In conclusion, it would seem highly plausible that the relatively high concentration of immigrant students in some German localities, their underrepresentation in academic secondary schools, and their unfavorable social position are related to their unsatisfactory progress through the educational system, as compared with the experiences of immigrant students in the United States and all but one of the other countries participating in the IEA Reading Literacy Study. In remains to be seen how much each of these factors contributes to the observed achievement gaps.

5.   Differential Reading Achievement Between Immigrant Groups

One approach to studying the contribution of the specific situations in which immigrant students live is to look at differences between groups that are relatively homogeneous within but subject to different impacts of tradition, culture, and environment. Table 7 lists the scores on the IEA reading literacy test for the language groups in the United States.

Table 7. Reading literacy scores by language group: Populations A and B, United States

Scale	English (reference group)	Spanish	Asian	European	Other
Population A					
Narrative	557	523	591	541	533
Expository	541	511	569	530	521
Documents	554	508	561	537	526
Total score	551	514	574	536	527
Population B					
Narrative	547	498	537	520	486
Expository	548	506	564	521	477
Documents	534	500	529	512	486
Total score	543	501	543	518	483

SOURCE: IEA Reading Literacy Study, U.S. National Study data, 1991.

As was predicted in the previous section, difficulties with reading comprehension are most obvious among the students with Spanish as their mother tongue. Here, the most unfavorable conditions in the social environment, or their comparatively low degree of linguistic assimilation, or the cumulative effects of both appear to have operated against high test performance, and the tendency among Spanish-speaking immigrants to cluster in urban areas may have served to stabilize and reinforce these adverse processes. The latter is not incompatible with the observation that urbanization is even stronger among the students from the Other category, because these students appear to be generally less disadvantaged in terms of the other predictors considered previously. The Asian group represents the other extreme. These students, although very few in number in both samples, confirm the expectation of superior performance, motivated not only by common lore, but also by their generally favorable backgrounds (Table 4). In fact, both the relatively low performance of the Spanish-speaking students and the high position of the Asian group appear to imply that the observed effects are due to long-term processes, operating between at least two generations.

As a side observation, it may be interesting to note that in the older sample, the achievement gaps, where they exist, are least pronounced in the documents component of the tests and most strongly pronounced in the narrative domain. This suggests that linguistic proficiency and tacit cultural knowledge, although captured only indirectly by these distinctions, are essential components of what has been measured by the test and, at the same time, are likely to be less developed among immigrant students, particularly if they come from comparatively intact language and culture subcommunities.

This last observation is also confirmed by the German data, as are the general patterns emerging from the comparisons between different language groups (Table 8).

Table 8. Reading literacy scores by language group: Populations A and B, former West Germany

Scale	German (reference group)	Turkish	Eastern European	Mediterranean	English/ French	Other
Population A						
Narrative	499	432	451	458	468	442
Expository	506	432	448	453	488	450
Documents	528	463	492	485	487	469
Total score	511	442	464	466	481	453
Population B						
Narrative	525	438	444	459	528	450
Expository	531	448	456	470	536	465
Documents	540	457	484	493	553	476
Total score	532	448	461	474	539	464

SOURCE: IEA Reading Literacy Study, West German National Study data, University of Hamburg, 1991.

As was the case with respect to their relative social position, the Turkish (or Kurdish) students are again in a relatively unfavorable situation concerning test performance. So the tentative explanations posited above are also well in line with the test results observed in the German samples. In the special case of the Turkish group, other factors, not considered so far, are also present in the data and may well have increased the difficulties for these students to adapt themselves to the fundamentally monocultural (i.e., not only monolingual) characteristics of the German educational system. The most obvious of these factors is the Turks' Muslim religion which, for many of them, introduces elements of visible group characteristics (e.g., religiously motivated clothing regulations) and tendencies to claim exemptions from normal curricular (physical education, religious education) as well as extracurricular (e.g., class excursions) activities. The present data are insufficient, however, to pursue these effects further.

That there are very distinct additional differences between the various immigrant groups can be inferred from data not shown here. In most groups, the frequency of using German as a language in the home increases over time since the first entry into Germany, but levels off after a period of some 3 or 4 years. Only in the case of immigrants from Eastern Europe, many of whom are legally considered German citizens, does the process of linguistic assimilation continue unrestrictedly. It is likely that the expectation to gain and strengthen an identity indistinguishable from the majority's self-definition plays an important role here, and it may well be part of the explanation for this group attaining a state of reading literacy on par with the Mediterranean group, which, on average, has been in the country for a much longer period.

6. Determinants of the Achievement Gap Between Immigrant and Nonimmigrant Students

The previous analytical steps have shown that in both the United States and Germany, immigrant status is clearly related to social disadvantages. These effects are significantly stronger in Germany as a country with a short but intensified tradition of immigration that in 1991 (the year of testing) was beginning to stretch the existing system of social and financial support for these groups to the point of menacing its affordability. Given, then, that the educational disadvantages of immigrant students are so closely interwoven with the empirically well-established adverse effects of social disadvantages, ways to disentangle the unique contribution of the specific immigrant situation from more general social effects, however closely these two are interrelated, should be sought.

Multiple regression analysis once again offers a technique to arrive at reasonable estimates of how well an educational system succeeds in dealing with the specific disadvantages of students from migrant families. In a fashion similar to the previous analyses, Table 9 presents the respective results.

Table 9. Beta coefficients[+] from multiple regression analyses with reading achievement (international total score) as dependent variable: Two populations from the United States and former West Germany

Predictor	United States		Former West Germany	
	Population A	Population B	Population A	Population B
Size of community	-.06 **	-.06 *	-.02 n.s	.02 n.s.
Parents' SES	.17 ***	.18 ***	.13 **	.10 ***
Parents' advanced-skill orientation	.17 ***	.09 ***	.05 n.s.	-.04 n.s.
Type of school (high = private)[++]	.08 ***	.04 n.s.	-.04 n.s.	-.05 ***
Student gender (high = female)	.04 *	.04 n.s.	.04 n.s.	-.02 n.s.
Student age	-.14 ***	-.18 ***	-.13 ***	-.10 ***
Student voluntary reading	.03 n.s.	-.01 n.s.	.16 ***	.06 ***
Student educational aspirations	-	.22 ***	-	.55 ***
Immigrant status (high = nonimmigrant)	**.06 ****	**.09 ****	**.16 ****	**.15 ****
R²	.14	.23	.13	.45

[+]Statistical significance levels are indicated, incorporating design effects as given in the footnote to Table 3: not significant (n.s.); significant at 10 percent level (*); significant at 5 percent level (**); significant at 1 percent level (***).

[++]For West Germany, secondary school track, high denotes Academic.

SOURCE: IEA Reading Literacy Study, U.S. and West German National Study data, 1991.

When looking at these data, it is interesting to note that the pattern of *unique* influences on reading achievement (independent of underlying substantial covariances) varies between the two countries investigated. In the United States, the parents' socioeconomic status and their orientation towards advanced skills play a prominent role, surpassed only by the subjective indications of students' educational aspirations. For Population B, in (West) Germany some of these effects appear to be mediated by student affiliation to a given secondary school track, which in itself is a good measure of the expected eventual educational attainment. Apart from this, the data show both commonalities and dissimilarities between the two countries. Among the American schools, the well-known inner-city problems are clearly demonstrated, whereas Germany appears to have a more homogeneous achievement distribution once the influence of social variables is controlled for. The American data also show the known relative superiority of private schools, which is not the case for Germany (but the number of private schools in the sample is much too small to bear strong assertions as to this point). Gender effects are present in both samples, but at the Population B level in Germany, the absolute superiority of females in reading achievement is small

111

and, as it seems, entirely mediated by the motivational factors of which voluntary reading is an indicator. Incidentally, it was already apparent from Table 6 that in this respect the immigrant students do not differ greatly from their nonimmigrant peers. The negative association of student age with reading achievement is present in all four samples. It is, of course, not a causal relationship in the strict sense, but a selection effect due to late school entry and grade repetition. Once again, the fact that it is smaller for the German secondary school sample can be explained by the fact that grade repetition is more frequent in the lower tracks of secondary school, and that it also often precedes a transfer from a higher track to a lower one.

Bearing all that in mind, it is most remarkable that the residual effects for immigrant status are still present in all data sets, but they are still substantially higher for Germany than for the United States. Accordingly, the attempt to explain the achievement gap between immigrant and nonimmigrant students on the basis of an underlying syndrome of social disadvantages has only been partially successful. Social disadvantages—concentration in urban areas, lower affinity to education, lower standards of living—contribute to the gap, but there are indications that other factors related to the immigrant status add a very specific component to the unfavorable situation of immigrant students, and that this component is more pervasive in Germany.

7.   Conclusion

At this point, the discussion of how best to understand—and subsequently alleviate—the situation of immigrant students is usually characterized by the introduction of very broadly defined terms difficult to handle empirically. References to specific historical and political circumstances, allegations as to the effects of a bicultural identity on career planning, and hypotheses on possible interferences in the (almost) simultaneous acquisition of a first and second language all carry a certain plausibility and are not totally void of empirical evidence. At the present state of knowledge it would seem hopeless, however, to develop these lines of thinking to a point where a convincing explanation for the quantitative differences between the American and the German situations seems likely.

The above analyses have produced some results, however, that could guide further studies in the search of a fuller understanding of the processes involved. The first of these observations concerns the possible consequences of a distinctly bilingual socialization with the original language as the dominant means of communication in the home and an exclusive use of the majority language in the school. While the IEA data contain some information on the language use in the home, it is improbable that this factor shows a very clear *unique* contribution to the explanation of reading achievement. The required more advanced techniques, such as commonality analysis, are, unfortunately, not applicable here because of the (proportionately) small number of immigrant students in the respective combined categories. It is highly recommended that such research be conducted with appropriate designs in the future because of its obvious implications. If it can be shown that slow linguistic assimilation in combination with related factors is detrimental to the children's progress through the educational system, it may be advisable to provide the parent generation with incentives to acquire a sufficient command of the majority language. This is common practice in Sweden, for instance, where the right to reside in the country eventually depends on passing a language examination.

Similar implications concern the potential effects of heavy local concentrations of immigrant students. This aspect has two different facets, which have to be studied separately and dealt with at different political levels. Clearly, residential patterns are not greatly influenced by educational planning, but it is highly desirable to investigate their effects on student achievement. Again, the present data do not permit carrying out the required analyses. Specialized studies designed to demonstrate the interactions between residential patterns and other factors, however, could conceivably show the extent to which closed neighborhoods affect educational development. Here, the second facet comes into play. Since schools (especially primary schools) are often neighborhood schools, one would expect that the resulting variation in the relative frequencies of immigrant students in classrooms is closely interacting with environmental effects. It is known, of course, that mean achievement in classrooms with a high density of immigrant students is relatively low. One would have to have very precise knowledge of the "ecological effects" of such concentrations in schools, however, before imaginable countermeasures—such as changes in the recruitment patterns of schools—are justifiable.

A final set of open questions concerns the specific influence of linguistic factors. There is a rapidly growing body of research in this area motivated by the rather direct practical implications: Early instruction in the mother tongue, bilingual education, or total immersion programs are options to be considered, but it will be impossible to interpret their relative merits without reference to potentially complex interactive processes with social factors involved. The IEA Reading Literacy Study tests were not constructed to furnish, nor do they provide, the linguistic information to study the issues, nor do the background questionnaires render sufficient information to pursue such aims. The available data do show some of the questions, however, that must be addressed if the current disadvantages of immigrant students are to be understood to a degree where rational decisions between existing policy options are possible.

References

Crawford, J. (1991). *Bilingual education: History, politics, theory, and practice.* Second edition. Los Angeles, CA: Bilingual Educational Services, Inc.

Elley, W.B. (1993). *The IEA Reading Literacy Study. The international report.* Oxford: Pergamon Press.

Hakuta, K. (1986). *Mirror of language. The debate on bilingualism.* New York: Basic Books.

Kish, L. (1965). *Survey sampling.* New York: Wiley.

Comparison of Reading Literacy Across Languages
in Spanish Fourth Graders

Guillermo A. Gil
Instituto Nacional de Calidad y Evaluación, Spain

Keith Rust, Marianne Winglee
Westat, Inc., USA

1.   Introduction

This paper discusses the results of a comparative language study for fourth grade students among regions (called autonomous communities) in Spain. The study of Spanish languages was conducted as part of the IEA Reading Literacy Study in Spain, which consisted of three components:

1.   An international component for comparisons across countries; that is, the relative performance of Spanish students in comparison with students from other countries (see Elley 1992);

2.   A Spanish component designed to study the proficiency levels of reading comprehension and reading habits for Spain as a whole and to compare results among the country's autonomous communities; and

3.   A language component to study and compare the reading proficiency in the different Spanish languages.

The international and Spanish regional components of the study involved samples of students from the whole of Spain. Students selected for these components were administered the IEA reading literacy test in Castilian. The Spanish languages component, however, involved only three autonomous communities—Catalonia, Galicia, and Valencia. Within these autonomous communities, an additional group of students was selected, and these students were administered the reading literacy test in the language of the community, which was Catalonian, Galician, or Valencian.

In the Spanish terminology, the terms "state," "nation," and "country" each mean the whole of Spain, formed by 17 different autonomous communities that are denominated. Depending on the circumstances, "nations," "countries," "principalities," or "autonomous communities" are approximate equivalents of the states that form the United States of America in relation to the Federal Union. Spain has a semifederal political structure and has been, since 1978, in a general and continuous process of decentralization of political powers, with a trend to becoming a state with a political federal structure. In the rest of this article, "state" will be used to mean the whole of Spain and "autonomous communities" refers to the various territories.

Section 2 of this paper briefly reviews the characteristics of the autonomous communities and languages spoken in the different communities. Section 3 outlines the aims of the study and issues addressed in the study, and Section 4 describes the sample design used to select schools and students and the characteristics of students in the sample. Section 5 discusses the differences in students' reading literacy in Castilian and in the languages of the autonomous communities and examines the influence of students' characteristics on reading literacy. Section 6 discusses the results of this study.

2.   Characteristics of the Spanish Languages

Several Spanish languages are used in Spain and around the world. Castilian, usually and internationally known as Spanish, is the official language for the whole of Spain. It is also the Spanish language used in the Philippines, most countries in South America, Central America, and Mexico, and by a sizable Hispanic population in the United States. There are about 400 million people who speak Spanish, and 330 million of them speak the Castilian Spanish as their first language.

The other Spanish languages are Catalonian, Galician, Basque, and Valencian. Each of these languages is also the official language of its respective nation: the Catalonian nation, the Galician nation, the Basque country, and the Valencian country. The Basque language (Euskera in Basque) was not included in the study because of translation problems that arose with a substantive group of the reading subtests. Figure 1 shows the locations of Catalonia, Galicia, and Valencia, and Table 1 provides some demographic and economic data on these three communities.

Figure 1.   Locations of the autonomous communities of Catalonia, Galicia, and Valencia

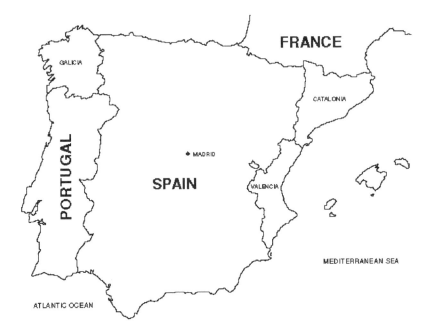

Table 1. **Demographic and economic data for the antonomous communities of Catalonia, Galicia, and Valencia: 1991**

Population characteristic	Catalonia	Galicia	Valencia	Whole of Spain
Number of inhabitants.................................	6,059,496	2,731,671	3,857,235	39,100,000
Per capita income[1]	1,601,300	1,038,800	1,325,400	1,315,900
Percent of population in employment sector:				
Agriculture..	4%	3%	8%	10%
Industry...	35	26	35	30
Services...	61	71	57	60
Percent unemployed[2]	13	13	15	17

[1]Per capita income in pesetas.
[2]Percent unemployed in relation to the total active population.
SOURCE: Anuario El País, Spain, 1993.

The Spanish languages included in this study— Castilian (Spanish), Catalonian, Galician, and Valencian—are all Latin-based romance languages. Because of the common root, the languages of the autonomous communities are close to Castilian, although each is clearly a different language. Table 2 summarizes the relationship between Castilian and the languages of the autonomous regions and the different governments' efforts to promote the language.

Table 2. **A comparison of the languages of autonomous communities relative to the Castilian language (Spanish)**

Characteristic	Catalonian	Galician	Valencian
Linguistic and structural features............................	Close to Castilian; Clearly a different language	Close to Portuguese and to Castilian; Clearly a different language	Close to Castilian; Sometimes considered a dialect of Catalonian
Government's effort to promote language	Strong	Mild	Moderate

Catalonian is spoken in Catalonia, an economically wealthy autonomous community in northeast Spain, south of France and north of Valencia. Nearly half of the population of Catalonia are immigrants, mainly from other parts of Spain. Catalonian has been the language of the upper bourgeoisie, the native Catalonian upper and middle classes, and the home servants and peasantry for centuries. From the 1940s to the 1970s, Catalonian was not widely and publicly used by the immigrant middle class, nor by the lower class workers who were mainly recent immigrants. Since 1978, the government of Catalonia has strongly promoted the use and the learning of the Catalonian language by all the population living in Catalonia through a widely extended and government-supported school-based program of linguistic immersion and other political measures.

In 1991, the time of data collection for the IEA Reading Literacy Study, the teaching at primary levels was done under seven modalities of schools that offered different levels of immersion in Catalonian and Castilian. In one extreme modality, there were schools that taught all subjects in Catalonian, except for the Castilian language subject-matter. In the other extreme modality, schools taught all subjects in Castilian, except for the Catalonian language subject-matter. By 1994, the seven modalities were to be phased out, and the huge majority of schools in Catalonia were supposed to be teaching primarily in the Catalonian language. Currently, most students at the end of compulsory education in Catalonia are bilingual in Castilian and Catalonian.

Galician is spoken in Galicia, an autonomous community that is relatively poor in comparison with the overall economic wealth of the state. Galicia is a region of Spain with a high rate of emigration and almost no immigration. The Galician language has some similarities to the Portuguese language and some similarities to Castilian and has traditionally been the usual home language, especially of the peasantry.

Valencian is spoken in Valencia, an economically wealthy, autonomous community in eastern Spain, south of Catalonia and north of Murcia. The Valencian language is considered by most linguists and a small segment of the population as a dialect of the Catalonian language. However, a substantial segment of the population and the different Valencian political parties argue that early literature written in Valencian preceded the Catalonian literature. Therefore, they consider Catalonian to be a product of the early Valencian language and argue that Valencian is a different language. From a political point of view, there is the fear that placing Valencian as a dialect of Catalonian may put Valencia in a situation of cultural and political dependency on Catalonia. Officially, Valencian is considered a different language. The Valencian language has been traditionally the language of the peasantry, and it has not been widely used by the middle and upper classes.

Table 3 shows the results of a recent survey on the percentage of people who use the Castilian language and the languages of the autonomous communities in which they live, people's attitude about the language that they believe should be used for education, and people's preferred language for reading.

Table 3. **Political and social status of the languages of autonomous communities in comparison to the Castilian language (Spanish): Percentage of population with characteristic: 1994**

Characteristic	Catalonia	Galicia	Valencia
Currently understands and speaks the language of the community...	73%	85%	54%
Currently has the language of the community as the main language	50	56	34
Currently has Castilian as the main language.....................	49	40	65
Believes that compulsory teaching has to be done in Castilian	27	63	81
Believes that compulsory teaching has to be done in the language of the community	62	23	8
Prefers Castilian for reading	34	51	67
Prefers the language of the community for reading.............	29	10	7

Note: "Not known" and "equal" answers are not included in the percentages.
SOURCE: Centro de Investigaciones Sociologicas, Spain, 1994.

In all three autonomous communities, the teaching and learning of Castilian and the language of the respective autonomous community are compulsory in schools. The political importance of the languages of the autonomous communities, however, has undergone some recent changes. Since the Constitution of 1978, the use of the language of the autonomous communities was promoted by their different governments. The most vigorous promotion has been in Catalonia, less so in Galicia and Valencia. Currently, most school children are bilingual in Castilian and the language of the autonomous community. Catalonian, Galician, and Valencian are usually spoken in the parliaments of their autonomous communities.

3.   Objectives of the Regional Study

The situations in the three autonomous communities provide different socioeconomic and political backgrounds for comparing factors that affect reading literacy in the different languages in Spain. Within each community, factors that influence students' reading proficiency in the language of the community and in Castilian may be influenced by the social and political importance of the languages in the region.

The goal of the Spanish languages study, therefore, is to compare the reading proficiency of fourth grade students tested in Castilian with that of students tested in Catalonian, Galician, and Valencian. Students in grade 4 are typically 9 or 10 years of age. The specific issues addressed in the analysis are as follows:

- Within Catalonia, Galicia, and Valencia:

    - How do literacy scores in Castilian compare with scores in their own language?

    - How do student characteristics affect literacy in Castilian? Do they affect literacy in their own language in the same manner?

- Across the three autonomous communities, are there variations in students' literacy scores in Castilian?

- Can the autonomous community differences, if there are any, be related to

    - The economy and industry of the region,

    - The linguistics and structural features of the languages,

    - The political and social importance of the language in the autonomous communities?

4.   Samples of Schools and Students by Autonomous Community

In Spain, as in other countries in the IEA Reading Literacy Study, students for the international component of the study were selected using a stratified equal probability sampling scheme with probabilities proportional to measures of size (i.e., number of students at grade level). In the first sampling phase, the country was stratified into eight domains—Catalonia, Valencia, Galicia, Andalucia, Canary Islands, Basque Country, M.E.C. (those communities administered by the Ministry of Education and Science), and Navarra. Within each domain, representative samples of fourth grade schools were selected, and one entire classroom of students was selected per school. For the Spanish state and Spanish languages studies, a stratified unequal probability sampling scheme was used to secure representative samples per community. The sample design resulted in approximately equal numbers of students per community in spite of the differences in their size.

In Catalonia, Valencia, and Galicia, two samples of schools and classes of students were selected for the Spanish state and language study. The objective was to have two comparable groups of students within each autonomous community, one being tested in Castilian and another in the own language of the community. Table 4 shows the number of schools and students in each region tested in the Castilian language and in the language of the respective communities.

Table 4. Number of schools and students in language study

Autonomous community	Test language	Number of	
		Schools	Students
Catalonia..	Castilian	39	1,021
	Catalonian	34	1,026
Galicia	Castilian	39	988
	Galician	37	907
Valencia..	Castilian	37	976
	Valencian	28	699

SOURCE: IEA Reading Literacy Study, Spanish National Study data, Spanish Ministry of Education and Science, 1991.

Given the sample design, the two samples of students within each autonomous community were expected to have comparable characteristics. In general, we found this to be true with small differences due to sampling error. In all three autonomous communities, the average age of students in both study groups was about 10 years. The average number of books at home for both groups was between 50 and 100, and both groups reported a similar number of items in home and student possessions. Also, both groups reported spending an average of 2 hours per day watching TV and similar frequencies in voluntary reading at home. The slight observed differences between test language groups in these characteristics are solely due to sampling variations in the selection of schools. However, in comparing students' literacy in the two test languages, it is important to take into consideration the contribution of these factors. This is addressed in the next section by including them in the regression models.

The characteristics that were different for the study groups were related to the language in which they were tested: the frequency of using test language at home, and the frequency of being read to in the test language. Tables 5 and 6 show the average scores on these characteristics. In Catalonia and Galicia, students reported speaking Castilian more frequently than the language of the autonomous community. In Valencia, however, both Castilian and Valencian were used with similar frequencies. Across the three autonomous communities, the frequencies with which fourth grade students spoke Castilian were very comparable (means of 3.8, 3.9, and 3.8 for the three communities, respectively).

Table 5. Average frequency[1] in using different languages at home

Language	Community		
	Catalonia	Galicia	Valencia
Castilian...	3.8	3.9	3.8
Language of the autonomous community...............	3.1	3.0	4.1

[1]Based on a 5-point scale where 1 = never, 5 = always.

SOURCE: IEA Reading Literacy Study, Spanish National Study data, Spanish Ministry of Education and Science, 1991.

A second difference between the study groups was the frequency with which people read to the student in a test language at home (Table 6). In Catalonia and Galicia, students were being read to more frequently in the language of the autonomous community than in Castilian. This difference, however, was not found in Valencia.

Table 6.   Average frequency[1] of being read to at home, by language

Language	Community		
	Catalonia	Galicia	Valencia
Castilian	1.5	1.5	1.7
Language of the autonomous community	2.4	2.8	1.9

[1]Based on a 4-point scale where 1 = never, 4 = daily.
SOURCE: IEA Reading Literacy Study, Spanish National Study data, Spanish Ministry of Education and Science, 1991.

5.   Reading Proficiency in Castilian and the Languages of the Autonomous Communities

Table 7 shows the average reading proficiency scores for students tested in Castilian and for students tested in the languages of the autonomous communities. In all three autonomous communities, the scores for students tested in Castilian were higher than those for students tested in the language of the community. In Catalonia, the mean reading proficiency score for students tested in Castilian was 516 and the score for students tested in Catalonian was 484, a difference of 32 points between the two test groups. In Valencia, the difference was 58 points, and in Galicia, the difference was 44 points. This means that in all three communities, students are better at reading Castilian than the language of the community.

Table 7.   Mean reading performance score in test language, by autonomous community

Test language	Catalonia	Galicia	Valencia
Castilian	516	521	524
	(83)[1]	(77)	(82)
Language of the autonomous community	484	477	466
	(112)	(116)	(112)
Both...	500[2]	500[2]	500[2]
	(100)	(100)	(100)

[1]Numbers in parentheses are standard deviations.

[2]Scores were scaled separately in each community and so cannot be used for comparisons across communities.

SOURCE: IEA Reading Literacy Study, Spanish National Study data, Spanish Ministry of Education and Science, 1991.

The scores shown in Table 7 were scaled using a three-parameter IRT model. A separate model was developed for each autonomous community such that the mean score for both language test groups was set at 500 and the standard deviation at 100. Since the scores for each region were standardized separately, they cannot be used to compare student's performance across communities.

Table 8 shows students' performances in Castilian scaled for state comparisons of all communities. With this scale, the national average for all autonomous communities was set at 500. The communities were listed in order of performance, and Catalonia ranked higher than both Valencia and Galicia. In Catalonia, the average score was 513 points, 13 points above the state average. The performance of children in Valencia and Galicia were very close to the state average, at 502 and 499, respectively. This result indicates that even in view of the Catalonian government's effort to promote the language of the autonomous community, Catalonian students' reading performance in Castilian is above the national average.

Table 8.   Reading performance in Castilian, by autonomous community

Rank	Autonomous community	Mean	Standard deviation
1	Navarra...	523	99
2	Basque Country..	518	95
3	Catalonia..	513	88
4	M.E.C.[1]..	512	97
5	Valencia..	502	98
6	Galicia	499	99
7	Andalucia..	469	102
8	Canary Islands..	463	106
	All..	500	100

[1] Territory administered by the Ministry of Education and Science.
SOURCE: IEA Reading Literacy Study, Spanish National Study data, Spanish Ministry of Education and Science, 1991.

To evaluate the effect of student characteristics on the reading literacy of the two languages in a community, multivariable linear regression models were used (Neter, Wasserman, and Kutner 1985). Separate models were specified for each autonomous community. The models were:

$$y_i = \beta_0 + \beta_1 x_{1i} + \ldots + \beta_p x_{pi} + \alpha_0 z_i + \alpha_1 x_{1i} z_i + \ldots + \alpha_p x_{pi} z_i + \varepsilon_i \tag{1}$$

where y_i was the reading literacy performance of student i in the community, x_{pi} was the pth student characteristic for student i, and z_i was 1 if student i was tested on the language of the autonomous community, and 0 if tested on Castilian. The β's are the regression coefficients for the main effect parameters, the α's are the coefficient for the interaction effects between the two languages used in the community, and ε_i was the error term.

The statistical procedure SUDAAN (Shah et al. 1992) was used to compute the regression estimates and conduct the hypotheses' testing. In this study, the sampling procedure involved a multistage design in which whole classes of students were selected within schools. When calculating the variance estimates for the regression parameters, SUDAAN took into consideration the clustering of students within schools and the stratifications used in the selection of schools.

Two hypotheses were tested with the model. One hypothesis tested was that the overall model fitted for students tested in Castilian is the same as the model fitted for students tested in the other languages (H_0: $\alpha_0 = \alpha_1 = \alpha_2 = \ldots = \alpha_p = 0$ against an alternative H_1: not so). A second analysis then assessed the hypothesis that students' differences in reading proficiency by language differed only in the mean, and not in its relationship to other characteristics (H_0: $\alpha_1 = \alpha_2 = \ldots = \alpha_p = 0$ against H_1: not so). Both hypotheses were rejected in all three communities suggesting that different equations should be used for the two test language groups. Therefore, the fitted equations for the two language groups were:

Castilian language group: $\bar{y}_i = b_0 + b_1 x_{1i} + \ldots + b_p x_{pi}$, and

Community language group: $\bar{y}_i = (b_0 + a_0) + (b_1 + a_1) x_{1i} + \ldots + (b_p + a_p) x_{pi}$ \hfill (2)

where the b's and a's are estimates of β's and α's in equation (1).

Before presenting the results, it should be noted that students with extreme performance scores (scores 3 standard deviations from the mean) were excluded from the model because they may have undue influence on the parameter estimates. Table 9 shows the percentages of students excluded. In general, very few students (ranging from 0 to 0.4 percent), scored higher than 800 points. The percentage who scored below 200 was also small when the test language was Castilian, about 0.1 percent. However, when the test language was the language of the autonomous community, a higher percentage of students scored below reasonable levels of proficiency. In Catalonia, about 3.6 percent of the students tested in the Catalonian language were completely improficient in the language. In Galicia and Valencia, the percentages were 7.3 and 7.6, respectively. The apparently lower percentage in Catalonia is probably due to the strength of the linguistic policy of the Catalonian government promoting the language of Catalonia.

Table 9. Percentage of extreme performers in assessment, by community and language

Autonomous community	Test language	Percentage scoring	
		< 200	> 800
Catalonia..	Castilian	0.1	0.1
	Catalonian	3.6	0.4
Galicia	Castilian	0.1	0.0
	Galician	7.3	0.0
Valencia..	Castilian	0.1	0.1
	Valencian	7.6	0.0

SOURCE: IEA Reading Literacy Study, Spanish National Study data, Spanish Ministry of Education and Science, 1991.

Tables 10 through 12 show the regression equations estimated for the test language groups by autonomous communities. The student characteristics that have a significant influence on reading literacy in Castilian (at $\alpha = 0.05$ level for a two-tailed test) and characteristics that are significantly different between the two test languages (significant interaction effects) are identified.

The results of the regression analyses showed that the student characteristics that affect reading literacy in Castilian had limited effects on the reading literacy of the language of the autonomous community. Student characteristics that had a significant effect on reading literacy in Castilian for all three populations were *age of student, number of books at home,* and *frequency of being read to.* Other characteristics were found to be significant in different communities. For example, in Catalonia *hours of TV watching* was also found to be significant, although no TV effect was observed in the other two autonomous communities. In Galicia, *use of test language* and *frequency of voluntary reading* were significant. In Valencia, *student possessions* was a significant variable. The characteristic *home possessions* was not significant in any of the three autonomous communities, probably because of a relatively high correlation with the item *number of books at home.*

Table 10. Regression estimates of the effect of student characteristics on reading literacy in Castilian and Catalonian: Catalonia

Student characteristic	Castilian language (b_i)	Interaction with language (a_i)
Age	-0.76	+1.08
Age^2	-0.32*	+0.24**
Number of books at home	14.24*	-17.22**
Home possession items (1 unit on 2-point scale)	11.08	-1.04
Student possession items (1 unit on 2-point scale)	-3.19	+4.79
Infrequent user of test language (1=yes, 0 otherwise)	12.77	-8.31
Frequent user of test language (1=yes, 0 otherwise)	6.64	+9.36
Hours watching TV	-4.10*	+3.17
Frequency of voluntary reading (1 unit on 4-point scale)	2.06	-4.99
Frequency of being read to (1 unit on 4-point scale).............	-9.58*	+11.88**
R^2	0.09	

*Statistically significant effect on Castilian (0.05 level).

**Statistically significant interaction effect with language (0.05 level).

NOTE: Scale has standard deviation of 100.

SOURCE: IEA Reading Literacy Study, Spanish National Study data, Spanish Ministry of Education and Science, 1991.

Table 11. Regression estimates of the effect of student characteristics on reading literacy in Castilian and Galician: Galicia

Student characteristic	Castilian language (b_i)	Interaction with language (a_i)
Age	-0.96*	+0.52
Age^2	-0.24*	+0.24**
Number of books at home	12.33*	-8.64**
Home possession items (1 unit on 2-point scale)	0.92	+1.44
Student possession items (1 unit on 2-point scale)	1.39	+0.90
Infrequent user of test language (1=yes, 0 otherwise)	-2.11	+1.87
Frequent user of test language (1=yes, 0 otherwise)	18.54*	-14.69
Hours watching TV	-0.73	-2.52
Frequency of voluntary reading (1 unit on 4-point scale)	7.21*	5.63
Frequency of being read to (1 unit on 4-point scale).............	-9.83*	+9.24**
R^2	0.10	

*Statistically significant effect on Castilian (0.05 level).

**Statistically significant interaction effect with language (0.05 level).

NOTE: Scale has standard deviation of 100.

SOURCE: IEA Reading Literacy Study, Spanish National Study data, Spanish Ministry of Education and Science, 1991.

Table 12. **Regression estimates on the effect of student characteristics on reading literacy in Castilian and Valencian: Valencia**

Student characteristic	Castilian language (b_i)	Interaction with language (a_i)
Age	0.00	+0.96
Age^2	-0.29*	+0.20**
Number of books at home	12.79*	-5.40
Home possession items (1 unit on 2-point scale)	10.50	-13.33
Student possession items (1 unit on 2-point scale)	15.63*	-14.48
Infrequent user of test language (1=yes, 0 otherwise)	10.73	-7.68
Frequent user of test language (1=yes, 0 otherwise)	11.87	-6.83
Hours watching TV	0.04	+0.14
Frequency of voluntary reading (1 unit on 4-point scale)	2.43	-4.83
Frequency of being read to (1 unit on 4-point scale)	-16.67*	+18.55
R^2	0.16	

*Statistically significant effect on Castilian (0.05 level).

**Statistically significant interaction effect with language (0.05 level).

NOTE: Scale has a standard deviation of 100.

SOURCE: IEA Reading Literacy Study, Spanish National Study data, Spanish Ministry of Education and Science, 1991.

In all three autonomous communities, significant interaction effects were found between the test language and the student's age and frequency of being read to. In Catalonia and Galicia, significant interaction effects between language and number of books at home also were observed.

To interpret the interaction effects, the following six figures plot the adjusted reading performance for students in the two test language groups by the student characteristics *age of student*, *frequency of being read to*, *number of books at home*, *use of test language at home*, *TV watching*, and *frequency of voluntary reading*. The adjusted reading performance is calculated as $\hat{y} = b'x$ with certain x's in the regression model set to specific values for evaluation; the remaining x's set to their mean values. The b's are the estimated regression coefficients. These adjusted mean scores allowed us to examine the effects of each student characteristic after holding constant the contribution of other characteristics in the regression equation.

Effect of Age on Reading Literacy

Age of the student is expected to have a curvilinear effect on reading literacy performance because the older children at a grade level are typically repeaters of the grade who tend to have lower performance. For grade 4 in Spain, the mean age of students is about 10 years old, and most students who are 11 years or older at this grade level (over 85 percent) are grade repeaters. To capture the curvilinear effects of age, a second-order model was used in the regression analyses; that is, age was entered in the regression equation as both a linear term (x) and a quadratic term (x^2). The coefficients of the quadratic parameter of age were significant in all three autonomous communities.

The adjusted means in Figure 2 show that the effect of age differed by the test language. For literacy in Castilian, performance increased with age until about 10 years old (the average age for grade), and declined thereafter. This trend was observed for all three autonomous communities. However, the effect of age on the language of the autonomous communities was different. The trend appears much more

Figure 2. Reading performance by autonomous community, language, and age of student

Language: ● Castilian   ○ Language of autonomous community

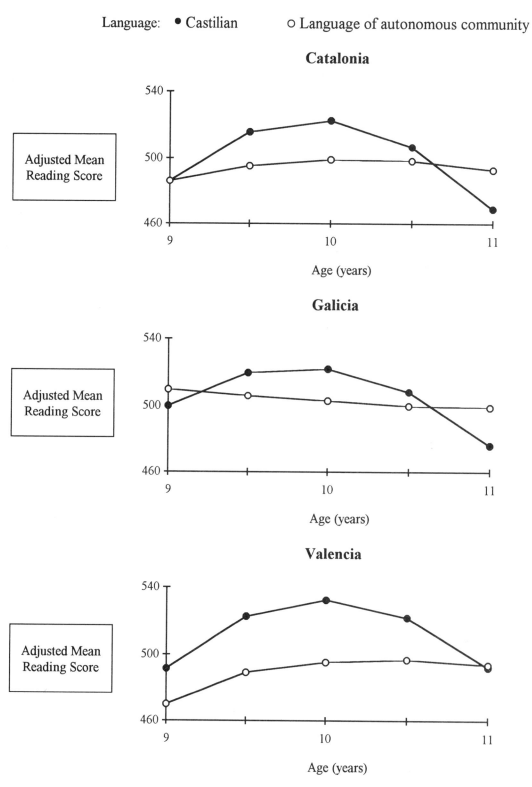

SOURCE: IEA Reading Literacy Study, Spanish National Study data, Spanish Ministry of Education and Science, 1991.

linear with age in each case, and generally speaking age does not have a strong relationship with reading proficiency in the autonomous languages.

Effect of Number of Books at Home

The characteristic *number of books at home* had different effects by test language and by autonomous communities. As shown in Figure 3, there was a positive association between reading literacy in Castilian and the number of books in all three autonomous communities; the slope of improvement appeared greatest in Catalonia. The number of books at home probably reflected the families' interest in reading, but also served as a measure of family possessions and family wealth. Therefore, the increasing performance as the number of books increased probably reflects the effect of sociocultural class in the level of achievement in reading.

The effects of number of books at home on the languages of the autonomous communities was less intuitive. In Valencia, performance in the Valencian language appears to improve with increases in the number of books. In Catalonia and Galicia, the number of books at home showed no significant relationship to reading proficiency in the autonomous language. Unfortunately, the questionnaire did not ask students the language in which the books at home were written, making it difficult to interpret these results on any great depth.

Frequency of Being Read To

In each autonomous community, the characteristic *frequency of being read to* had different effects on literacy in Castilian and literacy in the language of the community. The trends were comparable for the three autonomous communities, however (Figure 4). For literacy in Castilian, students who were being read to frequently had lower performance in Castilian than students who were rarely read to. The negative association between being read to and reading literacy performance at this age level has also been found in other countries, including the United States. A possible explanation is that by fourth grade, students who are frequently read to are likely to have some reading dysfunction and therefore are low reading achievers. The frequency of being read to, however, has no significant effect on the reading literacy in the languages of the autonomous communities. Again, a limitation of this measurement was that students were not asked to indicate the language used for reading.

Use of Test Language

The characteristic *use of test language* was entered in the regression equation as two dummy variables: *frequent user of test language* and *infrequent user of test language*. The variable *frequent user of test language* was set to 1 for students who responded "always" and "almost always" to the item about the use of test language at home and 0 otherwise. The variable *infrequent user of test language* was set to 1 for students who responded "never" or "almost never," and 0 otherwise. Students who answered "sometimes" had values of 0 on both variables.

Figure 3. Reading performance by autonomous community, language, and number of books at home

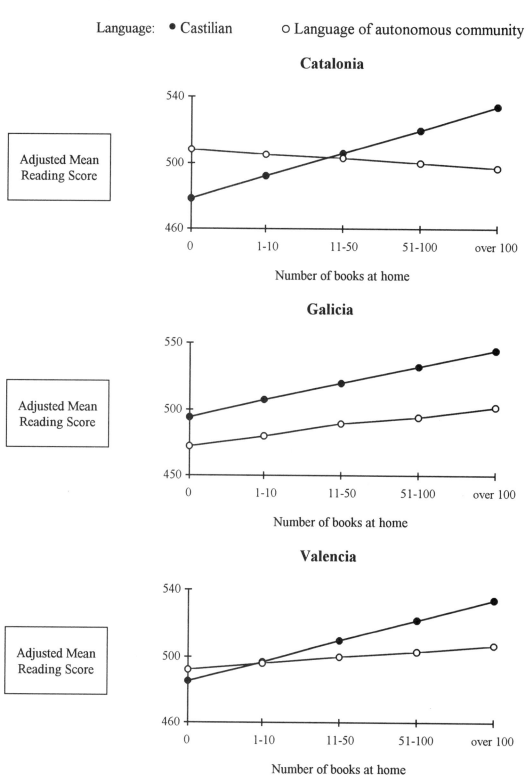

Language: ● Castilian   ○ Language of autonomous community

Catalonia

Adjusted Mean Reading Score

Number of books at home

Galicia

Adjusted Mean Reading Score

Number of books at home

Valencia

Adjusted Mean Reading Score

Number of books at home

SOURCE: IEA Reading Literacy Study, Spanish National Study data, Spanish Ministry of Education and Science, 1991.

Figure 4. Reading performance by autonomous community, language, and frequency of being read to

Language: ● Castilian   ○ Language of autonomous community

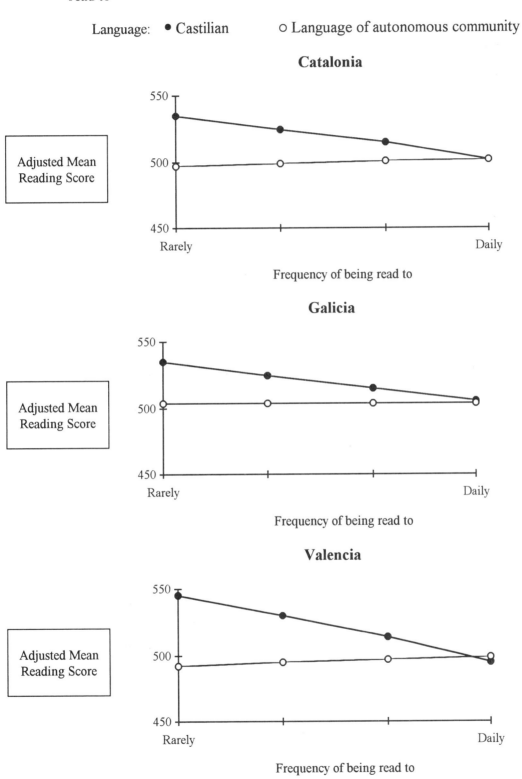

Catalonia

Adjusted Mean Reading Score

Frequency of being read to

Galicia

Adjusted Mean Reading Score

Frequency of being read to

Valencia

Adjusted Mean Reading Score

Frequency of being read to

SOURCE: IEA Reading Literacy Study, Spanish National Study data, Spanish Ministry of Education and Science, 1991.

Figure 5. Reading performance by autonomous community, language, and use of test language at home

Language: ● Castilian   ○ Language of autonomous community

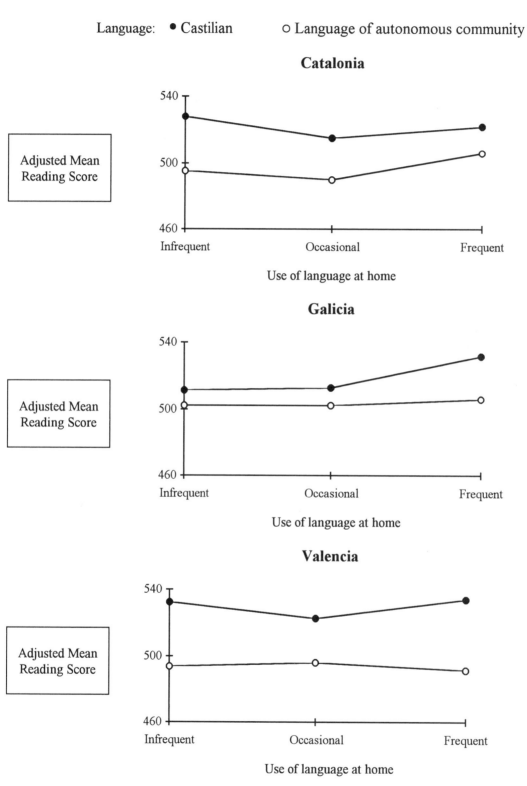

Catalonia

Adjusted Mean Reading Score

Use of language at home

Galicia

Adjusted Mean Reading Score

Use of language at home

Valencia

Adjusted Mean Reading Score

Use of language at home

SOURCE: IEA Reading Literacy Study, Spanish National Study data, Spanish Ministry of Education and Science, 1991.

These variables were used because in a bilingual community, *frequent users* of one language implies *infrequent users* of the alternative language. In Catalonia, for example, when the test language was Catalonian, frequent users of the test language were students from Catalonian-speaking families, and infrequent users of the test language were students from Castilian-speaking families. When the test language was Castilian, frequent users of the test language were students from Castilian-speaking families, and infrequent users of test language were students from Catalonian-speaking families. Students who sometimes used the test language may have been students from homes with mixed language backgrounds, in which two or more languages were used.

The results showed that the frequency of use of the test language at home had limited relationship to reading literacy (Figure 5). There was a positive association between frequent usage and literacy of Castilian in Galicia, but no such association was found for the other autonomous communities and for the other languages.

Hours of TV Watching

The effects of TV watching also differed by language and by region (Figure 6). In Catalonia, an increase in the number of hours per day watching TV was associated with a negative performance in Castilian, but no such effect was observed in the other autonomous communities. TV watching also had no adverse effects on the literacy of the languages of the autonomous communities, although a slight (but not statistically significant) negative trend is observed with the Galician language.

In order to understand the effect of TV watching, it was useful to examine people's preference about the language on television. Table 13 shows the percentage of the population that preferred watching television in the two languages of each community. In Catalonia, the chance that people favored TV watching in Castilian was about 1 in 4; the chance was about 1 in 3 in Galicia, and 1 in 2 in Valencia. In contrast, the chances that people preferred the language of the autonomous communities were 1 in 3 in Catalonia, 1 in 6 in Galicia, and 1 in 8 in Valencia. These rates of preference suggest that in Galicia and in Valencia, an increase in the number of hours watching TV was probably associated with an increase in exposure to the Castilian language. For Catalonia, the exposure to language through TV was relatively mixed; not dominated by any one language. Taken together, the results suggest that when the increase in TV watching was not associated with an increase in exposure to Castilian, TV watching had a negative effect on reading literacy of the language.

Table 13.   Preferred language on TV, by autonomous community

Preferred language on TV	Autonomous community		
	Catalonia	Galicia	Valencia
Castilian......................................	24%	34%	51%
Own language	33%	17%	12%
Both	43%	48%	36%

NOTE: Percentages may not add to 100 due to rounding.

SOURCE: Centro de Investigaciones Sociologicas, Spain, 1994.

Figure 6. Reading performance by autonomous community, language, and hours per day watching television

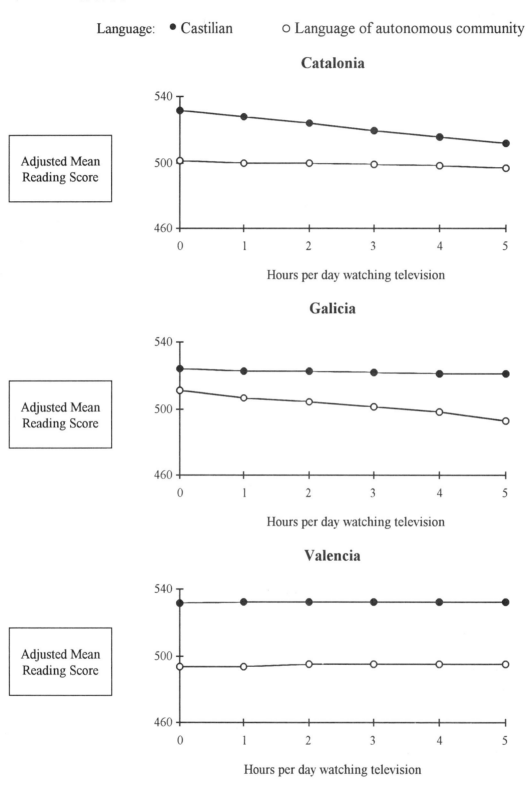

Language: ● Castilian   ○ Language of autonomous community

Catalonia

Adjusted Mean Reading Score

Hours per day watching television

Galicia

Adjusted Mean Reading Score

Hours per day watching television

Valencia

Adjusted Mean Reading Score

Hours per day watching television

SOURCE: IEA Reading Literacy Study, Spanish National Study data, Spanish Ministry of Education and Science, 1991.

Frequency of Voluntary Reading

The characteristic *frequency of voluntary reading* had a positive effect on reading literacy of Castilian in Galicia. No such effect was observed in the other autonomous communities (see Figure 7). Frequency of reading also had no effect on the literacy of the languages of the autonomous communities.

6. Discussion

This study compared reading literacy in different Spanish languages in the autonomous communities Catalonia, Galicia, and Valencia for fourth grade students. Two representative samples of students were involved in each community. One sample was given a reading literacy test in Castilian, the Spanish language spoken throughout the world, and a second sample was given the same test in the language of the autonomous community. The results showed that student characteristics that typically affected literacy in Castilian tended to have a limited effect on literacy of the languages of the communities. Literacy in the languages of the autonomous communities may be more heavily influenced by the social and political status of the languages and the linguistic policies of those communities.

In Spain, the languages of the autonomous communities may be regarded as minority languages that face potential disuse over time. To ensure that the language stays in functional use by the people, the governments of the autonomous communities have undertaken active measures to educate and promote their own languages. Government support is especially relevant in Catalonia, where there is a high rate of immigration. There are also strong incentives on the immigrants to learn Catalonian because of the high social status of the language. Immigrants need to know Catalonian for social upgrading and for the purpose of employment in the future. The need to promote the language of the community is less for Galicia and Valencia because there is low immigration. In these communities, there is less danger that the language of immigrants (almost exclusively Castilian) can become the main and dominant language, resulting in the long term in a disuse of their own languages.

The language immersion programs in Catalonia appear to have been successful in promoting literacy in the Catalonian language without unduly compromising literacy in Castilian. In Catalonia, relatively few students are completely illiterate in the Catalonian language despite the high influx of immigrants who speak Castilian. The situation in Catalonia suggests that literacy in a dominant language such as Castilian is unlikely to be adversely affected by the introduction of a second language.

In summary, it seems unlikely that there are general rules regarding the performance of reading when two languages are used together in a community. The achievement in reading literacy in each language probably depends strongly on a number of factors:

- The different social statuses and political strengths of the languages;

- The real and functional use of a language—for oral and written communication, conversational discourse, interchange of technical ideas, and other purposes;

- The situation in which the language is used—in communication media, school, work environment, or political settings;

- The preferences of the people and their attitude about the relevance of a language; and

- The linguistic policy of the governments that can exert a different degree of pressure on the population to study and learn a language.

Figure 7. Reading performance by autonomous community, language, and frequency of voluntary reading

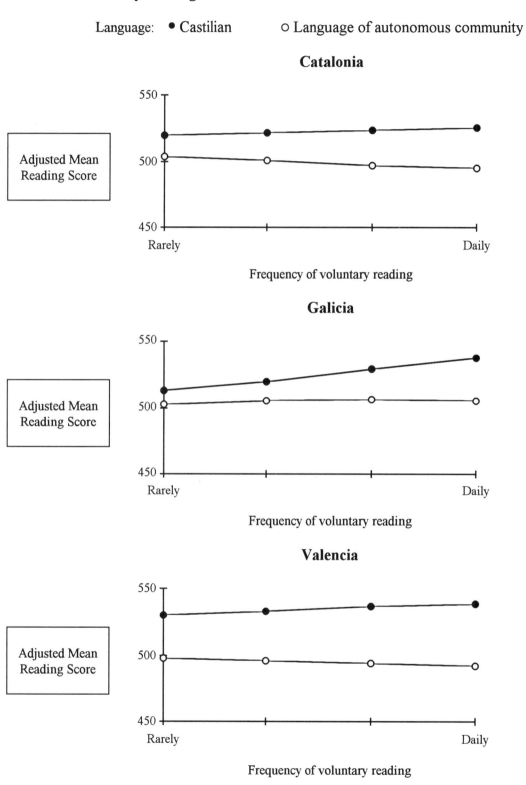

Language: ● Castilian   ○ Language of autonomous community

Catalonia

Adjusted Mean Reading Score

Frequency of voluntary reading

Galicia

Adjusted Mean Reading Score

Frequency of voluntary reading

Valencia

Adjusted Mean Reading Score

Frequency of voluntary reading

SOURCE: IEA Reading Literacy Study, Spanish National Study data, Spanish Ministry of Education and Science, 1991.

References

Elley, W.B. (1992). *How in the world do students read?* The Hague: The International Association for the Evaluation of Educational Achievement.

Neter, J., Wasserman, W., and Kutner, M.H. (1985). *Applied linear statistical models. Second edition.* Homewood, IL: Irwin.

Shah, B.V., Barnwell, B.G., Hunt, P.N., and LaVange, L.M. (1992). *SUDAAN User's manual, Release 6.0.* Research Triangle Park, NC: Research Triangle Institute.

SECTION B: INSTRUCTIONAL PRACTICES IN READING

- **Teaching Reading in the United States and Finland**
  Marilyn R. Binkley and Pirjo Linnakylä

- **A Nine-Country Study: How Do Teachers Teach Reading to 9-Year-Olds?**
  Emilie Barrier and Daniel Robin

Teaching Reading in the United States and Finland

Marilyn R. Binkley
National Center for Education Statistics, USA

Pirjo Linnakylä
University of Jyvaskyla, Finland

1.   Introduction

It seems almost trite to draw attention to the importance of literacy in the world today. Clearly, most national economies are based on the existence of a highly literate work force. All over the world, from their very inception, schools have been given the task of developing the literacy abilities of their students. As the school population grew and as compulsory schooling became widespread, the level of literate functioning necessary has increased exponentially.

The recent IEA Reading Literacy Study gave researchers an opportunity to compare literacy proficiency among nations and to consider other differences related to literacy, such as the organization of instruction. In such a large-scale international study, one can find a wide spectrum of teaching traditions, beliefs, values, and principles that guide school instruction. However, sometimes the educational, cultural, and social environments of the participating countries are so dissimilar that the differences found in instructional practice may only reflect the various prevailing stages of economic, social, or cultural development. It is obvious that the instructional activities most useful at certain developmental stages of educational evolution may not function at other stages of national development.

In this paper, we compare the instructional cultures of two of the highest achieving countries in the IEA Reading Literacy Study—the United States and Finland. The focus is on two highly industrialized nations that are very similar in a number of respects, but that also have differences. Both Finland and the United States allocate a lot of resources to education in general and to teacher education specifically. Both nations have populations that can be considered exceptionally literate. Both provide their students with easy access to books and other texts in homes, nearby libraries, bookstores, and schools. Likewise, both have lengthy teacher education programs and a strong academic tradition.

Cultural and educational differences, of course, also exist in such arenas as language and orthography, literacy and teaching traditions, school organization and starting age, and principles of child rearing at home and at school (cf. Elley 1992; Lundberg and Linnakylä 1992). Finland, as a Nordic country, has educational roots in Scandinavian, German, and Baltic traditions that contrast with the Anglo-American tradition predominant within the United States. Despite this difference in tradition, teachers from both countries are likely to be familiar with the newer theories of reading and instruction, even though such theories tend to originate primarily from research in North America.

There are also many common features of reading that pervade the entire world. For example, the cognitive processes in reading comprehension are considered basically universal. Texts have many common elements in their function, content, structure, and textual characteristics (Purves 1991). If this were not so, an international reading assessment would not be possible.

In considering how reading is taught, one can begin by thinking about how teachers approach the subject. Do reading teachers have an implicit theory that structures their thoughts, decisions, and actions?

Are there differences in theoretical approaches that reflect national cultures? Are there some common universal traits characteristic of the act of reading itself, or are the instructional features nationally and culturally constructed? These questions are the driving focus of this paper.

To examine the two teaching cultures, we used the empirical data gathered with the IEA Reading Literacy Study Population A Teacher Questionnaire (teachers of the 9-year-old students). The questionnaire was constructed from the perspective of an implicit general instructional model as held by each of the National Research Coordinators in the IEA study. We, however, wanted to explore teachers' instructional thinking as it explicitly related to reading theories. Thus, our main tasks were

- Develop an overview of reading theories;

- Explore the structure of the teachers' beliefs, activities, and assessment practices to provide a tentative picture of teachers' implicit theories as they compare to existing reading theories;

- Describe and contrast the instructional features and their theoretical connections in two different national teaching cultures;

- Compare the teachers' preferences regarding instructional beliefs and activities; and

- Explore the unity and diversity in the teaching of reading.

2. Developing an Overview of Reading and Reading Instruction Theories

2.1. The Relationship Between Reading and Reading Instruction Theory and More Generalized Theories of Teaching and Learning

Although the prime purpose of this section is to develop an overview of reading theories and reading instruction, it is important to note that theories of reading instruction are more than just theories of reading—they also intersect with more general theories of instruction and learning. This is especially true in the case of primary education, where the classroom teacher probably follows the same implicit theory while teaching all or most subjects. As depicted in Figure 1, issues of cultural diversity and cognitive unity also have a strong impact on how teachers organize their beliefs, activities, and assessments of student learning. Given that the impact of these other aspects is likely to be consistent across all teaching within the primary school classroom, the attributes of each theoretic stance in terms of reading instruction may often be consistent with our understanding and theories of instruction in other specific academic disciplines.

2.2. The Process of Teaching

Based on the large body of research related to how instruction and learning takes place, it is possible to construct a model of the teaching process. For example, according to some cognitive theories of instruction, the process is seen as an activity involving teachers and students working together (Shulman 1986; Clark and Peterson 1986). This collaborative work involves both thinking and acting on the part of all participants. Three significant attributes of each of the participants—capacities, actions, and thoughts—serve as potential determinants of the teaching and learning that takes place in the classroom.[1]

---

[1] *Capacities* are defined as relatively stable characteristics of ability, *actions* compose the purposive activities of teachers or students, and *thoughts* are the cognitions, emotions, beliefs, and intentions that guide the observable actions.

140

Figure 1: The structure of teaching reading in the United States and Finland

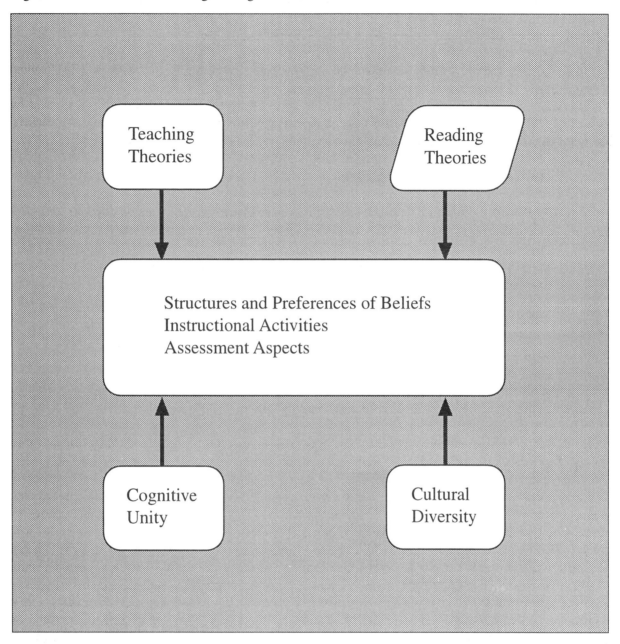

Research focusing specifically on teachers' thoughts and actions indicates that there is a reciprocal relationship between these attributes (Clark and Peterson 1986). Teachers' actions are to a great extent guided by their knowledge and beliefs, which in turn are affected by the teachers' instructional actions and students' behavior.

Research on the cultures of teaching focuses particularly on teachers' knowledge, values, and beliefs for action (Feiman and Floden 1986). In the same vein, the ethnographic and process-tracing studies have shown that teachers' instructional activities are in general guided by an implicit theory of action that has been shown to be well integrated and internally consistent (Marland and Osborne 1990).

Research on classroom processes has led to the development of a model for studying the teaching process (Bennett 1988; Yorke 1987). In brief, teachers' strategic classroom activities and actions are based on their belief system. However, the enactment of teachers' and students' classroom activities serves as a test of the implicit hypotheses of the teacher. If the students' actual outcomes differ from those the teacher intended, then the teacher will revise or modify his/her own implicit belief system or even the strategic planning and activities. This interactive model is depicted in Figure 2. If we assume that this model provides a good picture of what really goes on within classrooms, schools, and nations, then we can use this framework for comparing instructional systems across nations.

While constructing a frame for studying teachers' implicit or practical theories of reading instruction within different national school systems, it is important to note that the research on teaching in general accentuates the reciprocal nature of the relationship between teachers' instructional *beliefs* and purposive *activities*. It is believed that the two reflect the main determinants of the teaching process. Consequently, we hypothesize that there should be some consistency between teachers' beliefs and the instructional practices they frequently employ. Further, we hypothesize that this unity is based on definable theoretic stances.

2.3.   Common Features of Reading Theories

Because theories of reading have been promulgated for centuries, they are quite numerous. Logically there are certain attributes common to all theories of reading. We have identified seven:

- Reading theories are evolutionary. No reading theory stands on its own; each draws upon previous conceptualizations and modifies these to suit particular ends. Parallel with these reading theories is a concurrent evolution of larger, more inclusive theories of thinking and learning.

- Reading theories are partial. Given the complexity of reading, new insights into its nature are constantly adding piece by piece to the extant knowledge.

- Each reading theory has a specific focus. For example, some theories concentrate on word-recognition processes (Gough 1972, 1985; LaBerge and Samuels 1974, 1985; Stanovich 1991; Rumelhart 1985), while others focus on comprehension, almost to the exclusion of letter-level processes (Just and Carpenter 1985; Kintsch and van Dijk 1978).

Figure 2: A hypothetical model of the teaching process

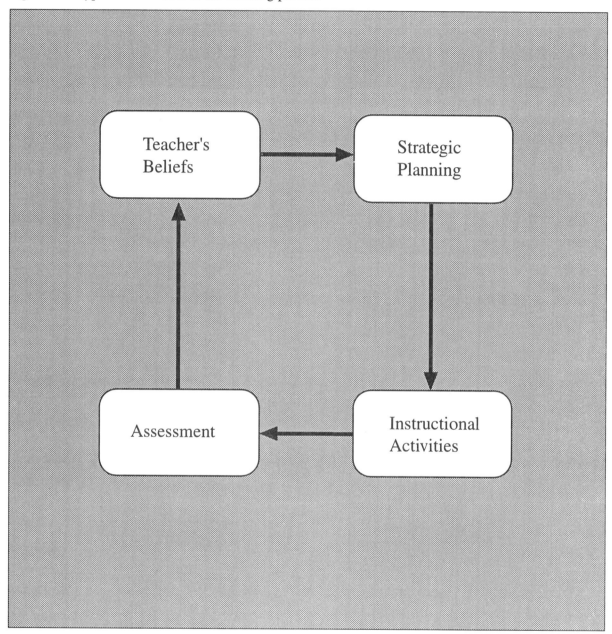

- Reading theories with the same focal phenomenon take variant positions. For instance, within the group of word recognition theories some emphasize strict linear processing (Gough 1972, 1985), while others emphasize the interaction of multilevel processes (e.g., Rumelhart 1985; Stanovich 1991; LaBerge and Samuels 1974, 1985).

- Versions of each reading theory may range from moderate to extreme. For example, some proponents of natural acquisition theories of reading argue that teaching children to read any more than they are taught to speak is a cause of reading failure (Goelman, Oberg, and Smith 1984). Others maintain that while learning to read is natural, some instruction can promote reading failure just as other instruction can help to prevent it (Applebee and Langer 1983).

- Reading theories are complementary, tending to be different rather than contradictory. Because they concentrate on a different aspect of the same phenomenon, different theories tend to contribute to an understanding of different aspects of reading. Taken together, they provide a more comprehensive view than any one theory alone would.

- Not all reading theories look equally closely at reading. Word-recognition theories generally tend to be local and microscopic in their examination of reading, while comprehension theories tend to be more global and macroscopic.

The lack of a common focus makes it hard to contrast reading theories. However, there seem to be certain positions regarding distinctive attributes of reading theories that have had salience at different points in time. To classify reading theories, we have relied heavily on a categorization system originally presented by Straw (1990) that distinguishes among five periods based on three criteria: locus of meaning, nature of knowledge needed to be literate, and purpose of literacy. We have extended his descriptors by focusing also on the attributes of theories of reading acquisition, instruction, and cognitive and affective processes that would likely be associated with his periods. None of the reading theories fit neatly into one and only one of these categories, nor into any one period of time. Given the evolutionary nature of reading theories and instructional practice, remnants of earlier periods and conceptions of reading continue to hold a very important place in both theory and practice.

2.4. The Progression of Reading Theories

The categorization system that we use divides conceptualizations of reading theories into four periods. It combines Straw's first two periods, transmission and translation, into one that we label "information transfer" consistent with the terminology put forth by Harste (1985), and it maintains the remaining three: interaction, transaction, and social construction.[2]

2.4.1. Information Transfer

As defined by Straw, during his transmission period the meaning of text rests with the author, and the knowledge (intention) incorporated into a text by an author is to be reproduced by the reader. This

---

[2]While Straw designates specific dates for each period, these designations are not important for our purposes. Rather, we are more interested in the progression across time and the way in which these periods correspond to notions of acquisition, instruction, and processes. Further, we believe that while many might disagree with his time periods, few would argue with the progression.

conceptualization of reading supports conceptions of teaching and learning that cast the teacher as the source of knowledge and the student as the recipient of that knowledge.

He contrasts this with the translation period, where meaning lies in the text, which is seen as independent of its author. The reader is a decoder of text, not of authors' intentions. To decode text the reader needs knowledge about reading and literature. Emphasis is placed on the entertainment value of text as well as on the information found in it (Just and Carpenter 1980; Davis 1944; Gough 1972; LaBerge and Samuels 1974).

From our perspective, we see the two as similar because in both instances the meaning of the text rests outside of the reader, and in both cases the reader is expected to reproduce someone else's meaning and knowledge as represented in the text. Consequently we have consolidated the two periods into one—information transfer (according to Harste 1985).

In this period, which strongly represents a behavioristic view of thinking and learning, the cognitive and affective processes are presented as separate domains (Bloom, Hastings, and Madaus 1971). The period clearly emphasizes an information transfer from the text to the mind of the reader, and the affective domain is clearly underestimated in the theoretical models (Mathewson 1985).

Consistent with that stance, one would expect stage models of reading acquisition that assume that human development progresses through a series of qualitatively different stages that are hierarchically ordered, and that higher stages cannot be reached without going through the ones below (Chall 1983; Gough and Hillinger 1980; Mason 1980). While each of the theories associated with this period might include a different number of stages of development, there is agreement that an understanding of the alphabet is basic to reading acquisition (Juel 1991).

Given the notion of a hierarchy, it also seems reasonable to see reading acquisition as the accretion of subskills or components that together make up reading (Barrett 1968; Gray 1960). In this view, reading is seen as a collection of discrete skills, such as letter recognition, ability to make letter-sound correspondences, word recognition, and sequencing ideas. Most basal reading series are structured upon such a model of reading acquisition.

Reading instruction during this period is very prescriptive. A central tenet is that students must be taught to use the single system of language properly. The definitions and rules of this system form the basis for what is to be taught. Teaching phonics before children have a concept of reading is the epitome of the prescriptive approach to reading literacy instruction. For instance, some theorists argue that first we should teach the code, and only then allow children to read (Balmuth 1982; Flesch 1955).

Reading theories of this period compare human mental processes to the mechanical operation of a computer. Discrete pieces of information that are taken in by the senses are processed by a series of discrete steps. The output for one processor becomes the input for the next one in a linear series of steps (Gough 1985). Variations in this view, which allow for information to be *chunked* into whole units (LaBerge and Samuels 1985; Ruddell and Speaker 1985; Rumelhart 1985), mark the bridge to the next period.

2.4.2. Interaction

During the interaction period, meaning resides with both readers and text. The theories of this period assume that three sources of knowledge are needed by readers: authors, text, and experience. The good reader is the one whose background knowledge fits the text. These theories also assume that meaning is determinate. Reading is seen as a means whereby authors and readers can share knowledge and experience (Frye 1957; Goodman 1970; Rumelhart 1977, 1985).

The interaction period stresses information processing. Reading is conceptualized as a series of linguistic and cognitive steps. Although most of the models neglect affective elements (Gough 1985; Rumelhart 1977, 1985; LaBerge and Samuels 1985), the later models by Ruddell and Speaker (1985) acknowledge its importance as one of many elements in knowledge utilization.

This period marks the beginning of a shift in views regarding instruction and cognitive processing. In contrast to the very prescriptive view previously held, we see the development of a psycholinguistic view where language is perceived as an instrument and the vernacular speech children bring to school is seen as an adequate base for learning to read. Spoken language is seen as the overt performance of underlying, abstract abilities involving phonological, syntactic, and semantic components of linguistic competence. The theme of building on those things the student already knows—linking the more formal language of school to the informal vernacular and the more disciplined academic understandings to the experientially acquired concepts already in place in the mind of the learner—fit the definition of interaction.

Learning to read is a matter of employing these components in the processing of meaning. Reading is much more than recoding visual symbols into their spoken equivalents. It involves readers in using their knowledge of oral language and their powers of conceptualization to derive meaning from print. The reader's knowledge of language includes familiarity with the syntactic order of linguistic elements and the semantic relationships among them. The reader's background experience with oral language is assumed to be a critical factor in reading development.

Psycholinguistic approaches to reading instruction recognize the principle of continuity between home and school in the young child's experience and language. Beginning readers encounter written materials as a natural part of their language development and are encouraged to read them fluently in terms of their own language and meanings, rather than precisely and accurately in terms of what appears on the printed page, as is required in the prescriptive approach. The graphic symbols are only part of the information that readers use; syntactic and semantic predictions supplement the visual display. These sources of information are available from the child's own linguistic competence acquired in the preschool years.

In the psycholinguistic view, language is a self-contained system to be acquired and refined by the individual. Psycholinguists are primarily concerned with the individual reader and how that reader establishes meaning for text. Of primary concern are the intrapersonal context, the background knowledge and skills that the reader brings to the task of interpreting a text, and individual differences in knowledge and skills.

Consistent with this psycholinguistic view, we see the development of schema-theoretic views where individuals are believed to possess cognitive structures called *schemata* (Anderson and Pearson 1984).

These schemata consist of organized sets of concepts, and understanding a piece of text occurs when stimuli from the text are fitted into one of these structures.[3]

2.4.3. Transaction

During the transaction period constructing meaning is considered to be a generative act in which the reader's role is most prominent. The meaning of text is indeterminate and is constructed by readers while reading. To do so, readers draw upon a variety of knowledge sources, including the text, knowledge of language, and experience. In contrast to the first two periods, which are communicative, theories associated with this period assume that reading is more than the reception or processing of information in text. The reader generates meaning in response to text, and the purpose of reading is actualization (Rosenblatt 1978; Tompkins 1980; Harste, Woodward, and Burke 1984; Straw 1990). Consequently, the reader's affective attributes (e.g., the attitudes, motives, interests, and intentions the reader brings to the setting) are actively engaged in text interpretation. Self-concept and self-regulation are crucial in terms of the degree of control the reader is ready to take and how much courage and willingness the reader has to interpret the text openly and individually (Harste 1985; McCombs and Whistler 1989).

This period is marked by the beginnings of a number of major shifts in the stances that theorists take. The stage models that prevailed in the two prior periods begin to be challenged by another conception—the nonstage model that assumes human development is continuous and reading does not require qualitatively different abilities for children and adults. Therefore, what is required of a child to read a piece of text is the same as what is required of the adult; the difference is that the adult has a broader base of knowledge on which to draw in making an interpretation (Goodman and Goodman 1979; Harste, Burke, and Woodward 1982; Smith 1973). In addition, the adult is likely to have a broader range of intentions for the reading (Harste 1985).

Reading acquisition is no longer necessarily based on formal, well-structured, sequential instruction. Theorists of this period maintain that reading acquisition is a natural activity analogous to learning to speak one's native language. Children learn to speak naturally, without formal instruction when reared in the context of other speakers of the language. Similarly, learning to read, just like learning to speak and to walk, emerges early in life from children's experiences with spoken and written language (Goodman 1986; Harste and Woodward 1989; Kastler, Rosen, and Hoffman 1987; Pearson 1985). Children learn to read earlier in the context of more diverse oral language use (Snow and Perlman 1985), and through more active engagement with written language (Cullinan 1989; Strickland and Morrow 1989; Sulzby 1985). Even within this group of theorists, however, there is often the acknowledgment that children profit from help (Ehri 1987; Goodman 1986; Harste and Woodward 1989).

As opposed to the subskill view that characterized earlier periods, we see the emergence of a holistic view that maintains that reading is more than the sum of its parts and involves more than a collection of skills (Goodman 1986; Harste and Woodward 1989). Every reading act, according to holistic theories, requires the integration of skill, background knowledge, purpose and intention, and attitudes.

Consequently, the characteristics of the reader and the text cannot be analyzed separately, as assumed by earlier reading theories. Reading emerges in the transaction between readers and text. In

---

[3]For example, a person's cognitive structure might contain a schema for DOG. The cognitive structure would consist of the relationship of this concept both to more general concepts (canines, four-legged creatures, mammals), and to more particular concepts (domestics, wild dogs, spaniels).

contrast to earlier interactive models, which assume that the text and readers are separable entities, both readers and texts are seen as aspects of a total event according to transactional theories of reading (Beach and Hynds 1991).

During the transaction period, the psycholinguistic views expand to include a somewhat more sociolinguistic position. From this perspective, language cannot be separated from its social context and reading is viewed not only as a set of cognitive processes, but also as social and linguistic processes (Wells 1986). As social processes, reading is used to establish, structure, and maintain social relationships among people. As linguistic processes, reading is used to communicate intentions and meanings between authors and readers (Olson, Torrance, and Hildyard 1985).

Both the psycholinguistic and sociolinguistic theories of the period lead to experiential learning or the achievement of linguistic abilities through engagement in language use. Children are encouraged and allowed to learn to read by reading for purposes that are personally meaningful. School reading programs provide opportunities for reflective appraisal of these communications (Moffett 1983). To this reflective repertoire could be added powerful tools of appraisal in the form of sociolinguistic understandings about such factors as the effects of certain kinds of audiences, situations, and purposes on meaning.

Learning to read is seen as a process of being socialized into the uses of written language. There is renewed interest in the home as a setting in which some children become literate and from which schools can learn how to establish settings that are more effective for general literacy teaching (Harste, Burke, and Woodward 1982).

2.4.4. Social Construction

According to Straw (1990), in the newly emerging period called social construction, knowledge is socially patterned and conditioned. The locus of meaning is in the social context, not with any person or object. As in the transaction period, the focus is on the construction of meaning, not by a single author or reader, but by the reader as a member of the larger social community (Vygotsky 1978; Hunt 1990; Hynds 1990). Social construction emphasizes the generation of meaning through social experience and interaction. The reader constructs meaning by using many types and levels of knowledge that are socially and culturally shared.

Social construction has its roots in pragmatism (Dewey 1938) and has been influenced by the ideas of Vygotsky (1978) and cultural psychologists who have developed and modified his views (Bruner 1985; 1990; Cole 1985). Like pragmatists, social constructionists consider reading literacy and literacy learning to be functional and social acts that are intentional and reflect shared knowledge, values, beliefs, and expectations on the part of the reader. Students act not only as individuals, but they are also influenced by their families, peers, teachers, the media, and the whole surrounding culture (McCarthey and Raphael 1989).

Cultural contents, myths, desires, intentions, commitments, and values, which are commonly shared in the social community, are also expressed in the texts children read. This is important because our culturally adapted way of life depends on shared meanings and shared concepts as well as on shared modes of discourse for negotiating differences in meaning and interpretation (Bruner 1990, 13).

Three basic assumptions undergird theories of social construction. First, knowledge is constructed by the interaction of the individual with the sociocultural environment. Second, higher mental functions including reading are social and cultural by nature. And third, knowledgeable members of the culture can assist others in learning (McCarthey and Raphael 1989, 21).

Reading, like other higher mental activities, requires voluntary self-regulation, conscious realization, reflection, and the use of signs for mediation. Because such acts are social by nature, they depend on communication across generations and between individuals. Consequently, reading acquisition begins in the interaction of an individual with parents, siblings, peers, or teachers and the surrounding media environment. The role of language and dialogue is critical, since it is through speech and social communication that the learner acquires new abilities. Through a more experienced person modeling and thinking aloud, students learn the role and functions of literacy within the culture and the different ways of actualizing the meaning in the texts. The dialogue itself is not merely facilitative, but actually formative in the development of the students' reflective and critical thinking in functional literacy (McCarthey and Raphael 1989).

Within the context of social construction theories, learning is considered an internalization of social interaction that occurs first between individuals and then within an individual. Internalization occurs in the *zone of proximal development*, defined as "the distance between the actual development level as determined by independent problem solving and the level of potential development as determined through problem solving under adult guidance or in collaboration with more capable peers" (Vygotsky 1978, 87). In this zone, learning awakens a variety of internal processes that are able to operate only when the child is interacting with people in his/her environment. Once these processes are internalized, they become part of the child's independent developmental achievement (Vygotsky 1978, 91).

In teaching reading, assisted instruction and student-teacher dialogue are emphasized. Assisted instruction has been compared to the scaffolding provided by the structuring of tasks through instruction, modeling, questioning, and feedback until the learner is able to function independently. The gradual release of responsibility moves toward a period of joint responsibility and ends with the student assuming control over learning (Pearson and Gallagher 1983).

The social construction period emphasizes the social nature of literacy practices in both society and the school. Because learners who operate in different literacy environments differ with regard to their reading experiences and their needs for functional literacy (Heath 1983), successful instruction is connected with the learner's everyday life and is placed in a broad, challenging, and growing context that addresses important needs of the reader both in and outside of school (Dewey 1938; Scheffler 1986).

Success or failure in reading may be due to cultural matches or mismatches between schools and homes. Sometimes the problems may exemplify a cultural mismatch between students' and teachers' values and intentions rather than a difference in ability (Anang 1982). Thus, during the social construction period, teachers have a responsibility to base their instruction on the backgrounds their students bring to the activity to be learned. Social construction assumes that the teacher has schema of the sociocultural development of literacy and that those schema are actually put into use in the planning of educational activities and in assessment (McCarthey and Raphael 1989).

2.4.5. Progression of Reading Theories Summarized

We arrive then at the definition of four dominant trends in reading theories:

- *Information transfer*, where the meaning of the text lies outside the reader who is expected to reproduce it; where teaching is based on a prescriptive view of language; instruction is hierarchical and subskill in nature; and processing is done in a linear fashion.

- *Interaction*, where the meaning of the text resides with both the text and the reader who is expected to have some background knowledge that fits the text; and where we see an interaction between the vernacular language of the student and the more formal language of school and text.

- *Transaction*, where meaning is generated by the reader while reading; where a reader of any age is expected to read in the same manner, albeit with differing levels of knowledge on which to base an interpretation; and in which the reading act is clearly considered to be holistic in nature and is tightly integrated into the socialization associated with active language use.

- *Social construction*, where knowledge is socially patterned and meaning is constructed through social experience and interaction; in reading instruction knowledgeable members of the culture play a prominent role in assisting in learning.

3. Exploring the Structure of Teachers' Beliefs, Instructional Activities, and Assessment Practices

3.1. Methodology

Within the IEA Reading Literacy Study, the teachers' beliefs and instructional and assessment activities were accessed through three question blocks related to teachers' beliefs, the activities that they have students do, and the things they test. Because of the difficulties in defining the total domain of classroom activities, it is hard to be sure that these items represent a full or representative sample of teachers' beliefs and instructional practices.

In most studies of this kind, and consistent with the way the data are gathered, researchers often report on an item-by-item basis. Although we could review each of the instructional variables in this way, we are not certain how it would help. To know that Finnish teachers do *x* more than American teachers do, or that American teachers do *y* more than Finnish teachers does seem somewhat trivial. Alternatively, researchers might define or derive a principal component and report on that in a comparative format. In this instance, the researchers are assuming a common definition of the latent variable across national contexts (see Lundberg and Linnakylä 1992).

For the purposes of this paper, however, we wished to ask a different question. We were more concerned with the web of instructional practices—the combinations that work to form an instructional network as they relate to a particular social milieu. Therefore, we considered it more useful to group these items into more meaningful and coherent units for analysis.

Based on the research findings regarding the process of teaching, one would expect that these units should, in principle, correspond to theories of reading—one hopes into those schools of thought we outlined above. Therefore, we engaged in exploratory factor analyses to examine the latent structure of responses to these items in both countries' data sets independent of the other. We looked at the data in this way because we believed the items might have differing interpretations related to the variation in instructional and cultural context.

3.1.1. Measurement Instruments

The measurement was focused on the teacher's beliefs, activities, and assessment approaches. Three omnibus questions—what teachers believe about reading instruction, what they have students do, and what they assess—included in the international instruments served as the basis of our inquiry.

What Teachers Believe. Teachers were asked to indicate their level of agreement with statements about issues in reading instruction (Table 1). This question addresses teachers' beliefs about reading theory and how instruction should be organized.

Table 1. What teachers believe

Below you will find a number of statements about issues in reading instruction. Please state your degree of agreement/disagreement with each statement by circling the appropriate number. *(Circle one number on each line.)*

		Strongly disagree	Disagree	Not certain	Agree	Strongly agree
a.	When my students read to me, I expect them to read every word accurately	1	2	3	4	5
b.	Teachers should keep careful records of every student's reading progress	1	2	3	4	5
c.	Students should not be encouraged to read a word they don't know	1	2	3	4	5
d.	All students should enjoy reading	1	2	3	4	5
e.	Most of what a student reads should be assessed	1	2	3	4	5
f.	Every day students should be read to by the teacher from a story book	1	2	3	4	5
g.	Reading aloud by students to a class is a waste of time	1	2	3	4	5
h.	Most students improve their reading best by extensive reading on their own	1	2	3	4	5
i.	Students should always understand why they are reading	1	2	3	4	5
j.	Teachers should always groups students according to their reading ability	1	2	3	4	5
k.	9-year-olds should not have access to books they will read in the next school year	1	2	3	4	5
l.	Class sets of graded reading material should be used as the basis for the reading program	1	2	3	4	5
m.	Students who can't understand what they read haven't been taught proper comprehension skills	1	2	3	4	5
n.	Every mistake a student makes in reading aloud should be corrected at once	1	2	3	4	5
o.	All students' comprehension assignments should be marked carefully to provide them with feedback	1	2	3	4	5
p.	Students should not start a new book until they have finished the last	1	2	3	4	5
q.	Parents should be actively encouraged to help their students with reading	1	2	3	4	5
r.	Students should learn most of their new words from lessons designed to enhance their vocabulary	1	2	3	4	5
s.	Reading learning materials should be carefully sequenced in terms of language structures and vocabulary	1	2	3	4	5
t.	Students should take a book home to read every day	1	2	3	4	5
u.	Students should be encouraged to read texts they have written	1	2	3	4	5
v.	Students should always understand what they are reading	1	2	3	4	5
w.	Students should always choose their own books to read	1	2	3	4	5
x.	A word recognition test is sufficient for assessing students' reading levels	1	2	3	4	5
y.	Teachers should carefully follow the sequence of the textbook	1	2	3	4	5
z.	Students should undertake research projects to improve their reading.	1	2	3	4	5

SOURCE: IEA Reading Literacy Study, Population A Teacher Questionnaire, 1991.

What Teachers Have Students Do. Teachers were asked how frequently they have students do certain reading activities (Table 2). This question looks at the kinds of assignments and activities teachers expect students to complete.

Table 2. What teachers have students do

How often are your <u>students</u> typically <u>involved</u> in the following reading activities? *(Circle one number per line only.)*	Almost never	About 1 or 2 times a month	About 1 or 2 times a week	Almost every day
a. Learning letter-sound relationships and/or phonics	1	2	3	4
b. Word-attack skills (e.g., prediction)	1	2	3	4
c. Silent reading in class	1	2	3	4
d. Answering reading comprehension exercises in writing	1	2	3	4
e. Independent silent reading in the library	1	2	3	4
f. Listening to students reading aloud to a whole class	1	2	3	4
g. Listening to students reading aloud to small groups or pairs	1	2	3	4
h. Listening to teachers reading stories aloud	1	2	3	4
i. Discussion of books read by students	1	2	3	4
j. Learning new vocabulary words systematically (e.g., from lists)	1	2	3	4
k. Learning new vocabulary from texts	1	2	3	4
l. Learning library skills	1	2	3	4
m. Reading plays or dramas	1	2	3	4
n. Playing reading games (e.g., forming sentences from jumbled words)	1	2	3	4
o. Dramatizing stories	1	2	3	4
p. Drawing in response to reading	1	2	3	4
q. Orally summarizing their reading	1	2	3	4
r. Relating experiences to reading	1	2	3	4
s. Reading other students' writing	1	2	3	4
t. Making predictions during reading	1	2	3	4
u. Diagramming story content	1	2	3	4
v. Looking for the theme or message	1	2	3	4
w. Making generalizations and inferences	1	2	3	4
x. Studying the style or structure of a text	1	2	3	4
y. Comparing pictures and stories	1	2	3	4
z. Student leading discussion about passage	1	2	3	4
aa. Reading in other subject areas	1	2	3	4
bb. Writing in response to reading	1	2	3	4

SOURCE: IEA Reading Literacy Study, Population A Teacher Questionnaire, 1991.

What Teachers Assess. Teachers were asked how frequently they assessed certain aspects of reading (Table 3).

Table 3. What teachers assess

How often do you assess these aspects of reading with all or most of your class? *(Circle one number per line only.)*					
	Never	About once a year	About once a term	About once a month	About once a week or more
a. Word recognition	1	2	3	4	5
b. Vocabulary	1	2	3	4	5
c. Text comprehension	1	2	3	4	5
d. Literary appreciation	1	2	3	4	5
e. Use of background knowledge	1	2	3	4	5
f. Sentence understanding	1	2	3	4	5
g. Phonic skills	1	2	3	4	5
h. Reading study skills	1	2	3	4	5
i. Amount of reading	1	2	3	4	5
j. Decoding	1	2	3	4	5

SOURCE: IEA Reading Literacy Study, Population A Teacher Questionnaire, 1991.

3.1.2. Sample

For the purposes of the Reading Literacy Study, it was decided to sample intact classes at the grade level in which the modal age of the students was 9 years. As a result, in Finland, third grade classes were sampled, while in the United States, fourth grade classes were chosen. The teacher of each participating class was asked to fill out the teacher questionnaire. In Finland, 71 teachers of 1,552 students responded. In contrast, in the United States 300 teachers of 6,729 students responded. Although the sample sizes differ, national probability samples of classrooms were selected in both cases. This means that, in each case, valid inferences can be made from the samples to the respective nation's teachers as a group.

In Finland, earlier studies have demonstrated relatively small differences between schools and classrooms as compared with differences within schools and classrooms. In such a relativity homogeneous educational system, the required sample size for making reliable national inferences is lower than in a system with wide variations between schools such as in the United States. In addition, within the United States, in schools where there was more than one fourth grade class, two classes were sampled, so that the sample of 167 participating grade 4 schools gave rise to the sample of 300 teachers who responded. In Finland, the 71 teachers were from 71 different schools. The two respective national samples are of sufficient size to enable us to make reliable comparisons of teachers' instructional practices and beliefs in reading. For more detail about the sample design used for the IEA Reading Literacy Study, see Elley (1992).

3.1.3. Data Analysis

With each group of items and for each country separately, we engaged in exploratory factor analyses to get at the latent structure of these items. As a general strategy, a principal factor solution was obtained, and, in the first instance, factors with eigenvalues greater than one were rotated to an oblique solution. In subsequent analyses, more or fewer factors were rotated until a solution was obtained that exhibited good simple structure and whose factors could be assigned meaning consistent with the theory and substance of reading and reading instruction.

3.2. The American Findings

3.2.1. What American Teachers Believe

As seen in Figure 3, we defined two factors from this question block. The first factor, labeled *sequenced instruction*, is characterized by sequencing, mastery of prior levels before moving on, accuracy, and heavy teacher direction. Although never specifically stated, one might read into this factor a belief in developmental stages that are carefully orchestrated by either the materials or the teacher. Sequence also may be related to beliefs about the logic of the subject matter moving from simple to more complex.

Although a number of the items in this factor are not specifically unique to the period, the items loading in this factor mostly characterize the theoretic stance underlying *information transfer*. "Accuracy" is representative of reproduction of an author's or text's message or knowledge. The necessity for correctness can easily be associated with a rule-driven or prescribed notion of language use. The controlled movement across graded sets of materials can be related to the idea of a hierarchy and stages of development. All of these attributes are characteristic of the information transfer period (Table 4).

In considering the distribution of teachers' responses to the items in this factor, the general picture that emerges is that at a minimum, 60 percent of the teachers appear to disagree with beliefs that are consistent with this factor. However, there are four items where this pattern is not as strong. Two items are related to the use of sequenced materials in class. Here teachers seem to be more evenly divided in their beliefs. Teachers also seem to be strongly supportive of providing feedback and monitoring student progress.

In contrast, the second factor, *extensive exposure to reading,* is characterized by students' active involvement in frequent extended reading, both at school and at home. It focuses most on what the student does. Here are elements of whole language approaches, with students being given a more central role in constructing meaning. Similarly, there is mention of the integration of reading and writing, where students are encouraged to read texts they themselves have written.

Although we see that all the items clustered in this factor need not be tied solely to a single particular period, we find that the underlying theme of the items in this factor would appear to be most closely associated with either the *interaction* or *transaction* periods. The movement between school and home, and between reading and writing, represents an integration between a psycholinguistic or sociolinguistic stance characteristic of these periods. These views are further developed by the statements of enjoyment and extensive independent reading.

Teachers appear to support the beliefs espoused in this factor, with more than 74 percent agreeing with all but one of the items. In that item, *students should always understand what they are reading,* teachers seem to be permitting students a bit more latitude and perhaps are leaving more room for students to be challenged by working at constructing meaning more interactively.

Table 4. American teachers' belief factors related to reading theories

| | Reading Theories | | | | Agreement |
	Information transfer	Interaction	Transaction	Social construction	
Sequenced instruction	*				-
Extensive exposure		*	*		+

NOTE: The asterisk indicates that the factor strongly represents the period.

SOURCE: IEA Reading Literacy Study, U.S. National Study data, National Center for Education Statistics, 1991.

155

Figure 3: What American teachers believe

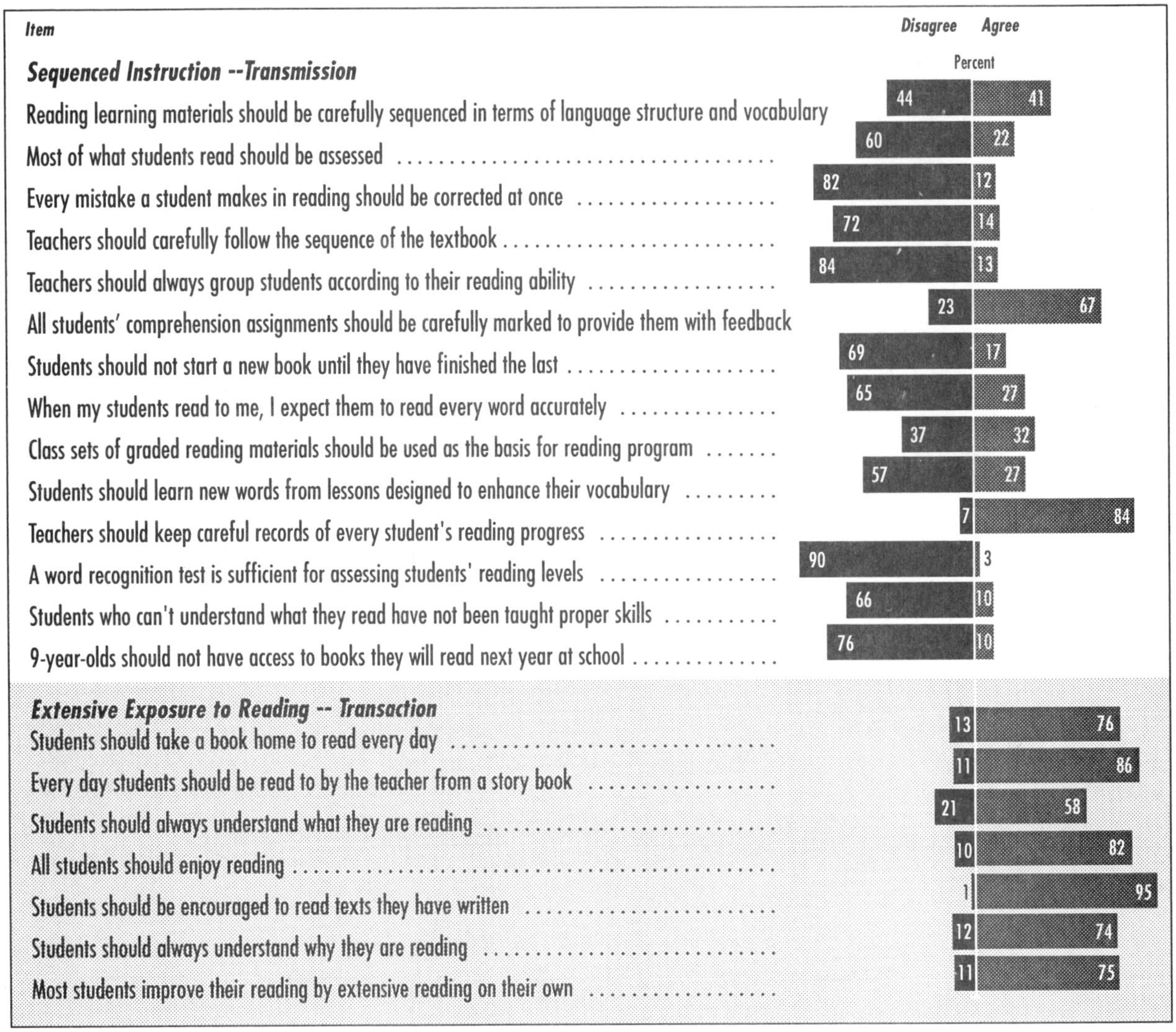

Item	Disagree	Agree
		Percent
Sequenced Instruction --Transmission		
Reading learning materials should be carefully sequenced in terms of language structure and vocabulary	44	41
Most of what students read should be assessed	60	22
Every mistake a student makes in reading should be corrected at once	82	12
Teachers should carefully follow the sequence of the textbook	72	14
Teachers should always group students according to their reading ability	84	13
All students' comprehension assignments should be carefully marked to provide them with feedback	23	67
Students should not start a new book until they have finished the last	69	17
When my students read to me, I expect them to read every word accurately	65	27
Class sets of graded reading materials should be used as the basis for reading program	37	32
Students should learn new words from lessons designed to enhance their vocabulary	57	27
Teachers should keep careful records of every student's reading progress	7	84
A word recognition test is sufficient for assessing students' reading levels	90	3
Students who can't understand what they read have not been taught proper skills	66	10
9-year-olds should not have access to books they will read next year at school	76	10
Extensive Exposure to Reading -- Transaction		
Students should take a book home to read every day	13	76
Every day students should be read to by the teacher from a story book	11	86
Students should always understand what they are reading	21	58
All students should enjoy reading	10	82
Students should be encouraged to read texts they have written	1	95
Students should always understand why they are reading	12	74
Most students improve their reading by extensive reading on their own	11	75

NOTE: Percentages do not add to 100; the shortfall is due to teachers checking "uncertain" as a response.

SOURCE: U.S. Department of Education, National Center for Education Statistics, *Reading Literacy in the United States: Technical Report.* Washington D.C.: 1994.

3.2.2. What American Teachers Have Students Do

As described above, in this question teachers were asked how frequently they have students do certain reading activities (Figure 4). Each of the three factors that emerge from this question reflects a theoretic position related to reading instruction.

In factor one, *schema-based activities*, students focus on the organization and interrelated aspects of text. They move back and forth from the detail to the overarching theme to make predictions and generalizations. They use what they know from experience and about the structure of text.

The instructional activities in this factor closely mirror the definition of the *interaction period*. The period focuses on reliance on background knowledge of the reader, which serves as a context for understanding. In activities such as making predictions, relating experiences to reading, and looking for the theme or message, students are calling forth the appropriate schemata for organizing the information gathered from the text.

For all but two of the items included in this factor, over 70 percent of the teachers report frequently having students do these things. In looking at the items, it is clear that they represent very common practices associated with a directed reading lesson that have been suggested and included in teaching manuals for years. With regard to the two remaining items—making generalizations and inferences, and studying the style or structure of a text—if one believed in a hierarchy of skills these would likely be considered beyond the range of a grade 4 student. Therefore, it is not surprising that fewer teachers reported frequent use of these activities.

In factor two, *integrated language arts activities*, the emphasis is on bringing all communication modes together. Students listen and discuss; they read and write as well as respond through other symbolic modes (drama, art). The items grouped in this factor share an underlying theme that is closely tied to the sociolinguistic theories characteristic of the *transaction period*, where reading and language more generally are situated in a social context. The heavy reliance on discussion, dramatization, and writing of text seems to indicate an emphasis on a more experiential approach to learning.

The social nature of the items in this factor suggest a possible precursor to the more current social construction period. Social activities are strongly represented. However, within the context of the United States, these items also describe very traditional activities historically occurring within other periods as well. Given that items associated with the active construction of meaning do not appear in this factor, we therefore more conservatively place it in the transaction period.

That there is a great deal of variability in the frequency with which teachers report using the instructional activities in this group is to be expected given the nature of these items. Having students dramatize stories or read plays or dramas is quite time consuming and possibly results in little added benefit given the heavy time commitment they require. Even if the teacher was highly committed to this type of approach, we would expect these kinds of differences among the items. However, in looking at those items that teachers report using frequently, we note that they need not be associated only with this type of program. Students are often asked to read aloud for diagnostic purposes. Students in any class frequently write something in response to reading. And, it is not uncommon to have teachers in any subject area draw students' attention to the accompanying pictures or diagrams and to make comparisons with the text. Given the dispersion of response rates, one would be very hard pressed to make any statement about teachers' commitment to this approach as a whole.

In the third factor, *skills-based activities*, the emphasis is on what is literally in the text. It is a very bottom-up orientation focusing on letters, words, sentences, and text-based understanding. This factor could most be associated with the *information transfer period*, where the teacher or the text organizes tasks to be accomplished that become increasingly more difficult and call forth increasingly more complex skills. The teachers surveyed seem to most frequently use the instructional activities

Figure 4: What American teachers have students do

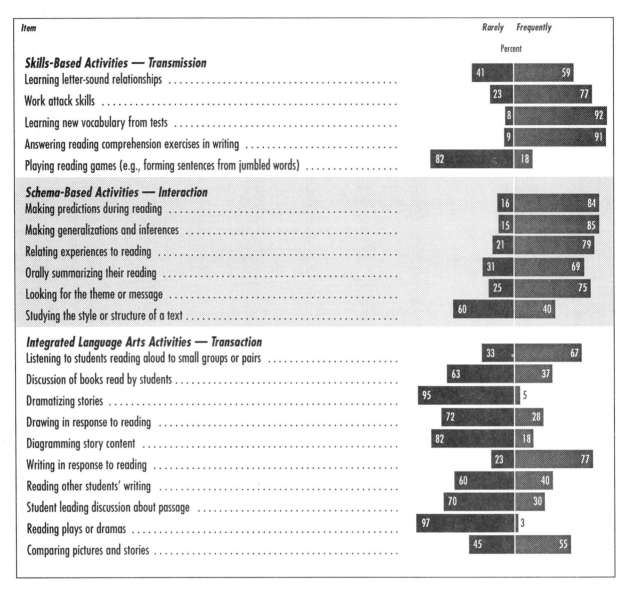

Item	Rarely	Frequently
		Percent
Skills-Based Activities — Transmission		
Learning letter-sound relationships	41	59
Work attack skills	23	77
Learning new vocabulary from tests	8	92
Answering reading comprehension exercises in writing	9	91
Playing reading games (e.g., forming sentences from jumbled words)	82	18
Schema-Based Activities — Interaction		
Making predictions during reading	16	84
Making generalizations and inferences	15	85
Relating experiences to reading	21	79
Orally summarizing their reading	31	69
Looking for the theme or message	25	75
Studying the style or structure of a text	60	40
Integrated Language Arts Activities — Transaction		
Listening to students reading aloud to small groups or pairs	33	67
Discussion of books read by students	63	37
Dramatizing stories	95	5
Drawing in response to reading	72	28
Diagramming story content	82	18
Writing in response to reading	23	77
Reading other students' writing	60	40
Student leading discussion about passage	70	30
Reading plays or dramas	97	3
Comparing pictures and stories	45	55

SOURCE: U.S. Department of Education, National Center for Education Statistics, *Reading Literacy in the United States: Technical Report.* Washington D.C.: 1994.

included in this factor. That only 58.5 percent report frequently teaching letter-sound relationships is not surprising, because these are teachers of grade 4 students who, in principle, should have moved beyond the rudimentary forms of this particular type of activity. Similarly, playing reading games would also be most likely to be associated with earlier grades—preschool, kindergarten, and first or second grade at the latest.

Because factor one, schema-based activities, involves drawing together background knowledge of both content and text structure to construct meaning, this factor would be characteristic of the *interactive period*. In contrast, the second factor, integrated language arts activities, includes activities that involve an integration of symbolic forms, an interaction with the texts, and peers to go beyond the text. Although it is probably most characteristic of the *transaction period*, it would also fit within the definition of the *interaction period*. The third factor, skills-based activities, only includes items that focus on small units of text—words, sentences. The very literal nature of these items places them in the *information transfer period* (Table 5).

Table 5. American teachers' activity factors related to reading theories

| | Reading Theories | | | | Agreement |
	Information transfer	Interaction	Transaction	Social construction	
Schema-based activities		*			+
Integrated language arts		*	*		-
Skills-based activities	*				+

NOTE: The asterisk indicates that the factor strongly represents the period.
SOURCE: IEA Reading Literacy Study, U.S. National Study data, National Center for Education Statistics, 1994.

3.2.3. What American Teachers Assess

Teachers were asked how frequently they assessed certain aspects of reading. According to the factor analysis, teachers appear to emphasize three different things in their assessments (Figure 5). As seen in factor one, *contextualized reading*, teachers are testing the entire process. The basics of decoding and vocabulary are given less emphasis in this factor than relating reading to what the student knows. The second factor, *reading skills,* focuses entirely on the basic subskills of reading–decoding, phonics. The third factor, *text-based understanding,* maintains a heavy text-based, bottom-up orientation. Teachers are focusing on what is specifically in the text.

One would be hard pressed to associate the assessment emphases with particular periods. Each has somewhat overlapping elements. For example, word recognition and vocabulary are very closely related, although the former is more strictly a decoding activity while the later includes some level of understanding. It seems reasonable, however, to say that *contextualized reading*, due to its more inclusive nature, would more likely be associated with either the *interaction* or *transaction periods* (Table 6). *Reading skills* implies a more subskill approach and an analytic organization of instruction, which would require someone outside the learner to structure. Consequently, a case could be made that this would best match the *information transfer* period. The third factor, *text-based understanding,* given the progression from word to sentence to text, appears to have elements of a hierarchy that are prevalent in both the *information transfer* and *interaction periods*.

What is most striking about this group of factors and the distribution of teacher responses to the items in each factor is that the teachers surveyed report frequently assessing everything, irrespective of the content implied in the factor, and perhaps irrespective of what they might be teaching.

Figure 5: What American teachers assess

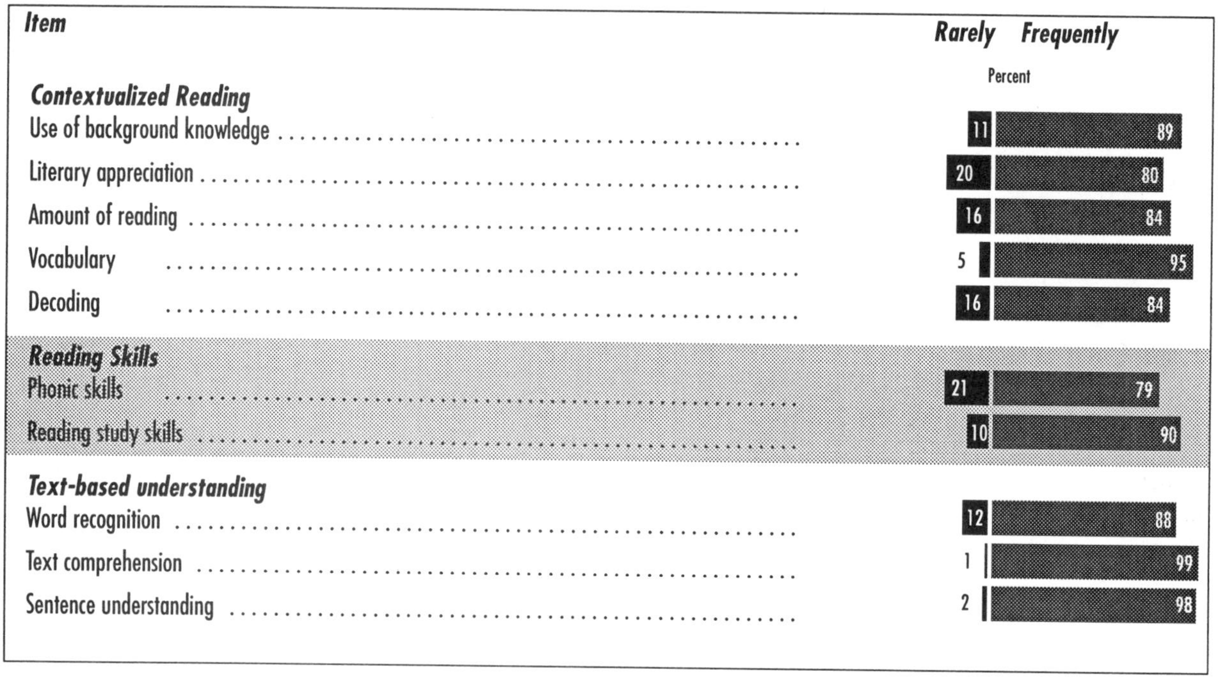

Item	Rarely	Frequently
		Percent
Contextualized Reading		
Use of background knowledge	11	89
Literary appreciation	20	80
Amount of reading	16	84
Vocabulary	5	95
Decoding	16	84
Reading Skills		
Phonic skills	21	79
Reading study skills	10	90
Text-based understanding		
Word recognition	12	88
Text comprehension	1	99
Sentence understanding	2	98

SOURCE: U.S. Department of Education, National Center for Education Statistics, *Reading Literacy in the United States: Technical Report.* Washington D.C.: 1994.

Table 6. American teachers' assessment factors related to reading theories

| | Reading Theories | | | | Agreement |
	Information transfer	Interaction	Transaction	Social construction	
Reading skills	*				+
Text-based understanding	*	*			+
Contextualized reading		*	*		+

NOTE: The asterisk indicates that the factor strongly represents the period.
SOURCE: IEA Reading Literacy Study, National Center for Education Statistics, 1994.

3.2.4. Can We Identify an Implicit Theory of Reading and Instruction that Underlies the Way that American Teachers Organize American Reading Instruction?

In principle, teachers might be expected to align their beliefs about instruction, what they have students do, and what they assess according to a consistent theory of either reading or instruction. As noted in the factors that emerged in the preceding sections, no clear and consistent theoretic stance emerged. Instead, in each of the three sets of items we found factors that related to groups of theories. In addition, across the questions there were factors that seemed to be related. In considering how they might fit together, we placed each of the factors into a grid (Table 7).

Table 7. Relating American teachers' factors to reading theories

| | | Reading Theory | | | | Agreement |
		Information transfer	Interaction	Transaction	Social construction	
What teachers believe	Sequenced instruction	*				-
	Extensive exposure		*	*		+
What teachers have students do	Skills-based activities	*				+
	Schema-based activities		*			+
	Integrated language arts		*	*		-
What teachers test	Reading skills	*				+
	Text-based understanding	*	*			+
	Contextualized reading		*	*		+

SOURCE: IEA Reading Literacy Study, U.S. National Study data, National Center for Education Statistics, 1994.

The table serves as a summary of the theoretical placement of these factors. What we see is that there is, in principle, the possibility for some consistency between teachers' beliefs, the activities they assign, and what they test. For example, teachers who believe in sequenced instruction could have students do activities that were skills based and might test reading skills knowledge and text-based understanding. Teachers who believe in an extensive exposure to reading might emphasize integrated language arts activities and test contextualized reading.

It is interesting to note that when one considers whether teachers support particular beliefs or activities according to a consistent theoretic framework, we find that the teachers' beliefs are in conflict with the activities they assign. For example, teachers disagree with belief statements related to information transfer. However, they frequently assign activities and test behaviors associated with this theoretic stance. Similarly, there is an inconsistency between beliefs and activities among teachers who express agreement with beliefs related to transaction. Few frequently assign associated activities.

To test whether the theoretic consistency in fact occurred, we conducted a second order factor analysis to identify broader second order constructs that might underlie the first order factors, thus reflecting a consistent implicit theory. This second order factor analysis resulted in three meaningful factors—one that captures all testing and two that distinguish between two schools of thought in instruction, as described below. Table 8 shows the second order factors.

Table 8. Theory and practice combined

Primary factor name	Agreement
Second order factor 1 – Interaction/Transaction	
Integrated language arts activities	-
Schema-based activities	+
Second order factor 2 – Information Transfer	
Sequenced instruction – teacher beliefs	-
Skill-based activities	+
Second order factor 3 – Assessment	
Contextualized reading assessment	+
Text-based understanding assessment	+
Skills assessment	+

NOTE: This table differs from the presentation in *Reading Literacy in the United States: Technical Report*. For the purposes of this paper and comparison with Finland, fewer items were used and a new analysis was done.

SOURCE: IEA Reading Literacy Study, U.S. National Study data, National Center for Education Statistics, 1996.

Assessment Emphasis. Second order factor 3, the easiest factor to describe, brings all the questions on assessment back together. Despite the fact that there are three possible emphases, assessment seems to run together. An American teacher who tests a great deal is likely to test everything frequently. A number of plausible explanations come to mind. It is much easier to test subskills where a correct answer is easily definable. Perhaps available testing materials support this type of approach. Alternatively, a large number of tests may be required by the district or the state. Often test scores serve as the basis of giving a term grade. However, no conclusion regarding why this practice has come about can be drawn from the data alone.

The other two factors that emerge are derived from the item blocks on beliefs and activities. One is associated with reading and learning theories based on a notion of information transfer from the teacher or the author to the student, and the other seems to be most related to notions of reading and learning as an interaction or transaction between the teacher or author and the student.

Information Transfer Emphasis. Instruction and reading theories that can be grouped under the heading of information transfer may be characterized as placing the meaning of the text outside the reader who is expected to reproduce it (Straw 1990), organizing teaching according to a prescriptive view of language (Balmuth 1982), providing instruction that is hierarchical and subskill in nature (Barrett 1968; Gray 1960), and processing that is done in linear fashion (Gough 1985). The first order factors that empirically fell into this category are strongly prescriptive and demand a high level of accuracy consistent with a view of language usage that is correct and that is known by the teacher and the authors of texts and materials.

What is interesting to note is that while the surveyed teachers' responses to the items on sequenced instruction tended to disagree with this position, the teachers frequently reported using materials-directed teaching practices that are consistent with this view.

Interaction/Transaction Emphasis. An interaction emphasis is characterized by a shared responsibility for generating meaning between the text, the author, and the reader. In contrast, a transaction emphasis may be characterized as having the meaning of the text generated by the reader while reading. Those who ascribe to an interaction emphasis believe that the reader would come to the task with the appropriate background knowledge necessary for understanding the intended meaning of the text. In contrast, those who ascribe to a transaction emphasis believe that readers of all ages are expected to read in the same manner, albeit with differing levels of knowledge on which they might base an interpretation. The act of reading is considered to be a holistic activity that is highly integrated into the socialization associated with language use.

The first order factors in this construct most strongly represent the transaction period. For example, the items subsumed under the factor integrated language arts stress the integration of communication modes. This integration is highly consistent with the sociolinguistic theories characteristic of the period. In contrast, the second factor, schema-based activities, includes items that could be characteristic of either the interaction or transaction schools of thought. Schema theory began with the interaction period but still remains a dominant force in later periods. Consequently, it seems reasonable to associate this second order factor with both interaction and transaction.

In this second order factor there is an inconsistency that may be associated with the transition between theoretic periods. Teachers agree with and frequently use activities related to schema theory. In contrast, they are less supportive of activities related to an integrated language arts approach. This may reflect the comparative newness of the intent of this approach as it relates to the construction of meaning. Alternatively, this may also be a reaction to older conceptions of language arts programs.

3.2.5. What Conclusions Can We Draw About How American Teachers Organize Instruction?

These data provide us with a reasonable glimpse at the current state of American teachers' instructional practices and beliefs. Although it is not easy to impose a systematic stance implied by the theoretical periods after the fact, doing so does help inform our understanding of instructional practices. Despite the fact that teachers may interpret the items in different ways, the factor analysis helps us to unravel these differences more easily.

We find that teachers' beliefs do not seem to line up with the instructional activities they are likely to assign. And, it is most evident that their assessment practices bear little relationship to their beliefs or instructional activities. On the basis of this finding, we might conclude that teachers do not integrate their instruction and assessment practices with their theoretic beliefs about reading.

Clearly there are other influences that may have had an even larger impact on instructional practice but were not included in the model assumed by the items in the questionnaire. For example, teachers may have been hampered in their attempts to teach in a manner consistent with a social constructionist point of view due to lack of appropriate materials. If teachers have access only to basal reading series with older copyright dates, the emphasis within the materials could preclude this emphasis. Alternatively, district- or state-level assessment programs might necessitate an emphasis on subskills. If this were the case, teachers might feel obliged to place a greater emphasis on these kinds of activities than they might otherwise be inclined to do. These are only two possible explanations, and the questionnaire did not include items that would allow us to systematically rule out these or other possible explanations.

Findings indicating an inconsistency between beliefs, activities, and assessments reinforce the underlying principle motivating systemic reform, that is, all parts of the system must interact in a consistent way simultaneously to bring about the most effective outcomes. However, what we see, even if only just glimpse, is that there is comparatively little coherence between beliefs and practice consistent with any theoretic stance.

At best these conclusions are tentative. First, the items were not specifically designed to measure the implementation of the described theories. Second, the data are based on teacher self-reports and might well be colored, at least to some degree, by notions of socially appropriate responses.

3.3.   The Finnish Findings

3.3.1.   What Finnish Teachers Believe

Just like their American counterparts who took part in the IEA Reading Literacy Study, Finnish teachers participating in the study were asked to identify their level of agreement with statements about issues in reading instruction. In contrast to the more straightforward dichotomy related to reading theory that seems to guide American teachers (see Figure 3), factor analysis of Finnish teachers' beliefs (Figure 6) indicates that more than one principle may be guiding their instructional thinking. However, an overriding principle related to general instructional guidelines plays a predominant role.[4]

In fact, the main structuring principle in teachers' thoughts may be directly tied to the control and responsibility of learning (Pearson and Gallagher 1983). Four out of seven factors are organized around the controlling element of instruction, i.e., teacher, student, or reading material. For example, the factors *teacher monitoring* and *teacher-directed correctness* both indicate a heavy hand on the part of the teacher, who in the first instance seems to constantly monitor, check, assess, and provide feedback to students, and in the second, expects thorough understanding by the students resulting from managed instruction provided by the professional teacher. Although the factor *sequenced instruction* focuses most on the organization of reading materials and tests as well as on grouping students according to their ability, control is shared between the materials and the teacher, who paces instruction appropriately. In the same vein, the factor *material-directed instruction* also has features of external direction, giving more emphasis to the roles of the materials and the outside expert who developed those materials than to the teacher.

In contrast to the factors discussed above, which placed control and responsibility for learning outside of the learner, the factors *enjoyment and interest, student-centered learning by reading,* and *extensive exposure to reading* emphasize the student's internal control of learning. The first factor appears to focus on the affective domain of reading, the second and third on the learning context. These factors seem to include motivational components as well (Roehler and Duffy 1991).

To place these factors within the framework of the reading theories developed earlier, we considered how the attributes of control fit those theoretic stances. *Teacher monitoring* and *teacher-directed correctness* reflect the *information transfer period.* The emphasis is on correct decoding and reproducing the determinate meaning of the words and text. There appears to be an underlying assumption indicating an explicit way to teach and to monitor correct comprehension. The teacher or the expert who designed the materials is considered to be the source of knowledge. Reading is seen as a collection of subskills that have to be taught properly and assessed frequently.

Similarly, the factors *sequenced instruction* and *material-directed instruction* reflect that a good reader is one whose background knowledge and skills are consistent with the content and difficulty of the text and, as such, can be placed in either the information transfer or interaction periods.

The factors *enjoyment and interest, student-centered learning,* and *extensive exposure to reading* refer to views characteristic of the *transactional* and possibly the *social construction periods.* In these instances the reader's personal motives and interests are considered significant in learning to read. In place of formal, stage-based, sequential instruction, these factors stress a natural learning environment and the reader's self-control. For example, *student-centered learning* refers to a social interaction through research projects, and *extensive exposure to reading* could refer to the assumption that reading develops at its best in a lifelike social environment. These particular aspects may be considered the precursors of a social construction view.

---

[4] This emphasis may in part be explained by the content of the questionnaire.

164

Figure 6: What Finnish Teachers Believe

Item	Disagree	Agree
		Percent
Teacher Monitoring — Information Transfer		
Most of what a student reads should be assessed	48	36
Teachers should keep careful records of every student's reading progress	50	38
Every mistake a student makes in reading aloud should be corrected at once	52	42
When my students read to me I expect them to read every word accurately	69	31
Comprehension assignments should be marked to provide students with feedback	31	56
Students should always choose their own books to read	59	35
A word recognition test is sufficient for assessing students' reading levels	32	36
Sequenced Instruction — Information Transfer or Interaction		
Reading materials should be sequenced in terms of language structures and vocabulary	45	40
A word recognition test is sufficient for assessing students' reading levels	32	36
Teachers should always group students according to their reading ability	46	33
Class sets of graded material should be used as the basis for the reading program	71	14
Students should not start a new book until they have finished the last one	45	40
Most students improve their reading best by extensive reading on their own	20	71
Nine-year-olds should not have access to books they will read in the next year at school	74	16
Employment and Interest — Transaction (Social Construction)		
All students should enjoy reading	12	85
Students should not be encouraged to read a word they don't know	92	6
Teachers should always group students according to their reading ability	46	33
Student-centered Learning — Transaction (Social Construction)		
Students should learn new words from lessons designed to enhance vocabulary	62	16
Nine-year-olds should not have access to books they will read in the next year at school	74	16
Every day student should be read to by the teacher from a story book	18	75
Student should undertake research projects to improve their reading	1	90
Students should read every word accurately	69	31
Teacher-directed Correctness — Information Transfer		
Students should always understand what they are reading	20	79
Students should always understand why they are reading	23	63
Parents should be actively encouraged to help their students with reading	3	93
Students who can't understand what they read haven't been taught proper comprehension skills	67	10
Teachers should keep careful records of every student's reading progress	50	38
Material-directed Instruction — Information Transfer or Interaction		
Teachers should carefully follow the sequence of the textbook	99	0
Students should be encouraged to read texts they have written	0	100
Class sets of graded material should be used as the basis for the reading program	71	14
Extensive Exposure to Reading — Transaction (Social Construction)		
Reading aloud by students to a class is a waste of time	91	7
Students should take a book home to read every day	41	48

NOTE: Percentages do not add to 100; the shortfall is due to teachers checking "uncertain" as a response.

SOURCE: IEA Reading Literacy Study, Finnish National Study data, University of Jyvaskyla, 1991.

Finnish teachers tended to agree with the items in the factor *enjoyment and interest*. On average, 75 percent of the teachers supported the views promulgated in these items, with slightly more than 85 percent emphasizing that "all children should enjoy reading." Finnish teachers also supported the items in the *student-centered learning* factor. On average, 65 percent of the teachers agreed with these items, with just under 90 percent expressing strong agreement with the statement that "children should undertake research projects to improve their reading."

On the other hand, Finnish teachers tended to disagree with the statements related to the other five factors. On average, almost 90 percent of the teachers disagreed with the items associated with *material-directed instruction*, 66 percent disagreed with items related to *extensive exposure to reading*, 51 percent disagreed with *teacher-directed correctness*, 49 percent with *teacher monitoring*, and 48 percent with *sequenced instruction*.

On the basis of these findings, we conclude that Finnish teachers appear to value the affective and functional domains of reading instruction. We derive this conclusion based on the level of support for *enjoyment and interest* and *student-centered learning*. Consequently, it appears that Finnish teachers would most strongly support reading theories associated with the transaction period and would probably adopt social construction views. Given that *material-directed* and *teacher-directed* were not favored, we conclude that Finnish teachers do not openly value the theoretic stance underlying either the information transfer or interaction views of reading. Table 9 serves as a summary of the relationship among the seven factors that typify Finnish teachers' beliefs and periods in reading theory.

Table 9. Finnish teachers' belief factors related to reading theories

	Reading Theories				Agreement
	Information transfer	Interaction	Transaction	Social construction	
Teacher monitoring	*				-
Teacher-directed correctness	*				-
Sequenced instruction	*	*			-
Material-directed instruction	*	*			-
Enjoyment and interest			*	(*)	+
Student-centered learning			*	(*)	+
Extensive exposure to reading			*	(*)	-

NOTE: The asterisk indicates that the factor strongly represents the period. The asterisk in parentheses (*) indicates that the factor is not strongly situated in the period, but elements of it are likely to be present.

SOURCE: IEA Reading Literacy Study, Finnish National Study data, University of Jyvaskyla, 1996.

3.3.2. What Finnish Teachers Have Students Do

Teachers were also asked how frequently their students participate in certain activities. The factor analysis of Finnish teachers' instructional activities in the reading classroom reinforces the position outlined above that there is not just one type of theory guiding the teachers' instructional activities (Figure 7). Although the Finnish teachers organize instruction based on general theories of learning, the structure of the classroom activities are more closely related to reading theories than to belief structure. This may be partly a function of the content of the questionnaire.

The main principles structuring the activities appear to be the *domains of reading, integration of reading,* and *control or responsibility of learning*. For example, the subareas or domains of reading are highlighted in the factors *literary comprehension, cooperative oral activities, independent silent reading, practicing subskills, expanding comprehension, enlarging vocabulary,* and *listening activities*. An alternative configuration comes through in the factors *integrating language arts, integrating literacy with other subjects, expanding comprehension, cooperative oral activities,* and *listening activities*. These

Figure 7: What Finnish Teachers have students do

Item	Rarely	Frequently
		Percent
Literary Comprehension — Interaction		
Looking for the theme or message	49	51
Making generalizations and inferences	50	50
Writing in response to reading	63	37
Studying the style or structure of a text	89	11
Integrating Language Arts — Transaction		
Diagramming story content	77	23
Drawing in response to reading	75	25
Orally summarizing their reading	49	51
Reading in other subject areas	20	80
Dramatizing stories	82	18
Silent reading in class	6	94
Cooperative Oral Activities — Transaction (Social Construction)		
Discussion of books read by students	82	18
Reading of plays or dramas	99	1
Playing reading games	96	4
Learning letter-sound relationships and/or phonics	75	25
Dramatizing stories	82	18
Listening to teachers reading stories aloud	16	84
Integrating Literacy with Other Subjects — Transaction (Social Construction)		
Reading other student's writing	75	25
Listening to students read aloud to small groups or in pairs	59	41
Reading in other subject areas	20	80
Making predictions during reading	82	18
Writing in response to reading	63	37
Independent Silent Reading — Interaction		
Silent reading in class	6	94
Answer reading comprehension exercises in writing	42	58
Independent silent reading in the library	43	57
Orally summarizing their reading	49	51
Practicing Subskills — Information Transfer		
Word-attack skills	17	83
Learning letter-sound relationship and/or phonics	75	25
Student leading discussion about passage	74	26
Learning new vocabulary from texts	43	57
Making predictions during reading	82	18
Dramatizing stories	82	18
Expanding Comprehension — Interaction		
Relating experiences to reading	54	46
Comparing pictures and stories	39	61
Making generalizations and inferences	50	50
Learning library skills	70	30
Independent Library Work — Interaction		
Learning library skills	70	30
Student leading discussion about passage	74	26
Independent silent reading in the library	43	57
Enlarging Vocabulary — Information Transfer		
Learning new vocabulary systematically	81	19
Learning new vocabulary from texts	43	57
Listening to teachers reading stories aloud	16	84
Orally summarizing their reading	49	51
Listening Activities — Interaction		
Listening to students reading aloud to a whole class	20	80
Reading in other subject areas	20	80
Playing reading games	96	4
Listening to teachers reading stories aloud	16	84

SOURCE: IEA Reading Literacy Study, Finnish National Study data, University of Jyvaskyla, 1991.

factors reflect an integration of communication and artistic modes or the integration of reading to other school subjects. The factors *independent silent reading* and *independent library work* emphasize students' own control and responsibility for learning, while the factor *cooperative oral activities* stresses shared control of instruction.

From the perspective of reading theories, the factors may be associated with the full range of theoretic paradigms outlined in Section 2 of this paper. The factors *practicing subskills* and *enlarging vocabulary* are characteristic of the *information transfer period* because decoding, separate skills, and literal understanding of words and text weigh heavily in these factors. The factors *literary comprehension, independent silent reading, independent library work, expanding comprehension,* and *listening activities* refer to features typical of the *interaction period*, where meaning is processed between the reader and the text.

The *transaction* period is somewhat represented in the factors focusing on integration such as *integrating language arts, integrating literacy with other subject areas,* and *cooperative oral activities*. These factors stress generating meaning into other modes of communication or through artistic expression. The students' own experience and open construction of meaning is emphasized in the actualization of comprehension.

The content of the integration factors—integrating literacy with other subjects and cooperative oral activities—may even include some features of the *social construction view*. At least some of the variables included in these factors seem to allow for the possibility of constructing socially and culturally shared meaning, while other variables indicate some socially controlled activity. Similarly, these integration factors reflect some motivational elements that are related to cognition and action.

On the one hand, Finnish teachers appear to most frequently use the activities related to listening activities (more than 80 percent of the teachers do three of the four associated activities frequently). Depending on the particular item, between 51 and 94 percent of the teachers report frequent use of activities related to independent silent reading, and more than half frequently use activities associated with expanding comprehension. The Finnish teachers particularly stress extended reading, with 94 percent frequently having students read silently in class and 84 percent frequently reading stories aloud to their classes.

On the other hand, teachers reported rarely using activities related to the other seven factors. For example, approximately 75 percent rarely had students participate in cooperative oral activities, 65 percent rarely assigned activities related to enlarging vocabulary; and more than half rarely engaged students in activities related to either literacy comprehension or independent library work.

This distribution of assigned activities leads to the conclusion that Finnish teachers prefer to emphasize listening and independent silent reading while downplaying activities that emphasize students' self-expression and active cooperation.

In considering how these factors relate to reading theory, it appears that Finnish teachers most emphasize activities characteristic of the interaction view. And there were some signs of movement toward activities consistent with a transaction view (i.e., expanding comprehension). Despite their expressed strong belief in the theoretic stance associated with both transaction and social construction views, Finnish teachers rarely used associated activities. Table 10 provides a summary of the relationship between the 10 factors that emerge from the Finnish teachers' responses to the activities items.

Table 10. Finnish teachers' activity factors related to reading theories

	Information transfer	Reading Theories Interaction	Transaction	Social construction	Agreement
Practicing subskills	*				-
Enlarging vocabulary	*				-
Listening activities		*			+
Independent silent reading		*			+
Independent library work		*			-
Literary comprehension		*			-
Expanding comprehension		*			+
Integrating language arts			*		-
Cooperative oral activities			*	(*)	-
Integrating literacy w/other subjects			*	(*)	-

NOTE: The asterisk indicates that the factor strongly represents the period. The asterisk in parentheses (*) indicates that the factor is not strongly situated in this period, but elements of it are likely to be present.

SOURCE: IEA Reading Literacy Study, Finnish National Study data, University of Jyvaskyla, 1996.

3.3.3. What Finnish Teachers Assess

The factor analysis of Finnish teachers' assessment practices indicates that the main structuring principle is the *sequence of instruction*. The first factor, *diagnosing basic skills*, has the highest loadings on word recognition, phonics skills, and vocabulary—skills commonly associated with beginning reading and instruction that takes place before actually beginning to read a selection. The factor *monitoring text comprehension* stresses study skills, sentence understanding, and use of background knowledge—all associated with comprehension development during instruction. The third factor, *surveying reading activity*, in contrast to the first two focuses on the affective domain, with most emphasis on interests and literary appreciation. This represents the outcome of reading instruction (Figure 8).

From the perspective of reading theories, these factors would be associated with a number of periods. Diagnosing basic skills seems to be related to the *information transfer* period. Monitoring text comprehension with high loadings in text features and reader's background knowledge could be associated with the *interaction* or *transaction* period, especially if the reader's personal background experience is considered significant in constructing text meaning. Surveying reading activity could be associated with either the *interaction* or *transaction* period and even possibly the *social construction* period. Minimally the variables amount of reading and literary appreciation could imply the readers' socially and culturally shared preferences and values after instruction, indicating potential for developing into an association with social construction themes.

The Finnish teachers' responses to the items in each of the different assessment factors indicate that teachers focus on all three aspects of assessment. The greatest emphasis is placed on *monitoring text comprehension* where, on average, 69 percent of the teachers report frequent assessment of sentence understanding (90 percent) and text comprehension (87 percent). Because all aspects of assessment seem to be utilized by Finnish teachers, it is hard to identify what their particular preference regarding assessment practices might be. This is in stark contrast to their stance with regard to beliefs and instructional pedagogy where only a few factors associated with specific periods were favored. These associations are summarized in Table 11.

Figure 8: What Finnish Teachers assess

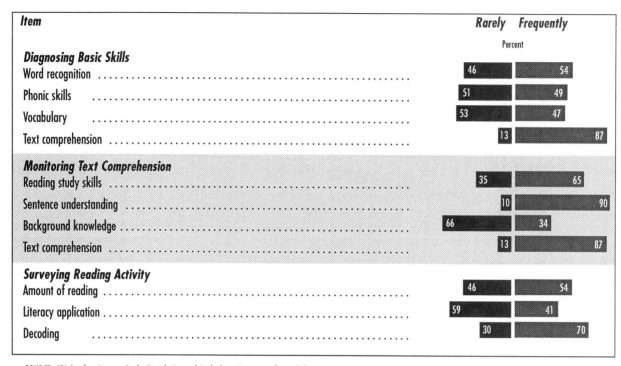

Item	Rarely	Frequently
		Percent
Diagnosing Basic Skills		
Word recognition	46	54
Phonic skills	51	49
Vocabulary	53	47
Text comprehension	13	87
Monitoring Text Comprehension		
Reading study skills	35	65
Sentence understanding	10	90
Background knowledge	66	34
Text comprehension	13	87
Surveying Reading Activity		
Amount of reading	46	54
Literacy application	59	41
Decoding	30	70

SOURCE: IEA Reading Literacy Study, Finnish National Study data, University of Jyvaskyla, 1991.

Table 11. Finnish teachers' assessment factors related to reading theories

	Reading theories				Agreement
	Information transfer	Interaction	Transaction	Social construction	
Diagnosing basic skills	*				+
Monitoring text comprehension		*	*		+
Surveying reading activity		*	*	(*)	+

NOTE: The asterisk indicates that the factor strongly represents the period. The asterisk in parentheses (*) indicates that the factor is not strongly situated in this period, but elements of it are likely to be present.

SOURCE: IEA Reading Literacy Study, Finnish National Study data, University of Jyvaskyla, 1996.

3.3.4. Can We Identify an Implicit Theory of Reading and Instruction that Underlies the Way that Finnish Teachers Organize Reading Instruction?

Similar to our interest in the alignment of American teacher beliefs, activities, and assessment practices, we questioned how things compared in Finland. As was the case with the American data, the factor structures of Finnish beliefs, activities, and assessment were not parallel or internally consistent. The main principle structuring Finnish teachers' beliefs appeared to be the *control of and responsibility for learning*. In structuring students' activities, the *domains of reading* and *integration of activities* were the most significant organizers. For assessment practices, the main structure may best be described as the sequence of instruction.

From the perspective of reading theories, the comparison of belief, activity, and assessment structures suggests that the Finnish teachers' thinking reflects many different discrete reading theories, which also vary in emphasis during different phases of instructional processes. The strongest implicit theoretical organizers in Finnish reading instruction seem to be either the interaction or transaction views (Table 12). In beliefs, three of the seven factors emphasize a position related to the transaction period, while two relate to interaction. Five of the 10 activities factors were related to interaction and 3 to transaction. In assessment, two of the three factors corresponded at least to some extent to the interaction paradigm with two related to transaction. Despite the heavy emphasis on either interaction or transaction, the behavioristic information transfer model was also evident in belief, activity, and assessment structures.

Table 12. Relating Finnish teachers' factors to reading theories

		Reading Theories				Agreement
		Information transfer	Interaction	Transaction	Social construction	
What teachers believe	Teacher monitoring	*				-
	Teacher-directed correctness	*				-
	Sequenced instruction	*	*			-
	Material-directed instruction	*	*			-
	Enjoyment and interest			*		+
	Student-centered learning			*	(*)	+
	Extensive exposure to reading			*	(*)	-
What teachers have students do	Practicing subskills	*				-
	Enlarging vocabularies	*				-
	Listening activities		*			+
	Independent silent reading		*			+
	Independent library work		*			-
	Literary comprehension		*			-
	Expanding comprehension		*			+
	Integrating language arts			*		-
	Cooperative oral activities			*	(*)	-
	Integrating literacy w/other subjects			*	(*)	-
What teachers test	Diagnosing basic skills	*				+
	Monitoring text comprehension		*	*		+
	Surveying reading activity		*	*	(*)	+

NOTE: The asterisk indicates that the factor strongly represents the period. The asterisk in parentheses (*) indicates that the factor is not strongly situated in this period, but elements are likely to be present.

SOURCE: IEA Reading Literacy Study, Finnish National Study data, University of Jyvaskyla, 1996.

Interestingly, a case could be made for the emergence of social construction views among Finnish teachers. With some latitude in interpreting, two of the belief factors, two of the activity factors and one of the assessment factors can be seen as precursors of that theoretic stance. This is particularly true if the theories associated with social construction are considered to be a social extension of the transaction model where reading reflects the intentions, attitudes, and values shared and promoted in the social and cultural learning context. However, it is also possible that the teacher questionnaire did not provide adequate representation of social construction in reading instruction.

The Finnish teachers fairly consistently held a negative view of information transfer theories. They more often disagreed with items that would be so classified, and they also rarely favored activities associated with the period. While the Finnish teachers did not subscribe to beliefs related to an interaction theory of reading, they nonetheless reported frequent use of activities that would characterize that stance. In contrast, the Finnish teachers espoused beliefs that typify the transaction period, but they rarely assigned activities associated with that stance.

It would appear that while Finnish teachers hold beliefs that are quite progressive, their instructional practices are less so. Finnish teachers believe that transaction and social construction views of reading—motivation, enjoyment and interest, as well as a highly student-centered active participatory environment—are important principles for the strategic planning of instruction. However, these principles do not seem to guide the selection of instructional activities. When it comes to selecting instructional activities, the Finnish teachers follow a more traditional model, one in which the student's role is more passive (the silent listener) and more isolated or independent (the lone reader).

A second order factor analysis was conducted to explore the underlying common constructs of the belief, activity, and assessment structures. As seen in Table 13, in Finland the second order analysis resulted in eight factors and indicated that the principles related to control and integration of learning are significant forces in instruction. Control and responsibility for learning is obvious in the factors *sequenced instruction, independent learning by reading,* and *cooperation.* It is evident that integration plays an important role in structuring the factors *integrating subskills, assessing learning by reading,* and *independent learning by reading.* In addition, the reading domains also structure the factors as is the case in *oral activities, learning vocabulary,* and *expanding comprehension.* An assessment emphasis is indicated in one factor—*assessing learning by reading*—that loaded heavily with *monitoring text comprehension* and *surveying reading activity.* However, the third assessment factor, *diagnosing basic skills,* was not loaded in this second order factor, which seemed to emphasize assessment of comprehension and learning by reading rather than diagnosing of basic skills.

When the second order factors are related to reading theories, the underlying theoretical approach seems to be in the interaction view, which is indicated in most of the factors (*integrating subskills, assessing learning by reading, sequenced instruction, oral activities,* and *independent studying by reading*). The signs of the more progressive transaction and social construction periods could be seen in the factors *assessing learning by reading, independent studying by reading, cooperation,* and *expanding comprehension.* However, these factors also reflect other theoretical views.

In brief, the second order factor analysis reveals that Finnish teachers follow many different practical theories, despite their emphasis on the interaction/information transfer stance. An interaction/transaction view can also be traced, and there are even signs of a combination of diverse stances indicative of either transaction or social construction views of reading.

Table 13. Theory and practice combined

Primary Factor Name   Agreement

Second order factor 1 – *Integrating subskills (information transfer/transaction)*

Practicing subskills	-
Literary comprehension	-
Teacher-directed correctness	-
Integrating language arts	-
Diagnosing basic skills	+
Integrating literacy with other subjects	-
Student-centered learning by reading	+

Second order factor 2 – *Assessing learning by reading (interaction/transaction)*

Monitoring text comprehension	+
Surveying reading activities	+
Independent library work	-
Integrating literacy with other subjects	-

Second order factor 3 – *Sequenced instruction (interaction/information transfer)*

Sequenced instruction	-
Teacher monitoring	-
Independent library work	-
Teacher directed correctness	-
Independent silent reading	+

Second order factor 4 - *Oral activities (interaction)*

Listening activities	+
Extensive exposure to reading	-
Enjoyment and interest	+
Cooperative oral activities	-
Student-centered learning by reading	+
Monitoring text comprehension	+

Second order factor 5 – *Independent learning by reading (interaction/transaction)*

Independent silent reading	+
Material-directed instruction	-
Integrating literacy with other subjects	-
Extensive exposure to reading	-

Second order factor 6 – *Learning vocabulary (information transfer)*

Enlarging vocabulary	-
Enjoyment and interest	+
Teacher monitoring	-
Extensive exposure to reading	-

Second order factor 7 – *Cooperation (transaction)*

Cooperative oral activities	-
Diagnosing basic skills	+
Student-centered learning by reading	+
Teacher-directed correctness	-

Second order factor 8 – *Expanding comprehension (transaction)*

Expanding comprehension	+
Surveying reading activity	+

SOURCE: IEA Reading Literacy Study, Finnish National Study data, University of Jyvaskyla, 1996.

3.3.5 What Conclusions Can We Draw About How Finnish Teachers Organize Instruction?

In ways that are similar to the findings about American teachers, we find that we do have a preliminary picture of how Finnish teachers organize instruction. The Finnish teachers appear to believe that the transaction view of reading—with an emphasis on motivation, enjoyment, and interest, as well as student-centered strategies and extensive exposure to reading – is important when planning and organizing instruction. However, these principles do not seem to translate into the instructional activities the teachers frequently choose to use. Instead, the instructional activities of choice appear to follow the more traditional views associated with the interaction period, where the student's role is that of a silent listener and a lonely reader rather than that of an active and self-expressive language user or cooperative participant in a social environment where meaning is generated based on shared values and views.

4. Comparing Reading Instruction in the United States and Finland

The most striking contrast between the underlying structures reflected in this survey of instruction in the United States and Finland is the difference in the number of factors that seem to tie instruction together. When the same rules for the identification of factors was applied, Finnish teachers' beliefs contained seven groups while American teachers only had two. Similarly, Finnish teachers seemed to use activities in ways that could be clustered into 10 factors, while Americans only segmented their activities into three clusters (Table 14).

American teachers appear to organize both their beliefs and instructional activities in accordance with the extensive and various programs that are readily available and form the mainstay of American instruction. In contrast, the Finnish teachers appear to structure both their beliefs and teaching activities into smaller units, separating teachers' and students' roles and responsibilities, sequencing instruction, materials selection, domains of reading, phases of instruction, and motivation. This may be attributable to the national curriculum, which specified the application of different methods flexibly in accordance with the differences among students and their differing needs. This position also pervades the guidelines and traditions of teacher training. Furthermore, Finnish teachers themselves choose the materials to be used within the class from among the various published or self-made options available. Consequently their decisions are made at a more microlevel and may result in greater diversity of texts within any one school or across schools.

The most striking similarity appears to be related to the organization of assessment practices. Here the teachers in both Finland and the United States seem to operate at the same level of generalization. Even though the Finnish schools do not have a tradition of standardized tests, there is a similar prevalence of models of testing that are comparable to the practices in America, where testing is an integral part of daily and weekly instructional programs.

When we look beyond the surface differences associated with the number factors and focus on the structuring principles underlying the belief factors of both the Finnish and American teachers, several similarities are readily apparent. The contrast between an external teacher- or material-directed instructional program and a more internal student-centered view are present in factor structures of both countries. The first set of principles can be connected with the external teacher and text control typical of the information transfer and interaction views. In contrast, the principles underlying the second set are more characteristic of the transaction view of reading. Control and responsibility for learning are significant discriminators in teachers' beliefs in both countries.

In quite a similar fashion, we note that both the Finnish and American teachers' preferences seem parallel. Neither agrees with the belief statements associated with the information transfer or interaction periods. Instead, the statements related to transaction or social construction are strongly preferred in both cultures.

Table 14. Instruction factors in Finland and the United States

Finland			United States		
Factor	Primary theory	Agreement	Factor	Primary theory	Agreement
Beliefs					
Teacher monitoring	Information transfer	-			
Teacher-directed correctness	Information transfer	-	Sequenced instruction	Information transfer/ interaction	-
Sequenced Instruction	Information transfer	-			
Material-directed instruction	Interaction	-			
Enjoyment and interest	Transaction	+	Extensive exposure to reading	Transaction	+
Student-centered learning	Transaction/social construction	+			
Extensive exposure to reading	Transaction/social construction	-			
Activities					
Practicing subskills	Information transfer	-			
Enlarging vocabulary	Information transfer	-	Skill-based activities	Information transfer	+
Listening activities	Interaction	+			
Independent silent reading	Interaction	+			
Independent library work	Interaction	-	Schema-based activities	Interaction	+
Literary comprehension	Interaction	-			
Expanding comprehension	Interaction	+			
Integrating language arts	Transaction	-	Integrated language arts	Transaction	-
Integrating literacy w/other subjects	Transaction/social construction	–			
Cooperative oral activities	Transaction/social construction	-			
Assessment					
Diagnosing basic skills	Information transfer	+	Reading skills	Information transfer	+
Monitoring text comprehension	Interaction/ transaction	+	Text-based understanding	Information transfer/interaction	+
Surveying reading activity	Interaction/ transaction	+	Contextualized reading	Interaction/ transaction	+

SOURCE: IEA Reading Literacy Study, U.S. National Study data, National Center for Education Statistics, and Finnish National Study data, University of Jyvaskyla, 1996.

Comparison of the activity factors reveals the same kind of unity and diversity. Both factor structures are mainly organized according to the domains, subareas, or cognitive processes of reading—skills, strategic activities, or integration with other language skills or even other subject areas. Despite the similarity in organizing principle, the American teachers' activity structure is global in nature, taking a large view of groups of instructional procedures, while the Finnish teachers are more specific in how they group the purpose and intent of activities.

The Finnish teachers focus on aspects of control and responsibility for learning that in the Finnish context may be teacher-directed, student-directed, or a shared responsibility. Furthermore, for Finnish teachers the learning environment and especially the integration with other language skills are important specifiers. For example, the Finns stress the role of listening, but this emphasis does not play a role in structuring American instructional activities. This may be related to the Finnish tradition of extensive practice of the auditive discrimination of phonemes, especially in the lower grades. Because the Finnish language has a very regular grapheme-phoneme correspondence, practicing auditive discrimination obviates the need for special spelling practice or memorization of spelling rules. The emphasis on listening may also have beneficial motivational effects. Many Finnish studies have shown that the teachers' reading aloud has both a strong motivational intention and effect. So, it is generally recommended both in the curriculum and in the teachers' training.

In both teaching cultures, teachers' instructional beliefs clearly are more progressive than their classroom activities (cf. Fishbein and Ajzen 1975; Lundberg and Linnakylä 1992). Both teacher groups appreciated beliefs reflecting a transaction view of reading while most frequently using instructional activities that reflected interaction model. Traditional attitudes on assessment were shared in both teaching cultures.

It was especially difficult to interpret Finnish teachers' instructional factors from the perspective of reading theory. This might be attributable to how the questionnaire was composed. It was not driven by the perspective of theory. And fortunately, at least according to the newer theories, meaning is relative and may vary across readers and cultures.

If the structuring principles of and the relations to reading theories are negotiated, it seems obvious that in reading instruction the control of and responsibility for learning, as well as the variety of reading domains and learning context and the integration of language and learning activities, are significant in defining the theory of reading instruction. We mainly followed Straw's categorization of reading theories. In his analysis, Straw (1990) used three perspectives for examination: locus of meaning, nature of knowledge needed to be literate, and purpose of literacy. This system was an adequate representation of the spectrum of reading theories. However, it was not quite as adequate when we consider theories of instruction. The vantage point must be expanded to include the control and responsibility of learning as well as the extent of integration in reading literacy.

Just like books, teaching to read books in different nations seems to be "...like mountain tops jutting out of the sea with an underlying universal intellectual geography" (Bruner 1990, ix). It seems to us that the unity of this intellectual geography is quite strong—as we saw when comparing the teaching cultures of two distant countries with quite different school systems, with different teaching traditions, and with very different languages. But even though the underlying intellectual basis was similar, there were also some differences. These do not pose a problem, but rather a possibility—a possibility to explore many new seas and to reach many new mountains.

References

Anderson, R.C., and Pearson, P.D. (1984). A schema-theoretic view of basic processes in reading comprehension. In P.D. Pearson (ed.), *Handbook of reading research*. Vol. 1, 255-291. New York: Longman.

Anang, A. (1982). *What is reading: A social theory of comprehension instruction*. Michigan State University. Institute for Research on Teaching. Occasional paper No. 62.

Applebee, A.N., and Langer, J.A. (1983). Instructional scaffolding: Reading and writing as natural language abilities. *Language Arts*, 60, 168-175.

Balmuth, M. (1982). *The roots of phonics*. New York: Teachers College Press.

Barrett, T.A. (1968). A taxonomy of cognitive and affective dimensions of reading comprehension. Outlined by Clymer, T.C. What is reading? Some current concepts. In H.M. Robinson (ed.), *Innovation and change in reading instruction*, 252-258. NSSE 67th Yearbook, Part II. Chicago: University of Chicago Press.

Beach, R., and Hynds, S. (1991). Research on response to literature. In R. Barr, M.L. Kamil, P. Mosenthal, and P.D. Pearson (eds.), *Handbook of reading research*. Vol. 2, 453-489. New York: Longman.

Bennett, N. (1988). The effective primary school teacher: The search for a theory of pedagogy. *Teaching & Teacher Education,* 4(1), 1993.

Bloom, B.S., Hastings, J.T., and Madaus, G.F. (eds.) (1971). *Handbook of formative and summative evaluation of student learning*. New York: McGraw Hill.

Bruner, J.S. (1985). Vygotsky. A historical and conceptual perspective. In J.V. Wertsch (ed.), *Culture, communication and cognition: Vygotskian perspectives*, 21-34. Cambridge, England: Cambridge University Press.

Bruner, J.S. (1990). *Acts of meaning*. Cambridge, MA: Harvard University Press.

Chall, J.S. (1983). *Stages of reading development*. New York: McGraw-Hill.

Clark, C.M., and Peterson, P.L. (1986). Teachers' thought processes. In M.C. Wittrock (ed.), *Handbook of research on teaching*. 3rd ed., 255-296. New York: Macmillan.

Cole, M. (1985). The zone of proximal development. Where culture and cognition create each other. In J.V. Wertsch (ed.), *Culture, communication and cognition: Vygotskian perspectives*, 116-161. Cambridge, England: Cambridge University Press.

Cullinan, B.E. (1989). Literature for young children. In D.S. Strickland and L.M. Morrow (eds.), *Emerging literacy: Young children learn to read and write*, 35-51. Newark, DE: International Reading Association.

Davis, F.B. (1944). Fundamental factors of comprehension in reading. *Psychometrika*, 9, 185-197.

Dewey, J. (1938). *Experience and education*. New York: Macmillan.

Ehri, L.C. (1987). Learning to read and spell words. *Journal of Reading Behavior*, 19, 5-31.

Elley, W. B. (1992). *How in the world do students read?* Hamburg: The International Association for the Evaluation of Educational Achievement.

Feiman, S., and Floden, R.E. (1986). The cultures of teaching. In M.C. Wittrock (ed)., *Handbook of research on teaching*. 3rd ed., 505-525. New York: Macmillan.

Fishbein, M., and Ajzen, I. (1975). *Belief, attitude, intention, and behavior: An introduction to theory and research.* London: Addison-Wesley.

Flesch, R. (1955). *Why Johnny can't read.* New York: Harper & Row.

Frye, N. (1957). *Anatomy of criticism.* Princeton, NJ: Princeton University Press.

Goelman, H., Oberg, A., and Smith, F. (eds.). (1984). *Awakening to literacy.* London: Heinemann.

Goodman, K.S. (1970). Behind the eye: What happens in reading. In K.S. Goodman and O.S. Niles (eds.), *Reading, process and program.* Urbana, IL: National Council of Teachers of English.

Goodman, K.S., and Goodman, Y.M. (1979). Learning to read is natural. In L.B. Resnick and P.A. Weaver (eds.), *Theory and practice of early reading.* Vol. 1, 137-154. Hillsdale, NJ: Lawrence Erlbaum Associates.

Goodman, Y.M. (1986). Children coming to know literacy. In W.H. Teale, and E. Sulzby (eds.), *Emergent literacy: Writing and reading,* 1-14. Norwood, NJ: Ablex.

Gough, P.B. (1972). One second of reading. In J.F. Kavanagh and I.G. Mattingly (eds.), *Language by ear and by eye,* 331-368. Cambridge, MA: MIT Press.

Gough, P.B. (1985). One second of reading: Postscript. In H. Singer and R.B. Ruddell (eds.), *Theoretical models and processes of reading.* 3rd ed., 687-688. Newark, DE: International Reading Association.

Gough, P.B., and Hillinger, M.L. (1980). Learning to read: An unnatural act. *Bulletin of the Orlon Society,* 30, 179-196.

Gray, W.S. (1960). *The major aspects of reading. Sequential development of reading abilities.* Supplementary Educational Monographs, No. 90. Chicago: University of Chicago Press.

Harste, J.C. (1985). Portrait of a new paradigm: Reading comprehension research. In A. Crismore (ed.), *Landscapes: A-state-of-art assessment of reading comprehension research 1974-1984,* 12:1-24, Final report. Indiana University, School of Education.

Harste, J.C., and Woodward, V.A. (1989). Fostering needed change in early literacy programs. In D.S. Strickland and L.M. Morrow (eds.), *Emerging literacy: Young children learn to read and write,* 147-159. Newark, DE: International Reading Association.

Harste, J.C., Woodward, V.A., and Burke, C.L. (1984). *Language stories and literacy lessons.* Portsmouth, NH: Heineman.

Harste, J.C., Burke, C.L., and Woodward, V.A. (1982). Children's language and world: Initial encounters with print. In J.A. Langer and M.T. Smith-Burke (eds.), *Reader meets the author: Bridging the gap,* 105-131. Newark, DE: International Reading Association.

Heath, S.B. (1983). *Ways with words: Language, life, and work in communities and classrooms.* Cambridge, England: Cambridge University Press.

Hunt, R.A. (1990). The parallel socialization of reading research and literary theory. In S.B. Straw and D. Bogdan (eds.), *Beyond communication: Reading comprehension and criticism.* Portsmouth, NH: Boynton/Cook-Heinemann.

Hynds, S. (1990). Reading as a social event: Comprehension and response in the text, classroom, and world. In D. Bogdan and S. Straw (eds.), *Beyond communication, reading comprehension and criticism.* Portsmouth, NH: Boyton/Cook Publishers, Heinemann.

Juel, C. (1991). Beginning reading. In R. Barr, M.L. Kamil, P. Mosenthal, and P.D. Pearson (eds.), *Handbook of reading research*. Vol. 2, 759-788. New York: Longman.

Just, M.A., and Carpenter, P.A. (1980). A theory of reading: From eye fixations to comprehension. *Psychological Review, 87*, 329-354.

Just, M.A., and Carpenter, P.A. (1985). A theory of reading: From eye fixations to comprehension. In H. Singer and R.B. Ruddell (eds.), *Theoretical models and processes of reading*. 3rd ed., 174-208. Newark, DE: International Reading Association.

Kastler, L.A., Rosen, N.L., and Hoffman, J.V. (1987). Understanding of the forms and functions of written language: Insights from children and parents. In J.E. Readance and R.S. Baldwin (eds.), *Research in literacy: Merging perspectives*, 85-92. Rochester, NY: National Reading Conference.

Kintsch, W., and van Dijk, T. (1978). Toward a model of text comprehension. *Psychological Review*, 85, 363-394.

LaBerge, D., and Samuels, S.J. (1974). Toward a theory of automatic information processing in reading. *Cognitive Psychology*, 6, 293-323.

LaBerge, D., and Samuels, S.J. (1985). Toward a theory of automatic information processing in reading: Updated. In H. Singer and R.B. Ruddell (eds.), *Theoretical models and processes of reading*. 3rd ed., 719-721. Newark, DE: International Reading Association.

Lundberg, I., and Linnakylä, P. (1992). *Teaching reading around the world*. The Hague: International Association for the Evaluation of Educational Achievement.

Marland, P., and Osborne, B. (1990). Classroom theory, thinking, and action. *Teaching & Teacher Education*, 6(1), 93-109.

Mason, J.M. (1980). When do children begin to read: An exploration of four-year-old children's letter and word reading competencies. *Reading Research Quarterly*, 15, 203-227.

Mathewson, G.C. (1985). Toward a comprehensive model of affect in the reading process. In H. Singer and R.B. Ruddell (eds.), *Theoretical models and process of reading*. 3rd ed., 527-557. Newark, DE: International Reading Association.

McCarthey, S.J., and Raphael, T.E. (1989). *Alternative perspectives of reading/writing connections*. Michigan State University. Institute for Research on Teaching. Occational paper No. 130.

McCombs, E.L., and Whistler, J.S. (1989). The role of affective variables in autonomous learning. *Educational Psychologist*, 24(3), 277-306.

Moffett, J. (1983). *Teaching the universe of discourse*. 2nd ed. Boston: Houghton Mifflin.

Olson, D.R., Torrance, N., and Hildyard, A. (eds.). (1985). *Literacy, language, and learning*. Cambridge, England: Cambridge University Press.

Pearson, P.D. (1985). Changing the face of reading comprehension instruction. *The Reading Teacher*, 38, 724-738.

Pearson, P.D., and Fielding, L. (1991). Comprehension instruction. In R. Barr, M.L. Kamil, P. Mosenthal, and P.D. Pearson (eds.), *Handbook of reading research*. Vol. 2., 815-860. New York: Longman.

Pearson, P.D., and Gallagher, M.C. (1983). The instruction of reading comprehension. *Contemporary Educational Psychology*, 8, 317-344.

Purves, A.C. (1991). Clothing the emperor. Notes towards a text-based typology of literacy. In T.I. Lundberg and T. Hoien (eds.), *Literacy in a world of change. Perspective on reading and reading disability*, 72-85, Center for Reading Research. Stavanger: Unesco.

Roehler, L.R., and Duffy, G.G. (1991). Teachers' instructional actions. In R. Barr, M.L. Kamil, P.B. Mosenthal, and P.D. Pearson (eds.), *Handbook of Reading Research*. Vol II. New York: Longman.

Rosenblatt, L.M. (1978). *The reader, the text, the poem: The transactional theory of the literary work*. Carbondale, IL: Southern Illinois University Press.

Ruddell, R.B., and Speaker, R. (1985). The interactive reading process: A model. In H. Singer and R.B. Ruddell (eds.), *Theoretical models and processes of reading*. 3rd ed., 751-793. Newark, DE: International Reading Association.

Rumelhart, D. (1977). Toward an interactive model of reading. In S. Dornic (ed.), *Theoretical models and processes of reading*. Newark, DE: International Reading Association.

Rumelhart, D.E. (1985). Toward an interactive model of reading. In H. Singer and R.B. Ruddell (eds.), *Theoretical models and processes of reading*. 3rd ed., 722-750. Newark, DE: International Reading Association.

Scheffler, I. (1986). Dewey's social and educational theory. In *Inquiries. Philosophical studies of language, science & learning*, 363-374. Indianapolis: Hackett.

Shulman, L.S. (1986). Paradigms and research programs in the study of teaching: A contemporary perspective. In M.C. Wittrock (ed.), *Handbook of research on teaching*. 3rd ed., 3-86. New York: Macmillan.

Smith, F. (1973). *Psycholinguistics and reading*. New York: Holt, Rinehart, and Winston.

Snow, E., and Perlman (1985). Assessing children's knowledge about book reading. In L. Galda and A. Pelligrini (eds.), *Play, language, and stories*, 165-189. Norwood, NJ: Ablex.

Stanovich, K.E. (1991). Word recognition: Changing perspectives. In R. Barr, M.L. Kamil, P.B. Mosenthal, and P.D. Pearson (eds.), *Handbook of reading research*. Vol. 2, 419-452. New York: Longman.

Straw, S. (1990). The actualization of reading and writing: Public policy and conceptualizations of literacy. In S.P. Norris and L.M. Phillips (eds.), *Foundations of literacy policy in Canada*, 165-181. Calgary, Alberta: Detselig.

Strickland, D.S. and Morrow, L.M. (eds.). (1989). *Emerging literacy: Young children learn to read and write*. Newark, DE: International Reading Association.

Sulzby, E. (1985). Children's emergent reading of favorite books: A developmental study. *Reading Research Quarterly*, 20, 458-481.

Tompkins, J.P. (1980). An introduction to reader-response criticism. In J.P. Tompkins (ed.), *Reader-response criticism: From formalism to post-structuralism*. Baltimore: Johns Hopkins University Press.

Vygotsky, L.S. (1978). *Mind in society* (1938). (eds. and trans. M. Cole, V. John-Steiner, S. Scribner, and E. Sonberman). Cambridge, MA: Harvard University Press.

Vygotsky, L.S. (1978). *Mind in society: The development of higher psychological processes*. Cambridge, MA: Harvard University Press.

Wells, G. (1986). *The meaning makers*. Portsmouth, NH: Heinemann.

Yorke, D.M. (1987). Construing classrooms and curricula: A framework for research. *British Educational Research Journal*, 13(1), 35-50.

A Nine-Country Study: How Do Teachers Teach Reading to 9-Year-Olds?

Emilie Barrier and Daniel Robin
Centre International d'Etudes Pedagogiques, France

The IEA International Reading Literacy Study conducted in 1990-91 showed between-nation differences in teachers' approaches to teaching reading (Elley 1992, 1994; Postlethwaite and Ross 1992; Linnakylä and Lundberg 1993). But differences also existed within countries. The aim of the present study is to determine the extent to which teaching practice within a given country is homogeneous, and to what extent practice within one country is like that within another. Is it possible to say that teaching practice is characteristic of cultural zones, as was shown to be the case for mathematics (Robin 1993; Robin and Barrier 1991), or are they characteristic of a given educational system?

The data analyzed here come from nine countries: Denmark, Finland, France, Germany, Italy, Spain, Sweden, Switzerland, and the United States. It comprises the answers given by the 1,803 teachers of 9-years-olds (Population A) surveyed in these countries.

1.   Method

Two groups of pupils were targeted by the study on reading: 9-year-olds and 14-year-olds. The sampled students were given reading tests and asked to complete a questionnaire on their backgrounds; their teachers completed a questionnaire on their points of view, their teaching practices, and their backgrounds. The teachers' geographical origins are shown in Table 1.

Table 1. Teachers' geographical origin

	Denmark	Finland	France	Germany	Italy	Spain	Sweden	Switzer-land	United States
Number of teachers	209	71	136	149	154	324	234	227	299

SOURCE: IEA Reading Literacy Study, 1991.

Table 2 displays the teachers' responses about the teaching of reading and their own teaching practices and methods. Taken together, these answers compose the "profile" of the teacher concerned. We have chosen to compare these profiles by calculating the distance between them by means of a Principal Component Analysis. This analysis makes it possible to bring out the principal factors accounting for the dispersion among the profiles (Table 3).

Together with the Principal Component Analysis, a Hierarchical Cluster Analysis of the teachers has been done. The distance measure chosen is Euclidean, and the criterion of aggregation is the maximization of variance. Two teachers with the closest profiles are combined and replaced by their center of gravity in a step-by-step fashion. A study of the histogram indicating the hierarchy makes it possible to determine the pertinent number of clusters needed to describe the typology. It is possible to describe a given cluster interpretation by its defining variables.

Table 2. Descriptive dimensions of teachers' strategies and methods

Dimension	Number of items
Reading activities with the students	28
Aims of reading instruction	12
Instructional strategies	13
Views with respect to issues in reading instruction	26
Methods to discover the students' needs in reading	9
Assessment of reading	9
Assessment methods	6

SOURCE: IEA Reading Literacy Study, 1991.

Table 3. Eigenvalues of the factors of the Principal Component Analysis

Factor	Eigenvalue	Percent of inertia	Cumulative percent of inertia
1	12.98202	12.483	12.483
2	5.53273	5.320	17.803
3	3.99929	3.845	21.648
4	3.13399	3.013	24.661

SOURCE: IEA Reading Literacy Study, 1991.

The Principal Component Analysis and the Hierarchical Cluster Analysis enabled us to identify four principal factors and a typology of teachers made up of 10 clusters.

2. Dispersion Factors

The Principal Component Analysis enables us to identify the main factors. The first four together account for almost 25 percent of the inertia (variance) of the cloud (Table 3). If the latter had no structure (hypersphere), the first four factors would account for less than 4 percent of the inertia (4 x 100 / 104). Tables 4, 5, and 6 enable us to interpret the first three of the factors.

Table 4: Interpretation of Factor 1: 12.5 percent of the variance

Variable	CTR
Positive end	
Frequency of the assessment of vocabulary	42
Frequency of the assessment of sentence understanding	42
Frequency of the assessment of word recognition	40
Frequency of the assessment of the reading study skills	36
Frequency of the assessment of text comprehension	35
Frequency of the assessment of phonic skills	34
Negative end	
No items	

NOTE: CTR is the relative contribution of the variable to the factor structure.

SOURCE: IEA Reading Literacy Study, 1991.

Table 5: Interpretation of Factor 2: 5.3 percent of the variance

Variable	CTR
Positive end	
When my pupils read to me, I expect them to read every word accurately	57
Every mistake a child makes in reading aloud should be corrected at once	56
All children's comprehension assignments should be marked carefully to provide them with feedback	48
Reading learning materials should be carefully sequenced in terms of language structures and vocabulary	47
Children should always understand what they are reading	36
Frequency of the assessment of vocabulary	32
Frequency of assessment of phonic skills	28
Frequency of assessment of word recognition	25
Negative end	
Most of what a child reads should be assessed	32
Activity: listening to teachers reading stories aloud	31
Instructional strategies: reading aloud to children	30
Activity : silent reading in class	26
Informal observation to discover the students' needs	22

NOTE: CTR is the relative contribution of the variable to the factor structure.
SOURCE: IEA Reading Literacy Study, 1991.

Table 6 : Interpretation of Factor 3: 3.8 percent of the variance

Variable	CTR
Positive end	
Children should always understand what they are reading	38
Children should always understand why they are reading	29
When my pupils read to me, I expect them to read every word accurately	27
Every mistake a child makes in reading aloud should be corrected at once	26
Negative end	
Frequency of the assessment of literary appreciation	71
Frequency of the assessment of text comprehension	65
Frequency of the assessment of the use of background knowledge	53
Frequency of the assessment of vocabulary	48
Frequency of the assessment of decoding	46
Frequency of the assessment of sentence understanding	42
Frequency of the assessment of word recognition	40

NOTE: CTR is the relative contribution of the variable to the factor structure.
SOURCE: IEA Reading Literacy Study, 1991.

The first factor contrasts the Spanish and American teachers, who emphasize methods of assessment, to the Finnish, German, and French teachers, who make textual understanding the basis of their approach. The former give more importance to the elements of a document—vocabulary, words, sentences—than to the document as a whole.

The second factor contrasts the Spanish and Swiss teachers to the Italian and American teachers. The Spanish teachers tend to insist on reading that is perfectly correct from a formal point of view and on an immediate assessment, whereas the others put greater emphasis on reading aloud by both teacher and pupil, although they do not deny the importance of assessment. Assessment of elements is less important than in the first case (in which vocabulary, knowledge of phonics, and word recognition are assessed frequently). The second factor also involves the assessment of pupils but opposes two types of methods.

The third factor contrasts the Swedish, Danish, and, to a lesser extent, the Swiss teachers to the Italian and Spanish teachers. It also contrasts the comprehension of the documents read, together with correctness in reading, to understanding of the text, together with appreciation of its literary qualities, with the exploitation of previously acquired knowledge. This second approach may also include the verification of detail, such as the vocabulary.

Taken together, the factors that distinguish the teachers in this way put the emphasis on the contrast between learning (and an assessment) based on a pointillist point of view and learning (and an assessment) that is global, with more attention paid to understanding than to precision in reading.

From this initial analysis can be seen certain national tendencies that can be linked very generally and approximately with the national averages of the pupils in Population A. The countries that place greater emphasis on comprehension generally have better results, but this emphasis does not in itself imply that little importance is given to precision in reading.

3.   Typology of Teaching Practice

This analysis of the factors does not make clear the differences that can exist within countries. It cannot be assumed that in each of these countries the teachers form a homogeneous group and use a single method or approach to the teaching of reading. But it does allow comparisons between national tendencies as it can be seen in Figure 1. One can see a grouping composed of Spain (SPA) and the United States (USA), a group formed with Finland (FIN), France (FRA), Germany (GER), and another with Sweden (SWE), Switzerland (SWI), and Denmark (DEN). Italy (ITA) is relatively isolated.

Figure 1 : Countries position on the first factorial plan

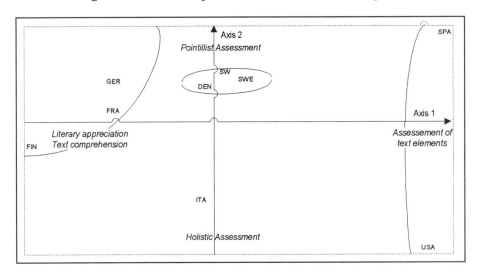

In order to indicate the extent to which the teachers as a whole form an unique group, a typology that divides them into 10 groups has been defined. The teachers within the same cluster have more characteristics in common than they have in common with the teachers in the other clusters. It is possible to see which countries they come from and to check the extent to which practices within a country are the same.

Figure 2 shows the resulting classification. The vertical lines between two clusters measure the "distance" between these clusters. In each of the clusters the percentage of teachers from a given country is indicated. Thus, cluster 1 (which includes 4.7 percent of all the teachers), is made up almost exclusively of Swedish teachers, and 32 percent of the Swedish teachers are in this cluster. Most of the other teachers from this country are in cluster 2 (44 percent), but there is also a minority in clusters 7 (7 percent) and 10 (9 percent). It is to be noted that clusters 1 and 2 are formed very early, and for this reason they form very homogeneous groups. Cluster 1 contains mostly Swedish teachers, and in cluster 2 most are either Swedish or American.

Table 7 indicates the percentage of teachers from each country to be found in each cluster. As shown, most of the German teachers can be found in clusters 7 and 4, the Spaniards in 3 followed by 9, the Americans in 10, 5, and 2, the vast majority of the Finns in 8, a majority of the French in 8 followed by 9, the same number of Italians in 6 and in 3, the Swedes in 2 and 1, and the Swiss mainly in 7. It should also be noted that some countries are not represented at all in certain clusters.

Table 7: Partition in 10 clusters: Percentage of teachers in each cluster, by country

Country	Cluster 5 7.0 %	Cluster 6 4.0%	Cluster 3 15.9%	Cluster 1 4.7%	Cluster 7 15.1%	Cluster 8 8.7%	Cluster 2 11.6%	Cluster 9 11.0%	Cluster 10 10.1%	Cluster 4 11.9%
Denmark	0	0	2	0	**23**	2	7	4	2	**58**
Finland	0	0	6	0	1	**82**	3	0	3	6
France	2	0	8	1	6	**48**	6	**19**	4	6
Germany	1	1	8	1	**38**	2	2	12	3	**33**
Italy	6	**40**	**39**	0	1	1	2	6	4	1
Spain	3	3	**51**	0	3	0	0	**31**	8	1
Sweden	2	0	2	**32**	7	1	**44**	2	9	1
Switzerland	2	0	8	2	**53**	5	4	13	4	9
USA	**31**	0	3	0	3	3	**21**	1	**35**	2

SOURCE: IEA Reading Literacy Study, 1991.

Four wider groupings emerge from the typology as a whole: clusters 5 and 6, cluster 3, clusters 1, 7, 8, 2, and 4, and clusters 9 and 10. Each of these groups is characterized by certain general themes: the development of a critical attitude for the first (clusters 5 and 6), constant assessment (cluster 3), noncognitive aims for clusters 1, 7, 8, 2, and 4, and immediate understanding for clusters 9 and 10.

The Development of a Critical Attitude

Encouraging children to read, guided inference, and a critical attitude (cluster 5: 31 percent of the Americans). This group consists almost entirely of Americans, with a small number of Italians. The priority appears to be given to the attempt to encourage the pupils by every possible means (the reading of stories by the teacher, the opportunity to take books home, the help of parents), together with the amount of attention given to exact pronunciation and to monitoring progress. It is more important to develop a critical attitude than to widen the pupil's horizons or his or her emotional development. This explains the search for comparisons, generalizations, inferences, and messages, as well as the structure of the text. It also explains the importance given to testing all aspects of the text, from decoding to the understanding of ideas. The teachers in this group get the pupils to work on ideas, following the text as closely as possible, by inference.

Figure 2. Resulting classification

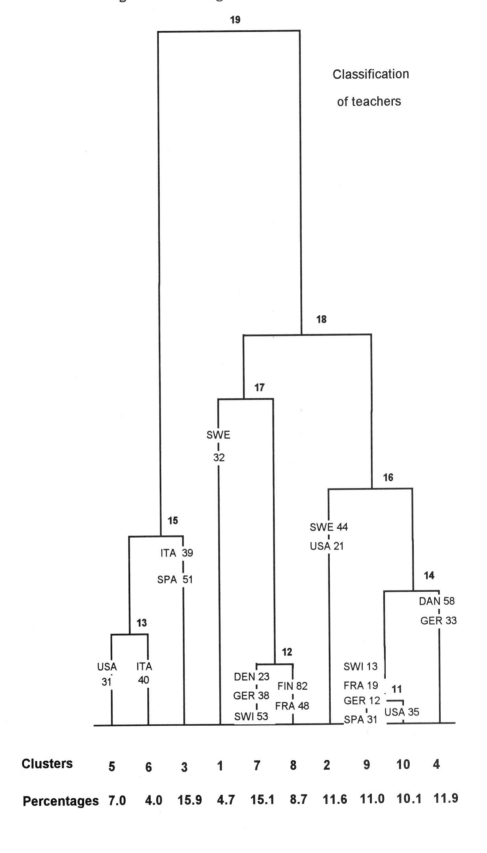

Change of language and critical attitude (cluster 6: 40 percent of the Italians). This cluster is made up almost entirely of Italians, with few teachers from any other country included. As in the preceding cluster, the development of a critical attitude is considered to be important, but emphasis is placed directly on the techniques necessary to understand the text, and in particular on those that involve a change of language, i.e., drawing, oral summaries, discussion, games, and scenarios. Much attention is paid to correcting mistakes. The teachers in this group use various representations or images of the idea to develop a critical attitude in their pupils. They base their approach on a living culture.

Constant Assessment

Oralization and assessment (cluster 3: 51 percent of the Spaniards, 39 percent of the Italians). This cluster differs from the others because of the importance given to correctness in oral work and to constant assessment, especially of vocabulary. Encouraging a love of reading or widening pupils' range of choice are secondary considerations. Nevertheless, reading is the pretext for various activities such as games, oral summaries, written commentaries, and identification of the themes or the plan. The parents are also encouraged to help their children.

Noncognitive Aims for Reading

The pleasure of reading, above all (cluster 1: 32 percent of the Swedes). This cluster consists almost entirely of Swedish teachers. It will be noted that it is very isolated on Figure 2, which indicates that it is a particularly homogeneous group, and one that has a very different profile from the others.

The main aim of these teachers is to make their pupils like reading by appealing to their emotions. They reject the idea of immediate and constant assessment and activities based on working out the meaning or the vocabulary, but they do not emphasize understanding, either of the text or the sentences. Understanding is less important than enjoyment.

Widening the pupils' horizons through a structured learning without any particular means (cluster 7: 53 percent of the Swiss, 38 percent of the Germans, 23 percent of the Danes). This cluster includes teachers who reject the idea of constantly assessing the pupils, but consider that children should learn to read in a structured way and that the aim of teaching reading is to widen pupils' horizons, that is, to enrich their emotional development through vocabulary. Answering questions concerning comprehension, looking for the message, and making generalizations is given relatively little importance compared to their principal preoccupation.

Development of pupils' research ability and rejection of oral skills (cluster 8: 82 percent of the Finns, 48 percent of the French). To a certain extent, these teachers, like those in the preceding cluster, accord little importance to the systematic assessment of the pupils, even though they are attentive to their level. Developing the pupils' ability to research and study for themselves is considered to be fundamental. Acquiring vocabulary is less important than personal reading. Reading aloud to the pupils is thought to be a waste of time. What matters is the personal reaction to the text, individually rather than in a group context.

Priority given to getting the pupils to read (cluster 2: 44 percent of the Swedes, 21 percent of the Americans). The fundamental aim of the teachers in this group is to widen pupils' reading choice and to get them to like reading. Various strategies are used: the reading of stories by the teacher, discussions, compositions on the same theme, and the use of library. Parents are also encouraged to read to their children and to participate in reading-related activities. On the other hand, little importance is given to assessment, to pronunciation, to vocabulary, or even to comprehension.

Widening the Pupils' Horizons is the Only Aim

No particular encouragement is given to reading (cluster 4: 58 percent of the Danes, 33 percent of the Germans). A third of the German teachers and a majority of Danes consider that widening the pupils' horizons is fundamental. They give much less importance than their colleagues to correctness, comprehension, and work based on the text. Paradoxically, reading does not seem to be important in itself for these teachers.

Immediate Comprehension, with the Enjoyment of Reading not a Priority

Cluster 9: 31 percent of the Spaniards, 19 percent of the French, 13 percent of the Swiss, 12 percent of the Germans. The teachers in cluster 9—a third of the Spaniards and small numbers of the French, Swiss, and German teachers—give great importance to correctness in reading and in progressing to more and more difficult texts. Assessment is therefore constant. What is fundamental in their eyes is developing textual comprehension, with comprehension being immediately apparent. In fact, they do not work by generalizations or by inferences, the theme of a text is not identified, and there is no discussion of the book. They do not try to develop literary appreciation. No importance is given to the enjoyment of reading.

Cluster 10: 35 percent of the Americans. As in the preceding cluster, even though comprehension is a priority, teachers are not very demanding in this respect, whereas monitoring pupils' progress by assessment is considered to be important. The pupil has a personal activity (reading on his own) to do, but he is not asked to do any work on the text, such as to make a plan or a summary. The teacher is very active and very directive. Enjoyment of reading is not the main aim.

4. Conclusions

In most countries, it is clear that teachers do not make up a completely homogeneous group as far as their approach to reading is concerned, even if certain tendencies are stronger in some countries. Only in Finland do teachers make up such a group (82 percent of them are in cluster 8). For them, developing pupils' ability to research questions is the main aim of their teaching.

The German teachers are mainly concerned with widening their pupils' horizons through reading, and to this end use either highly structured teaching of the language (38 percent) or work of a literary nature (33 percent). The Danes have a very similar approach (23 percent and 53 percent, respectively). German and Danish teachers approach reading in a very similar way, their aims being cultural rather than cognitive.

The Spaniards' teaching is centered on monitoring procedures. Some give more importance to oral work (51 percent), others to immediate comprehension (31 percent).

The approach of the Americans is the most varied. Some teachers are not very demanding, aiming at immediate comprehension and not giving any particular importance to enjoyment (35 percent), others strongly encourage pupils to read and develop a critical attitude (31 percent), while a third group is eclectic in its approach (21 percent).

The French teachers are divided between two contrasting groups, one developing the ability to research questions concerning the texts (48 percent), the other demanding immediate comprehension without trying to get pupils to enjoy reading (19 percent).

Some of the Italians emphasize a living culture in which comprehension and oral work are most important (40 percent), whereas others (39 percent) also give great importance to oral work, together with constant assessment, particularly of the vocabulary.

The Swedish teachers consider that love of reading is the most important issue. Some try to achieve it through encouragement (32 percent), others by the widening of the field of reading (44 percent).

The last group, the Swiss teachers, consider that it is essential that the teaching be structured. A majority of them (53 percent) use reading as a means of widening pupils' horizons, others (13 percent) use it to achieve immediate comprehension, closely monitored through assessment.

It is therefore possible to speak of national tendencies in the approach to reading that go beyond the differences that may exist. Although we cannot speak of cultural zones, as was seen in the teaching of mathematics, it does seem that most countries adopt consistent approaches within their educational systems.

References

Elley, W.B. (1992). *How in the world do students read?* Hamburg: The International Association for the Evaluation of Educational Achievement.

Elley, W.B. (ed.). (1994). *The IEA study of reading literacy: Achievement and instruction in thirty-two school systems.* Oxford: Pergamon/Elsevier.

Linnakylä, P., and Lundberg, I. (1993). *Teaching reading around the world.* The Hague: The International Association for the Evaluation of Educational Achievement.

Postlethwaite, T.N., and Ross, K.N. (1992). *Effective schools in reading. Implications for educational planners.* The Hague: The International Association for the Evaluation of Educational Achievement.

Robin, D. in L. Burstein (ed.). (1993). *The IEA study of mathematics III: Student growth and classroom processes.* Oxford: Pergamon Press.

Robin, D., and Barrier, E. (1987). L'enseignement des mathématiques dans le contexte international. Contribution à la réflexion. *Revue Française de Pédagogie*, 80, 5-15.

SECTION C: SCHOOL CLIMATE

- **Consistencies in the Quality of School Life**
  Trevor Williams and Stephen Roey

- **Quality of School Life in the Finnish- and Swedish-Speaking Schools in Finland**
  Pirjo Linnakylä and Viking Brunell

- **Analysis of the Williams and Batten Questionnaire on the Quality of School Life in Spain**
  Guillermo A. Gil

Consistencies in the Quality of School Life

Trevor Williams and Stephen Roey
Westat, Inc., USA

Some schools are dull, depressing, even terrifying places, while others are lively, comfortable, and reassuring ... such differences are enormously important... eliminating these differences ... would do a great deal to make the quality of children's (and teacher's) lives more equal. Since children are in school for a fifth of their lives, this would be a significant accomplishment.

This observation was made in connection with a study of inequality in American schools (Jencks et al. 1972, 256) at a time when most interest was directed at the cognitive outcomes of schooling—as it is now. Nothing much has changed since that time; affective outcomes are recognized and their importance acknowledged, but no one pays much attention to them.

Work on the affective outcomes of adults' lives—measures of *quality of life, happiness,* or *well-being*—is further advanced. The discussion that follows briefly examines the conceptualization and development of a measure of the qualities of school life that draws on these more general "quality of life" models, the results of applying this measure in the schools of eight nations, and the consistencies of students' responses across these nations. More specifically, we consider whether this view of life in schools has application outside the United States, in the schools of Denmark, Finland, France, Germany, Italy, Spain, and Switzerland,[1] and whether one could think of some universal dimensions of school life students take into account in evaluating their life at school.

1.   Affective Outcomes of Schooling

Much of what we know about the affective outcomes of schooling appears to have evolved as an interest in the motivational components of achievement. The main thrust of this argument is that students who are happier, more enthusiastic, and more engaged in life within schools are, all things equal, likely to learn more and perform better on achievement tests. However, as Epstein and McPartland (1976, 15) point out, there has been little systematic study of the aspects of school life that evoke these feelings. Despite a general acceptance that such affective outcomes are important, they tend to be seen more as an (affective) means to a (cognitive) end rather than an end in themselves.

The literature in question seems to see the affective outcomes of schooling in two main ways: as *school climate,* the aggregate of individual values, beliefs, and behaviors into dimensions that characterize the school or classroom; and *attitudes to school,* essentially feelings about school in general. Measures of school climate consider schools as differing along some global dimension variously called climate, feel, or tone (see Pace and Stern 1958; Halpin and Croft 1963; Stern 1970; and Moos 1978). Anderson and Walberg (1974), Fraser (1980), and Anderson (1982) provide reviews of this literature.

---

[1] The data on which these analyses are based were obtained as part of the IEA International Reading Literacy Study in which some 30 nations took part. Consistent with the purpose of this volume, the analyses are restricted to information on eight of these nations.

The interest in student attitudes has been more extensive. While some has been concerned with the development of these attitudes (Dreeben 1968, for example), most are concerned with effects on achievement and/or commitment to school. Some of the work takes a "mental health" approach—studies of neuroticism, introversion-extroversion, anxiety, self-concept, and the like are common; the extensive use of Rotter's (1966) internal-external control scale is a good example of the belief in attitudinal effects of this kind. The interest of sociologists in alienation and related constructs in schools and students also reflects this orientation; Stinchcombe (1964) and Otto and Featherman (1975) provide examples. Research into more general attitudes on life in schools and classrooms is also reasonably well represented in the literature; reviews by Jackson (1968) and Silberman (1971) capture the essence of this work.

The widely used Like-School scale created by IEA for use in their international comparative studies was developed within the latter tradition. The scale, reported in Husen (1967, 121), consists of 11 items of which the following are examples: *I generally like my school-work; I find school interesting and challenging.* While there is no explicit theoretical basis for the scale, it seems to be measuring general satisfaction with school and, in the context of these studies, is treated as a potential influence on achievement.

2. Quality of Life, Happiness, and Well-Being

Other attempts to think about this affective aspect of schooling have used work on the quality of (adult) life as a model[2] (see Gurin, Veroff, and Feld 1960; Bradburn and Caplovitz 1969; Cantril 1965; Bradburn and Caplovitz 1969; Campbell, Converse, and Rodgers 1976; and Andrews and Withey 1976). Gerson (1976) provides an overview of the theoretical perspectives adopted. Burt et al. (1978;1979) summarize the underlying models used, capturing this summary in a general model involving four dimensions: *general affect*—satisfaction with life as a whole; *positive affect* and *negative affect*—affect based on more immediate experiences; and *domain affect*—satisfaction with specific domains of life such as family, housing, neighborhood, education, leisure, the government, friendships, work, and so on.

3. Quality of Life and Quality of School Life

At least two measures of the quality of school life have their roots in models of this kind. Epstein and McPartland (1976) link their work to this perspective developing three dimensions: *general satisfaction with school, commitment to classwork,* and *reaction to teachers.* These seem to reflect, respectively, a measure of general affect and measures of satisfaction with two domains of schooling.

Parallel work by Williams and Batten (Williams and Batten 1981; Williams 1984) was based explicitly on the model proposed by Burt et al. (1978). These authors generalize the notions of general affect and of positive and negative affect for life as whole to life in schools in a relatively straightforward way. However, conceptualizing the nature of the domains of schooling that parallel those for life as a whole is less straightforward.[3] What is needed is some notion of the important aspects of schooling whose "quality" is likely to generate feelings of well-being in students. This amounts to developing a model of schooling from the perspective of students, something not addressed in any comprehensive way in the education literature. In

---

[2] Other work with similar concerns often identifies its focus as *happiness* or *well-being* rather than quality of life. However, since the focus is much the same in each case it seems reasonable to use *quality of life* as a generic term in this instance.

[3] In the quality of life literature, *education* is one of the domains of life.

the light of this fact, an attempt was made to develop a definition of the domains of schooling from first principles. The full argument is detailed in Williams and Batten (1981) and is summarized below.[4]

4.   Domains of School Life

Feelings of well-being in any domain are derived from two sources: the level of consumption of socially valued goods and services relative to socially prescribed norms, and the extent to which an individual can control his/her own well-being (Burt et al. 1978, 367). In the present context, the problem faced was one of defining the goods and services provided by schools and valued by students, goods and services to which students had different degrees of access and over which they had different degrees of control. These categories of goods and services define the domains of schooling in a way similar to that in which such factors as occupation, income, and health define the domains of quality of life in general.

The nature of these categories of valued goods and services—the domains—were developed by drawing on a theory of schooling that links social-structural and individual systems of action in schools. This theory is developed in several papers (Spady and Mitchell 1977; Mitchell and Spady 1977; Mitchell 1977; Spady 1979) and is used to support the existence of four domains of schooling: *status*, *identity*, *adventure*, and *opportunity*. These authors draw on both structural-functional and symbolic-interaction theory to construct a model of schooling that sees schools as action systems for integrating individual student expectations for personal fulfillment with societal expectations for what schools are about. The social-structural perspective is expressed as four broad expectations responsible for the creation and maintenance of schools. Schools are expected to

- Facilitate and certify the achievement of *technical competence*;

- Encourage and enhance *personal development*;

- Generate and support *social integration* among individuals; and

- Nurture each student's sense of *social responsibility*.

And, in response to these societal expectations, schools have developed

- *Certification* structures, which certify the student's technical competence;

- *Instruction* structures, which facilitate personal development through learning;

- *Socialization* structures, which promote participation in the school's social system; and

- *Supervision* structures, which promote the learning of social norms and values.

From the student's perspective, certification processes, which embody performance standards, are only attractive if they enable the student to qualify for desirable future *opportunities*—students evaluate their schooling in terms of its perceived relevance for their future well-being. Instructional effectiveness is best

---

[4] Even though presented in summary form, the argument is still an extended one. In good part this comes about because of the need to develop this conceptualization from first principles and because the basis for this development is somewhat unconventional and not well known.

realized when there is the experience of *adventure* in learning—high quality learning is that which is intrinsically rewarding and generates self-motivation. The product of successful social integration is *identity* formation, and students look at the quality of their school environment in terms of the extent to which it provides for the development of self-awareness in interaction with others within the school. Similarly, students see the quality of their school lives influenced by the extent to which schools encourage social responsibility, which, in turn, is fostered when students are given the opportunity to achieve *status* in the group.[5]

5.   Models and Items

The end result of this process is a model of the quality of school life based on the following dimensions: *general affect, positive affect, negative affect, opportunity, adventure, identity,* and *status*. In these terms one can think of the quality of life of students reflecting, respectively, their overall well-being, feelings of well-being and ill-being generated by recent events, and feelings of well-being generated by the extent to which the schools they attend provide for the satisfaction of students' needs for opportunity, adventure, identity, and status.

Items developed to tap general affect, positive affect, and negative affect were straightforward adaptations of those found in traditional quality of life measures, with the exception that they referred to life in school. The development of items to reflect the domains of schooling was, of necessity, undertaken from first principles. However, this process was assisted by a more detailed elaboration of the opportunity, adventure, identity, and status dimensions within the context of the original arguments of Spady and Mitchell.[6] This elaboration defined the scope of the domains, and hence the particular focus of the items, more precisely.

Each of the items was written as an extension of the stem *School is a place where....* and was designed to be responded to on a 4-point agree-disagree scale. Both teachers and students found the instrument to have high face validity in the sense that they saw it as addressing issues important in their lives at school. Trial testing and item-analysis procedures designed to elicit the latent structure of the item pool reduced the original pool of items to 29.[7] These procedures are described in detail in Williams and Batten (1981).

---

[5] This is not meant to imply that these are the *only* domains of schooling. These four aspects of schooling are a beginning and are consistent with a coherent argument about the nature of schooling. We expect that further work on the development of this model would produce other domains of schooling important to students and, hence, to the feelings of well-being that they express.

[6] See Williams and Batten (1981) for a more detailed development of the model that postulates some 20 domains in all, 5 separate constructs within each of the 4 domains noted here.

[7] See Table 1 for wording of the items in question.

6. Consistencies in the Quality of School Life

This 29-item measure has been used a number of times with samples of high school students in Australia and Canada and with university students[8] in the United States and Canada. In each instance, a slightly modified version of the theoretical structure used to generate the items has been supported by the data. The emergent structure to this measure of quality of school life differs in three ways from the model on which it is based. First, we are unable to distinguish positive affect from general affect, though negative affect retains its identity. Second, we were unable to find evidence of a latent variable we could identify as *adventure*. Third, students tended to respond in much the same way to any item to do with teachers with the result that it makes sense to talk about a *teacher's* construct as part of this model. The end result is six dimensions to this measure of the quality of school life: *general affect, negative affect, opportunity, teachers, identity,* and *status*.

In one of their first attempts to extend their international comparative studies beyond cognitive achievements, the IEA provided for the inclusion of these 29 items in student questionnaires administered in 1991 to national samples of 14-year-olds in the 30 nations taking part in the International Reading Literacy Study. In so doing, they provided the opportunity to examine the consistencies of student responses across nations rather less similar than are the United States, Canada, and Australia. Given fairly substantial cultural differences between these nations and the differences between their school systems, one would not confidently expect students to respond to these items in the same way. As a result we would not expect to find the same six-construct latent structure to these data in each nation. However, if the same latent structure did emerge in each nation, we would have grounds for claiming to have identified aspects of the quality of students' lives that were universal rather than culture bound.

In examining this proposition we limited our attention to the eight nations previously identified.[9] As a relatively simple test of the notion that student responses had the same latent structure in each of these nations, factor solutions[10] were obtained separately for each data set and six factors[11] rotated to an oblique structure.[12]

7. Statistically Consistent Latent Structures

The results of these analyses are summarized in Table 1, which shows rotated factor loadings and communalities for the eight nations. The presentation is compressed somewhat according to the following conventions.

1. Only factor loadings equal to or greater than .4[13] are considered to give substantive definition to factors.

---

[8]Item wording was modified to suit the differences between universities and high schools.

[9] Comparisons of the United States with the seven other nations are the overall focus of the analyses reported in this volume for reasons set down in the introductory section.

[10] A principle axes solution with iterated communalities was used in each case.

[11] Since the predicted latent structure was based on six constructs, we rotated six factors rather than use rule-of-thumb approaches like the eigenvalue-one criterion.

[12] Oblimin rotation criteria were used.

[13] Loadings are rounded to the first decimal place.

Table 1. Rotated factor loadings and communalities for items on quality of school life scale

School is a place where. . .	Rotated factor loadings								Communalities							
	DEN	FIN	FRA	GER	ITA	SPA	SWI	USA	DEN	FIN	FRA	GER	ITA	SPA	SWI	USA
General Affect																
I really like to go	.6	.7	.8	.7	.7	.7	.7	.5	.5	.6	.7	.5	.5	.4	.6	.4
I feel happy	.5	*	*	.6	.6	.4	.6	.4	.4	.4	.4	.5	.5	.4	.5	.4
I find that learning is a lot of fun	.6	.5	.5	.7	.5	.6	.7	.8	.5	.5	.4	.6	.5	.5	.6	.7
I get enjoyment from being there	.8	.6	.9	.9	.8	.8	.8	.9	.6	.6	.8	.7	.6	.7	.7	.7
I feel great	.6	*	S	.5	*	.4	.6	.4	.6	.4	.3	.4	.4	.4	.4	.5
Negative Affect																
I feel lonely	.7	.6	.6	.6	.7	.6	.6	.8	.5	.4	.4	.4	.5	.4	.4	.6
I feel restless	.6	.5	.6	.7	.6	.7	.6	.6	.4	.3	.3	.4	.4	.4	.4	.4
I feel depressed	.7	.7	.7	.7	.6	.7	.6	.7	.5	.5	.5	.4	.4	.5	.4	.5
I get upset	.4	*	.4	*	*	.7	*	.6	.2	.1	.3	.2	.1	.4	.2	.3
Status																
I feel important	.4	.6	.6	.4	.5	*	.5	.4	.3	.4	.4	.4	.3	.2	.3	.5
People have confidence in me	*	*	.6	I	*	.6	.4	.4	.3	.4	.4	.4	.3	.4	.4	.5
People come to me for help	.5	*	.4	*	*	.4	.4	.5	.3	.3	.2	.3	.2	.2	.3	.4
I know that people think a lot of me	.6	.8	.6	.6	.6	.5	.5	.8	.3	.6	.4	.4	.4	.2	.3	.5
People look up to me	.7	.8	.5	.6	.7	.6	.5	.8	.4	.6	.3	.4	.5	.4	.2	.6
Identity																
Mixing with other people helps me understand myself	.7	.6	.7	.7	.6	.7	.6	.7	.4	.4	.4	.4	.4	.4	.5	.5
I learn to get along with other people	.5	.4	.5	.7	.5	.5	.5	.6	.4	.3	.4	.4	.3	.4	.4	.5
I learn a lot about myself	.6	.5	.6	.5	.6	.5	.7	.4	.5	.4	.5	.4	.4	.4	.5	.5
I get to know myself better	.7	.5	.7	.5	.7	.7	.7	.4/G	.5	.5	.6	.4	.5	.5	.6	.6
I have learned to accept other people as they are	.4	*	.4	.4	*	*	*	*	.2	.2	.2	.3	.2	.3	.3	.3
Teachers																
Teachers are fair and just	.6	.7	.6	.7	.7	.7	.7	.8	.4	.6	.4	.5	.5	.5	.5	.6
Teachers help me to do my best	.5	.6	.6	.5	.6	.7	.6	.6	.3	.5	.4	.4	.5	.5	.5	.5
Teachers treat me fairly in class	.8	.9	.7	.8	.8	.7	.8	.8	.6	.8	.5	.6	.6	.6	.6	.7
Teachers give me the marks I deserve	.5	.4	.6	.5	.6	.6	.5	.5	.3	.4	.4	.3	.4	.4	.3	.4
Teachers listen to what I say	.5	.6	.6	.4	.5	.7	.5	.5	.4	.5	.4	.3	.4	.5	.4	.5
Opportunity																
I know how to cope with the work	*	*	*	*	.4	*	*	*	.1	.3	.1	.1	.3	.2	.2	.3
I know I can reach a satisfactory standard in my work	.6	.6	.7	.6	.6	.7	.5	.7	.4	.3	.5	.4	.4	.5	.4	.5
I know the sorts of things I can do well	.6	.6	.5	.5	.4	.6	.5	.8	.4	.4	.3	.4	.3	.4	.3	.6
I get satisfaction from the school work I do	G	G	*	*	.5	G	G	G	.5	.5	.3	.4	.4	.5	.4	.5
I know I can do well enough to be successful	S	.4	.6	.6	.6	.6	.4	.7	.4	.3	.4	.4	.4	.3	.3	.5

KEY: G= general affect; S = status; I = identity; * = variable has loading factor of less than .4 on any of the factors.
SOURCE: IEA Reading Literacy Study, 1991.

2. The normal 29x6 matrix of loadings is compressed into a 1x6 matrix. It may be easiest to think of this in the following terms. The items in the 29x6 matrix for each nation are arrayed construct by construct according to the a priori arguments: six items measuring *general affect*, followed by four items measuring *negative affect*, followed by four 5-item groups tapping *status, identity, teachers,* and *opportunity*. Assume that all loadings less than .4 are shown as blank cells. The six columns are then overlaid to create a single composite column. If good simple structure is achieved in the rotation, then one would have a column of 26 loadings greater than .4.

3. Where a variable fails to achieve a loading of .4 on any of the six factors, it is shown as an *. The second postulated indicator of *status* for Denmark, for example, failed to achieve a loading of .4 or better on any of the six factors.

4. Where an indicator achieved a loading of .4 or better, but on a factor other than the one hypothesized, the factor on which it did load is indicated instead of the loading. Thus, in the case of Denmark, the fifth and sixth hypothesized indicators of *opportunity* achieved loadings of .4 or better on *general affect* (G) and *status* (S).

5. Where an indicator achieved loadings of .4 or better on more than one factor, it is indicated by the loading and a pointer to the other factor—a situation that occurs once. In the case of the United States, the fourth item thought to tap *identity* loads .4 on *identity* and at this value or greater on *general affect*.

It may be helpful to illustrate the interpretation of these findings by examining the results for the United States. In the full 29x6 matrix of factor loadings for the United States, six items defined a priori as tapping *general affect* loaded on only one factor. Two other items also loaded (unexpectedly) on this factor—the fourth item under *identity*, and the fourth item under *opportunity*. Given this, it seems reasonable to think that *general affect* exists,[14] and we would be justified in labeling this factor accordingly.

In the case of the items hypothesized to tap *negative affect*, all four loaded on the one factor and on no other, giving us reason to suggest that this may well be a dimension to the quality of (U.S.) students' lives. The situation is analogous for the items defining, respectively, the *status* and *teachers* dimensions. The five *status* items load on one factor only, and the five *teachers* items load on another, and on only that one. There is justification then for thinking about these as legitimate dimensions to the quality of students' lives. The situation for *identity* and *opportunity* suggests that there is less of a fit between hypotheses and reality in this instance, though the fit is by no means bad. The fourth *identity* item loads on *general affect* as well, and the fifth item does not achieve the criterion value on this or any other factor. Similarly, the first item under *opportunity* fails to reach this same criterion on any factor. The fourth item does not load on *opportunity* at all, but rather seems to be a measure of *general affect*.

By most standards this would be seen as a very positive result. The model developed a priori and operationalized is supported by the data for the proposed latent structure. In the majority of cases, items hypothesized to define one of the six constructs load on a single factor and on no other. The criteria for simple structure are achieved, for the most part, in each of the eight nations, and items cluster to define factors in the way predicted. Not too surprisingly there are a few items that do not work in the way

---

[14]In the sense that hypothetical constructs or unobservable variables can be thought of as *existing*.

expected. The first item in *opportunity* is an example, since it does not load on any factor except in Italy. So, too, is the fourth item under *opportunity*, which seems to tap *general affect* rather than *opportunity*.

8.   Conclusion

Overall, though, we are looking at latent structures that are remarkably consistent across nations. This consistency is even more surprising if one considers that affective aspects of schooling are much more likely to be culturally bound than cognitive dimensions. Our predictions at the outset were that what seemed to be a fairly culturally specific model and instrument would present problems in translation at the outset and, more importantly, would call forth different kinds of responses in different cultures. This seems not to be the case overall. The data suggest that we may have identified dimensions of schooling that cross national boundaries—aspects of life in school that are important to students everywhere and, to the extent realized, influence student feelings of well-being.[15]

Students in Western European nations and the United States respond to life in schools in much the same way. They can express the extent of their happiness with life in school, and they can also see a negative side of schooling in general. At a less global level they consider their well-being in terms of the extent to which the school provides them with the chance to develop notions of their own status vis a vis that of their peers and teachers; provides the structures that facilitate social integration and the sense of identity that grows from this experience; provides for harmonious and equitable interactions between students and teachers; and provides the means by which student learning can be certified and in this way be seen by others as a recognizable investment in the future.

Clearly one could do more with this model and measure of the quality of school life, and the evidence presented here suggest that further effort would be warranted. More, and more refined, items could be developed for the model as it stands to strengthen the six dimensions talked about here. The items on positive and negative affect need to be more clearly defined as expressions of affect in the short term. The opportunity dimension is a little weak. And it may be possible to operationalize the hypothesized adventure dimension in such a way as to establish its identity as a separate construct. This would be particularly relevant given the current interest in student motivation and engagement, or the lack thereof.

Further, almost certainly there are other domains of school life to which students respond. The domains defined here were based on a particular model of what goes on in school, a model the authors certainly do not claim to be all inclusive. Conceptualizing what these other domains might be is a challenging task. It is probably a worthwhile task as well, since we seem to have been able to define and measure some aspects of schooling important to students everywhere.

---

[15] One might well object that this group of Western European countries and the United States are quite similar culturally and hence that these national similarities are not too surprising. However, analyses conducted on all 30 nations but not reported here do not support this view. Although there is some variation between nations in the patterns of loadings, it is much like we have seen here. In all, the same basic pattern emerges across all 30 nations.

References

Anderson, C.S. (1982). The search for school climate: a review of research. *Review of Educational Research,* 52, 368-420.

Anderson, G.J., and Walberg, H.J. (1974). Learning environments. In H. J. Walberg (ed.), *Evaluating educational performance: A sourcebook of methods, instruments and examples.* Berkeley: McCutchan.

Andrews, F.M., and Withey, S.B. (1976). *Social indicators of well-being.* New York: Plenum Press.

Bradburn, N.M., and Caplovitz, D. (1969). *The structure of psychological well-being.* Chicago: Aldine.

Burt, R.S., Fischer, M.G., and Christman, K.P. (1979). Structures of well-being: Sufficient conditions for identification as restricted covariance models. *Sociological Methods and Research,* 8, 111-120.

Burt, R.S., Wiley, J.A., Minor, M.J., and Murray, J.R. (1978). Structure of well-being: Form, content and stability over time. *Sociological Methods and Research,* 6, 365-407.

Campbell, A.P., Converse, P.E., and Rodgers, W.L. (1976). *The quality of American life.* New York: Russell Sage.

Cantril, H. (1965). *The patterns of human concern.* New Brunswick, NJ: Rutgers University Press.

Dreeben, R. (1968). *On what is learned in school.* Reading, MA.: Addison-Wesley.

Epstein, J.L., and McPartland, J.M. (1976). The concept and measurement of the quality of school life. *American Educational Research Journal,* 13, 15-30.

Fraser, B.J. (1980). Guest editor's introduction: Classroom environment research in the 1970's and 1980's. *Studies in Educational Evaluation,* 6, 221-223.

Gerson, E.M. (1976). On "quality of life." *American Sociological Review,* 41, 793-806.

Gurin, G., Veroff, J., and Feld, S. (1960) *Americans view their mental health.* New York: Basic Books.

Halpin, A.W., and Croft, D.B. (1963). *The organizational climate of schools.* Chicago: Midwest Administration Centre, University of Chicago.

Husen, T. (1967). *International study of achievement in mathematics.* Stockholm: Almqvist and Wiksell.

Jackson, P.W. (1968). *Life in classrooms.* New York: Holt, Rinehart & Winston.

Jencks, C., Smith, M., Acland, H., Bane, M.J., Cohen, D., and Gintes, H. (1972). *Inequality: A reassessment of the effect of family and schooling in America.* New York: Basic Books, Inc.

Mitchell, D. (1977). Expectation, evaluation and reward systems in schools. Unpublished manuscript.

Mitchell, D., and Spady, W.G. (1977). Authority and the functional structuring of social action in schools. Unpublished American Educational Research Association (AERA) symposium paper.

Moos, R. (1978). Toward a typology of classroom social environments. *American Educational Research Journal,* 15, 53-60.

Otto, L., and Featherman, D.L. (1975). Social-structural and psychological antecedents of self-estrangement and powerlessness. *American Sociological Review,* 40 , 701-719.

Pace, C., Stern, R., and George, G. (1958). An approach to the measurement of psychological characteristics. *Journal of Educational Psychology,* 49, 269-277.

Rotter, J.B. (1966). Generalized expectancies for internal-external control: Implications for past and future research. *Psychological Monographs,* 80, 1.

Silberman, M.L. (1971). *The experience of schooling.* New York: Holt, Rinehart & Winston.

Spady, W.G., and Mitchell, D.E. (1977). The uses of authority and power in the organization and control of school task performance. Unpublished American Educational Research Association (AERA) symposium paper.

Spady, W.G. (1979). Authority and the management of classroom activities. In D. L. Duke (ed.), *Classroom management.* Seventy-eighth Yearbook of the National Society for the Study of Education, Part 11. Chicago: University of Chicago.

Stern, G.C. (1970). *People in context: measuring person-environment congruence in education and industry.* New York: Wiley.

Stinchcombe, A.L. (1964). *Rebellion in a high school.* Chicago: Quadrangle Books.

Williams, T., and Batten, M. (1981). *The quality of school life.* Hawthorn, Victoria: Australian Council for Educational Research.

Williams, T. (1984). Measuring the quality of school life. In P. van den Eden and H. Oosthoek (eds.), *Multilevel aspects of the educational process.* London: Gordon and Breach.

Quality of School Life in the Finnish- and Swedish-Speaking Schools in Finland

Pirjo Linnakylä and Viking Brunell
University of Jyvaskyla, Finland

1.   Context of the Study

Finland is a bilingual country where 94 percent of the 5 million inhabitants speak Finnish and about 6 percent speak Swedish as their mother tongue. Finland's constitution decrees that the cultural and economic needs of Finnish- and Swedish-speaking populations are to be met on an equal basis. In principle, all forms of social services should be available in Finnish and Swedish in all bilingual areas of Finland.

Many countries where several languages are spoken have decided in favor of making the first school language the same for all students. In Finland, students are offered a choice for the first school language, and this language policy makes it possible for Finnish- and Swedish-speaking children to attend separate schools. Furthermore, the Swedish-speaking population is entitled to education in Swedish at all levels of the educational system from kindergarten to university. The Swedish schools have become the real cornerstone for the existence of the Swedish-language culture in Finland. Mother tongue and literacy instruction have an important position, especially in the early grades.

Language-minority students are often expected to have a lower performance level, particularly in literacy, and this was supported by the data from most countries in the 1990-91 cross-national IEA Reading Literacy Study. Children whose home language was different from the dominant language used in schools showed lower literacy levels in both populations (9- and 14-year-olds) (Elley 1994). Finland, however, has nearly avoided this problem and achieved an unusual level of literacy in both languages. In the IEA study in Finland, the Finnish-speaking students at both age levels showed the highest reading literacy levels in almost all domains. Likewise, in a parallel national study, the Swedish-speaking minority students demonstrated an almost equal performance level (Brunell and Linnakylä 1994).

In Table 1, the scores of the Finnish-speaking students are compared with their peers attending Swedish-speaking schools in Finland and also with those Swedish students who participated in the IEA study in Sweden (cf. Brunell and Linnakylä 1994). As shown, the Swedish-speaking students in Finland scored almost as high in reading literacy tests as their Finnish-speaking peers, who had the highest average scores in both populations (Elley 1994). In Population A, the performance level of the Swedish-speaking Finnish students came between that of Finnish-speaking Finns and Swedish students. In Population B, the performance levels of the two Swedish-speaking populations were the same. In all, the mean difference between reading literacy performance of the Finnish-speaking majority and the Swedish-speaking minority was rather marginal. Taking into consideration that the students of Sweden also performed very well in the IEA study, scoring third in both age groups in the international comparison, the performance level of Swedish-speaking minority students in Finland can be regarded exceptionally high.

Table 1.   Literacy scores of Finnish- and Swedish-speaking students in Finland and of Swedish students in Sweden: Populations A and B

Literacy domain and population	Mean percentage of correct answers	
	Population A (9-year-olds)	Population B (14-year-olds)
Documents		
Finland: Finnish	78	86
Finland: Swedish	78	82
Sweden	72	81
Expository		
Finland: Finnish	77	74
Finland: Swedish	73	71
Sweden	70	71
Narrative		
Finland: Finnish	79	79
Finland: Swedish	73	76
Sweden	72	77
Total		
Finland: Finnish	78	80
Finland: Swedish	75	77
Sweden	71	77

SOURCE: IEA Reading Literacy Study, Finnish National Study data and Swedish National Study data.

2.   Aims of the Article

The purpose of this article is to explore how the quality of school life in general appears in the two Finnish school systems, which seem to produce equally high cognitive achievement. Furthermore, the aim was to examine whether the quality of school life in Finland resembles the Nordic school culture and whether it has any correspondence to school life of Germany or the United States. The Finnish schools in this study are compared to the other Nordic schools and the German and U.S. schools because of the assumption that Finnish school system has partly followed the principles of the German and Baltic, later the Scandinavian, and most recently the U.S. school systems (Iisalo 1991).

Earlier international assessments on the satisfaction with their schools expressed by Finnish children and adolescents were not very flattering. In the 1970s, the IEA Six Subject Study, in which Finnish-speaking students participated, did not provide a very positive picture of attitudes towards the school and studying among Nordic students in general and Finnish students in particular. For example, among 14-year-old students in the nations included in that study, overall satisfaction with their schools was considerably lower in Finland, Sweden, and West Germany than in the United States, Hungary, and Japan. Negative attitudes towards school were exceptionally common in Finland. Particularly striking in these results was that Finnish students' relationship with the teachers indicated feeling of inferiority (low self-esteem); that is, 73 percent of the students said that "they felt little" in front of the teacher (Husen 1973; Fägerlind and Munck 1981).

What is the situation in Finland in the 1990s? How do Finnish children enjoy school? How do the Finnish-speaking majority schools and the Swedish-speaking minority schools differ in the quality of school life? And how do Finnish schools compare with the other Nordic schools as well as with the German and American schools? We use the extensive international data collected during the IEA Reading Literacy Study (Elley 1994) and the national data collected simultaneously in Swedish-speaking schools in Finland to address these questions.

3. Defining the Quality of School Life

When assessing schools, focus on cognitive achievements does not, of course, suffice. The development of the affective domain has to be evaluated as well. In the affective domain, motivation to learn has been most frequently assessed, since motivation is found crucial in energizing and directing learning (Gage and Berliner 1988). It sustains our attention and maintains our effort. It may be reinforced by extrinsic rewards or it may be a result of some intrinsic personal drive (Deci 1975). It seems to be supported by a complex system of thought and feelings to understand the causes of our performance. These attributions are related to subsequent behavior and also to our emotions (Weiner 1986). Motivation is also viewed in connection with enjoyment, an optimal experience, which usually occurs when a person's mind is stretched to its limits in a voluntary effort to accomplish something worthwhile (Csikszentmihalyi 1990).

Increasingly, interest has also been focused on the study of school ecology, school environment, school climate and milieu, social relations in school, school culture, and the quality of school life (Fraser 1986; Csikszentmihalyi 1990).

The concept of the quality of school life has been derived from a more general concept, "the quality of life" (Land and Spilerman 1975; Williams and Batten 1981; Csikszentmihalyi 1990). Quality of life means the level and versatility of social life experienced by individual members of society. From an individual's point of view, the quality of life is usually considered a general, holistic well-being or enjoyment, i.e., how life as a whole is experienced at a certain moment in a given environment. Evaluation is mainly focused on the positive—things that have brought happiness, pleasure, and satisfaction—but also on negative experiences and feelings. Furthermore, experiences are evaluated in some specific areas significant in the individual's life, such as family, friends, school, work, and leisure (Gerson 1976; Williams and Batten 1981).

The "quality of school life" is defined in this study as students' general well-being and satisfaction and their positive and negative experiences, particularly in activities typical of school life. According to Williams and Batten (1981, 9) the typical activities and functions of school environment are as follows:

1. To facilitate and certify the *achievement* and *technical competence* valued in the society;

2. To encourage and enhance an individual's *personal development;*

3. To support individuals' socialization, social relations, and *social integration;* and

4. To nurture and guide an individual's *social responsibility* for his or her own actions and for the groups to which he or she belongs.

To support these more general societal expectations, schools have created such structures and programs that translate these expectations into actions within the school (Williams and Batten 1981). Societal expectations can be met and schools structured successfully only if individuals approve and are attracted to the outcomes and studying processes that they embody. As shown in Table 2, there are four major areas of student motivational experiences corresponding to the four societal expectations and school structures (Williams and Batten 1981).

Table 2.   Domains of student experience of the quality of school life

Societal expectations	School structures	Student experiences
Technical competency	Certification	Opportunity (security, adequacy)
Personal development	Instruction	Adventure (adequacy, intimacy)
Social integration	Socialization	Identity (intimacy, worth)
Social responsibility	Supervision	Status (worth, security)

SOURCE: T. Williams and M. Batten, *The Quality of School Life*. ACER research monograph No. 12, 1981, p. 10.

From the student's point of view, obtaining competency is desirable if certification processes offer a secure basis for the future and new *opportunities* for personal development and for functioning and succeeding in society. From the perspective of individual growth, student experiences must include the experience of *adventure* in learning, i.e., a joyful experience that makes learning intrinsically motivating. The main motivating element of social integration is *identity* formation, the development of self-awareness in a school class and in relation to the larger society. Acquiring of social responsibility is dependent upon the student *status* and prestige in the group (Williams and Batten 1981, 10).

4.   Method

4.1   Measuring the Quality of School Life

A questionnaire with 29 items originally constructed and refined by Williams and Batten (1981, 36) was used as the instrument for measuring the quality of school life. The items operationalize the domains of the quality of school life mentioned above: general satisfaction, negative affect, and four central domains of student experiences—opportunities for success, adventure of learning, and the development of identity and status. Each domain was operationalized in five items with the exception of negative affect, which had only four questions (Schleicher and Siniscalco 1991).

In exploratory analyses of refining the instrument, the adventure items—the joy and self-motivation in learning—did not come out as a subscale of their own, but they were linked with opportunity questions. Therefore the adventure and opportunity items were combined when the questionnaire was revised. Furthermore, the student-teacher relationship linked to socialization was assessed as an independent domain, and even though it was not assumed to be an isolated factor in the original model, it already emerged in Williams and Batten's exploratory analyses (1981) and later also in Ainley's (1986; Ainley and Bourke 1989) empirical data as a distinctively essential domain in the quality of school life.

Table 3 shows the content of the items in the international questionnaire used in the IEA study, their hypothetical domain, and for the Finnish-speaking schools, the structure of the empirical data based on exploratory factor analysis (principal component with varimax rotation).

Students responded to the items by using the following scale: I definitely agree (4), mostly agree (3), mostly disagree (2), and definitely disagree (1). The results of the assessment are described and compared both variable by variable and factor by factor as the proportion of the students agreeing (definitely agree and mostly agree) with the items. In the factor and regression analyses as well as in the analysis of variance, the original ratings were used as an ordinal scale.

Factor analysis of the Finnish data indicated that the items of the questionnaire clearly clustered according to the assumed factor structure. Consistent with the theoretical structure, the item variables clustered into six factors, of which general satisfaction, teacher-student relations, student's status, and social identity were the most distinct. The variables related to the domains of opportunity for success and adventure and for developing oneself clustered into the same factor as in earlier analyses in Australia. Furthermore, the teacher-student relationship also formed a distinct domain of its own. The only item that did not behave as expected was the item "I feel happy": it did not fall into the factor of general satisfaction but got a rather strong negative loading and clustered into the factor of negative affect. After further analysis, the item variable was placed into the scale of negative affect and was reformulated as "I do not feel happy" in order to avoid negative loading.

Factor analysis was applied to confirm the *construct validity* of the instrument. It seems reasonable to argue for six construct dimensions within the theoretical context. Within the assessment of the quality of school life, the results were thus analyzed according to the factor scales focusing on the following domains: general satisfaction, negative affect, teacher-student relations, student's status in the school, social identity, and the student's view of opportunity for succeeding in school.

Coefficient alpha, a measure of the *reliability* (internal consistency) of the whole instrument was fairly high at .87. The six-factor solution explained 55 percent of the total variance. The alpha coefficients measuring the reliability of the different domains based on the factors were as follows:

- General satisfaction   .83
- Teacher-student relations   .83
- Student's status in school   .78
- Identity formation   .71
- Achievement and opportunity   .67
- Negative affect   .60

Table 3. The items measuring the quality of school life classified according to their theoretical and empirical factor (rotated principal component analysis) structure

Items	Theoretical classification*	1 (G)	2 (T)	3 (S)	4 (I)	5 (A)	6 (N)

School is a place where...

Items	Theoretical classification*	1 (G)	2 (T)	3 (S)	4 (I)	5 (A)	6 (N)
I really like to go to school	G	.62					
I get satisfaction from the school work I do	G	.62					
I get enjoyment from being at school	G	.62					
I find that learning is a lot of fun	G	.56					
Teachers treat me fairly in class	T		.81				
Teachers are fair and just	T		.68				
Teachers listen to what I say	T		.61				
Teachers help me to do my best	T		.58				
Teachers give me the marks I deserve	T		.44				
People look up to me	S			.74			
I know that people think a lot of me	S			.71			
I feel important	S			.55			
People have confidence in me	S			.41			
People come to me for help	S			.38			
Mixing with other people helps me understand myself	I				.60		
I get to know myself better	I				.51		
I learn to get along with other people	I				.47		
I learn a lot about myself	I				.46		
I have learnt to accept other people as they are	I				.33		
I know the sorts of things I can do well	A					.57	
I know I can reach a satisfactory standard in my work	A					.54	
I know I can do well enough to be successful if I try	A					.45	
I feel great	A					.40	
I know how to cope with the work	A					.39	
I feel depressed	N						.71
I feel lonely	N						.56
I feel restless	N						.51
I feel happy	G						-.38
I sometimes get nervous	N						.26

* G = general satisfaction
T = teacher-student relations
S = status in school
I = identity formation
A = achievement and opportunity
N = negative affect

SOURCE: IEA Reading Literacy Study, Finnish National Study data.

The coefficients indicate that the factors of general satisfaction and teacher relations are the most internally consistent. The factor of negative affect proved the least internally consistent.

In the negative affect scale, the lowest loading (.26; in contrast to .52 in the original Australian data) was in the item "I sometimes get nervous," which seemed to point to a translation problem. The item was orginally expressed in English as "I sometimes get upset," which may have a slightly, or even more than slightly, different meaning than in the Finnish item. The difference in item meaning may also cause some unreliability in the comparative assessment of this item.

In the Swedish-speaking schools, the instrument differed to some extent. Three international items were excluded and five national terms were included. Therefore, the factor structure of the data from the Finnish-speaking schools is used as the basis in the following factor scales.

4.2.   Who Participated in the Assessment?

The measurement took place in Finland in March 1991 in connection with the IEA Reading Literacy Study. The parallel national study was conducted in Swedish-speaking schools in Finland at the same time.

In the international study of the quality of school life the participating groups were those classes where the majority of students were 14 years old. In Finland, these students were eighth graders in comprehensive schools. Altogether, 1,379 eighth graders participated in this assessment in the Finnish-speaking schools. The Swedish-speaking schools were not sampled, but rather all schools and all eighth graders (3,318) participated in the national study.

The findings in both Finnish- and Swedish-speaking schools are compared with those from the other Nordic countries participating in the international assessment—Norway, Denmark, and Iceland. Sweden did not participate in the assessment of the quality of school life. Among the countries compared for this assesment, 24,732 students participated in the study (Table 4), including 14,772 students from the four Nordic countries. The data were collected by the national research coordinators in the compared countries under the supervision by the International Coordination Center at the University of Hamburg.

5.   Results of the Assessment

The results of the assessment on the quality of school life are described and compared below both by variables and by factor scales as the percentage of the students' agreement with the item statements (definitely agreeing plus mostly agreeing).

Figure 1. Percentage of students in Finnish-speaking schools in Finland agreeing with the statement

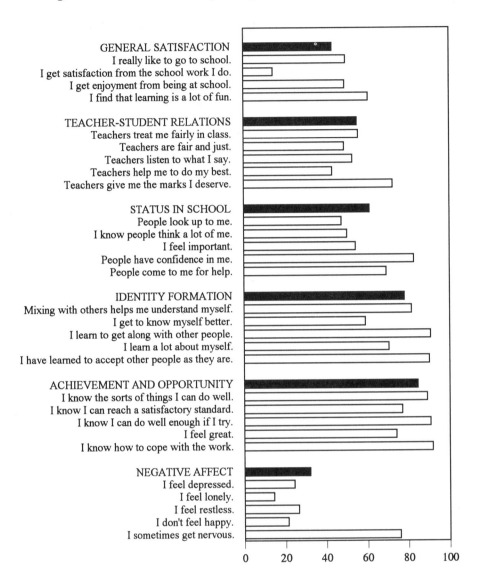

SOURCE: IEA Reading Literacy Study, Finnish National Study data.

Table 4. Number of students participating in this comparison

Countries compared	Number of students
Finland	
Finnish-speaking schools	1,379
Swedish-speaking schools (all schools, no sampling)	3,318
Total in Finland	4,697
Denmark	3,913
Iceland (all schools, no sampling)	3,855
Norway	2,307
Total in the Nordic countries	14,772
Germany/Western states	4,521
Germany/Eastern states	1,963
United States	3,476
Total in the combined countries	24,732

SOURCE: IEA Reading Literacy Study, Finnish National Study data.

5.1. How is the Quality of School Life in the Finnish-Speaking Majority Schools in Finland?

The results of students' self-assessment, as presented in Figure 1, show that Finnish 14-year-olds experience the comprehensive school as a learning and growing environment that is partly inspiring and partly depressing. However, *general school satisfaction* was clearly more common than was a negative attitude towards school. Nearly half (49 percent) of the Finnish students reported that they enjoyed school a lot. Another 49 percent said that they really liked to go to school. Nevertheless, few students (14 percent) agreed that they get satisfaction from the school work, even though 60 percent of the students generally liked learning.

Negative attitudes towards school were nevertheless quite common. As many as 24 percent of the students reported that they felt depressed at school, and even more (28 percent) felt restless. While 21 percent of the students were happy at school, loneliness was rarer (14 percent).

The students had a clear idea of how to *achieve at school*. Ninety-two percent of the students said that they could succeed at school if they tried. They did not, however, all claim to have achieved success: 77 percent of the students stated that they achieved satisfactorily, and 74 percent reported that they did well at school.

According to students, school was clearly experienced as a place for social growth. Ninety-one percent thought that they had learned to get along with other people at school, and 81 percent stated that they had learned to accept others the way they are.

The students also experienced their *social status* quite positively. Eighty-three percent of the students said that other people had confidence in them, and 69 percent reported that others asked for their help. Fifty-four percent felt important, 50 percent believed that people think a lot of them, and 47 percent believed that people look up to them.

The students' *relationship to the teachers* was less positive than their sense of social status. Even though 72 percent of the students thought that the teachers gave them the grades they deserved, only 49 percent of them stated that the teachers were fair and just. Furthermore, only 53 percent of the students reported that the teachers listened to what they said, 56 percent stated that the teachers treated them fairly in class, and 43 percent felt that the teachers helped them to do their best.

The results suggest that general well-being in Finnish schools is more common than general dissatisfaction, although one-fourth of the students found school depressing. However, most Finnish students seem to experience school as a place for many learning and achieving opportunities as well as a place for social growth. Particularly, they learn to socialize with other students. Unfortunately, the teacher-student relationship is not equally trustful, at least from the students' point of view.

5.2.   How is the Quality of School Life in the Swedish-Speaking Minority Schools in Finland?

The general profile of the quality of school life in Swedish-speaking schools in Finland was quite similar to the Finnish-speaking schools, as seen in Figure 2. The domains of social identity and achievement and opportunity were rather similar, as was negative affect. Only the item "I sometimes get upset," which may contain the translation error, showed significant dissimilarity.

Some differences in the profiles, however, could be found. The Swedish-speaking students experienced their school life altogether more positively than their Finnish-speaking peers. *General satisfaction* with school was more common (51 percent versus 43 percent) and negative affect clearly less usual (22 percent versus 32 percent) in the Swedish-speaking schools than in the Finnish-speaking schools. Particularly, learning was found to be more fun and school work more satisfying.

The *relationship between teachers and students* was also more positive in the Swedish- than in the Finnish-speaking schools. In particular, teachers were rated as more helpful (65 percent versus 43 percent). Furthermore, Swedish-speakers rated their *status in school* slightly more positively than their Finnish-speaking peers. Feelings of importance (69 percent versus 54 percent) and the belief that others have confidence in them were more common in Swedish-speaking schools.

In contrast, Finnish-speaking students' conceptions of potential *achievement and opportunities* at school were more positive than Swedish-speaking students' views. In particular, Finnish students more often felt great (74 percent versus 61 percent) and more of them believed that they could succeed if they tried (91 percent versus 83 percent). Furthermore, Finnish-speaking students found the school more influential on identity formation than did the Swedish-speaking students. Mixing with others seemed to help the students in Finnish-speaking schools (81 percent) understand themselves more often than was the case in the Swedish-speaking schools (62 percent).

The comparison between the Finnish- and Swedish-speaking quality profiles indicates significant unity but also some diversity. Diversity, however, also can be found within the Swedish-speaking schools if the profiles are drawn from the perspective of students with different language identity.

Figure 2. Percentage of students in Finland agreeing with the statement

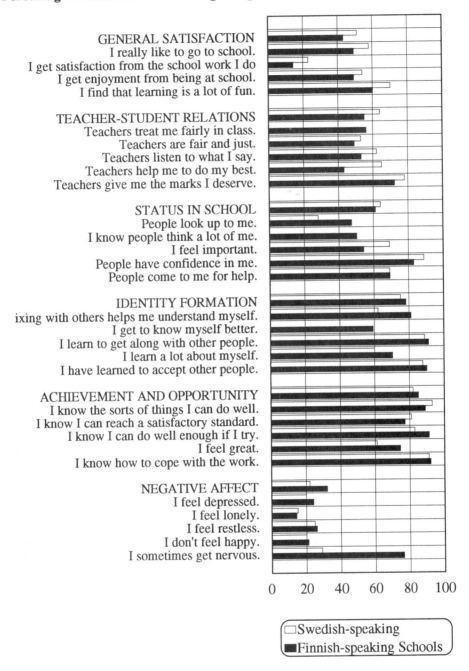

SOURCE: IEA Reading Literacy Study, Finnish National Study data.

213

5.3. Students' Language Identity and the Quality of School Life in the Swedish-Speaking Schools

In the Swedish-speaking schools in Finland, the students' home language may vary to great extent. The home language may be Swedish or Finnish, or the home may be bilingual. Likewise, the students' own language identity may vary. In this study, 62 percent of the students assessed themselves as Swedish-speakers, 36 percent thought they were bilingual, and 2.4 percent considered themselves as Finnish-speakers.

How did the students with different language identities experience the quality of school life in the Swedish-speaking schools? The comparison of the quality profiles in different language groups (Figure 3) indicates that the students with monolingual Swedish or bilingual identity experience the quality of school life more positively in almost all domains than do the students with the monolingual Finnish background. The most striking distinctions between language groups were in the domains of general school satisfaction, teacher-student relations, and achievement and opportunity. In negative affect, however, the differences between language groups were not significant.

In brief, the Finnish-speaking students in the Swedish-speaking schools seem to enjoy school life significantly less than do the monolingual Swedish-speakers and the bilingual students. This may be partly caused by the language deficiency, which may evoke problems in social integration and also in teacher-student interaction, both of which are strongly related to general school satisfaction (Linnakylä 1995).

5.4. Comparing Finnish Schools to the Other Nordic Schools

The students in the other Nordic countries participating in the study of the quality of school life—Iceland, Norway, and Denmark—shared the Finnish students' views that resulted in data showing general school satisfaction was stronger than general negative affect and that students had quite a distinct view of how to work and succeed in school (Figure 4). Moreover, students in the compared countries generally agreed that school was important in the growth of their social identity. However, there were some differences in the Finnish and other Nordic schools, and the differences between the other Nordic and Finnish schools were greater for the Finnish- than the Swedish-speaking schools in Finland.

The students in the other Nordic countries experienced their school life partly more and partly less positively than their Finnish peers. General satisfaction and good relationship between students and teachers were more common in the other Nordic countries than in Finland. Correspondingly, the negative attitude towards school was less common in the other Nordic countries. In contrast, students' views of potential achievement and opportunities at school were more positive in Finland than in the other Nordic countries. Likewise, the students' social status in school and identity development were assessed more positively in both types of Finnish schools than in the other Nordic schools.

The Swedish-speaking schools in Finland proved to some extent more similar to the other Nordic schools than to the Finnish majority schools. In three domains—general school satisfaction, teacher-student relations, and negative affect—the quality of school life in Swedish-speaking schools clearly resembled the Nordic profile. However, in three other domains—social status, social identity, and achievement and opportunity—the Swedish-speaking schools corresponded more closely to the Finnish-speaking schools.

214

Figure 3. Percentage of students in Finland agreeing with the statement, by students' language identity

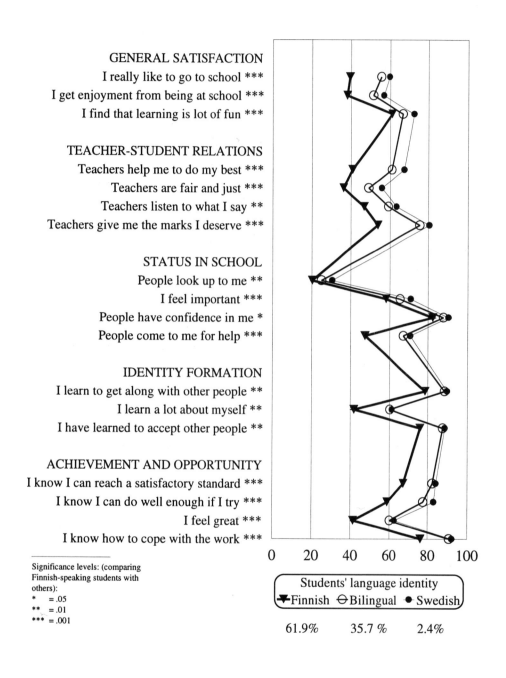

GENERAL SATISFACTION
I really like to go to school ***
I get enjoyment from being at school ***
I find that learning is lot of fun ***

TEACHER-STUDENT RELATIONS
Teachers help me to do my best ***
Teachers are fair and just ***
Teachers listen to what I say **
Teachers give me the marks I deserve ***

STATUS IN SCHOOL
People look up to me **
I feel important ***
People have confidence in me *
People come to me for help ***

IDENTITY FORMATION
I learn to get along with other people **
I learn a lot about myself **
I have learned to accept other people **

ACHIEVEMENT AND OPPORTUNITY
I know I can reach a satisfactory standard ***
I know I can do well enough if I try ***
I feel great ***
I know how to cope with the work ***

Significance levels: (comparing
Finnish-speaking students with
others):
*   = .05
**   = .01
*** = .001

0   20   40   60   80   100

Students' language identity
Finnish   Bilingual   Swedish

61.9%   35.7 %   2.4%

SOURCE: IEA Reading Literacy Study, Finnish National Study data.

Figure 4. Percentage of students in Finland and other Nordic countries agreeing, by factor scale

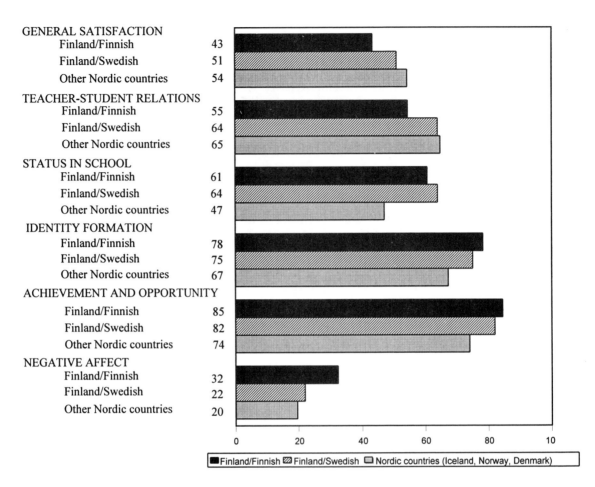

SOURCE: IEA Reading Literacy Study, Finnish National Study data.

Particularly, developing social status in class was more strongly agreed upon among the Swedish-speaking students than among their Finnish-speaking counterparts. Thus, the status domain distinctly deviated from the Nordic profile.

The comparison of the findings suggest that the Swedish-speaking schools in Finland partly reflect typical Finnish school culture with high achievement orientation and emphasis on students' social integration and identity development. The Swedish-speaking schools, however, reflect the Nordic quality of school life with more positive attitude toward school in general and a warmer relationship between students and teachers.

5.5.   Comparing Finnish Schools with German and U.S. Schools

The factor scales, as seen in Figure 5, indicate that school life in the countries compared here has both similarities and differences. The students of all countries shared the view that general school satisfaction was stronger than general negative affect, and that the students had quite a distinct picture of how to work and succeed in school. Moreover, students in the compared countries generally agreed that school was important in the growth of one's social identity.

However, there were some distinct differences in both general school satisfaction and different domains of school life. In general satisfaction, the American and other Nordic students were clearly more positive towards school life than Finnish students, particularly in the Finnish-speaking schools. However, German students in both the Eastern and Western states were even less satisfied with their schools. Accordingly, negative affect towards school was strongest in the Finnish-speaking schools in Finland and in the German schools. Dissatisfaction was clearly weaker in the United States, in the other Nordic countries, and in the Swedish-speaking schools in Finland.

The same profile favoring the U.S., Nordic, and the Swedish-speaking schools in Finland could be found in the teacher-student-relationship. Among the compared countries, students' relationships to their teachers were the most negative in Finnish-speaking schools in Finland and almost as negative in Germany. The most positive was the relationship in the United States.

A different type of profile, however, was found in the domains of achievement and opportunity, as well as in the domains of social identity and status in class. From the perspective of achievement and opportunity, the Finnish schools, particularly the Finnish-speaking system, were regarded by students most positively among compared school systems. In this area, Finnish students resembled Americans. A similar profile was found in the assessment of social identity. The Americans and the Finns in the Finnish-speaking schools assessed their status in class most positively; the Germans, least positively. Almost the same type of diversity also emerged in the domain of status in class. However, in this domain the U.S. and the Swedish-speaking schools in Finland had the most positive attitude. The most negative attitude was again found in Germany.

In all, Finnish students in both Finnish- and Swedish-speaking schools seemed to have some unity and also some diversity in their assessment of the quality of school life. Differences seemed to reflect two different school cultures—perhaps also different cultural codes—the more enjoyable Nordic and U.S. school culture as well as the less enjoyable German school life.

Finnish-speaking students' assessment of the quality of school life resembled German students' attitudes toward school both in general school satisfaction and negative affect, as well as in the domain

Figure 5. Percentage of students in Finland and all comparison countries agreeing with the statement, by general factor scales

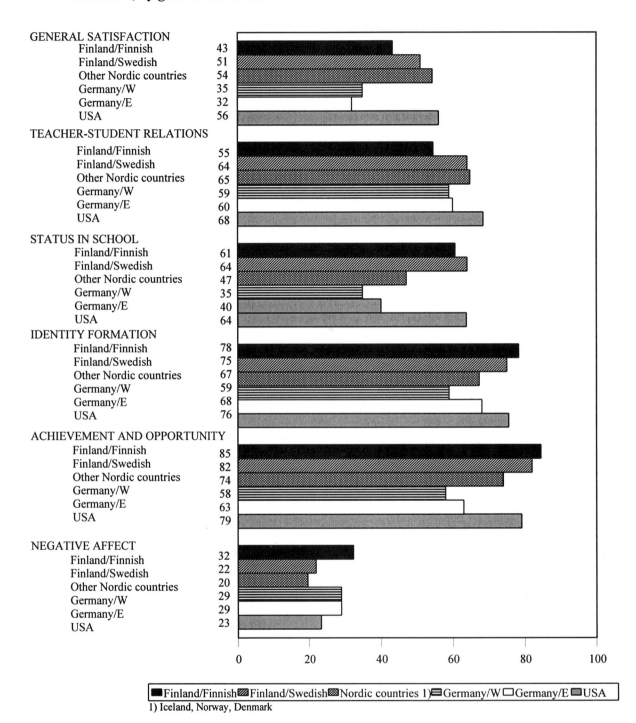

GENERAL SATISFACTION
Finland/Finnish 43
Finland/Swedish 51
Other Nordic countries 54
Germany/W 35
Germany/E 32
USA 56

TEACHER-STUDENT RELATIONS
Finland/Finnish 55
Finland/Swedish 64
Other Nordic countries 65
Germany/W 59
Germany/E 60
USA 68

STATUS IN SCHOOL
Finland/Finnish 61
Finland/Swedish 64
Other Nordic countries 47
Germany/W 35
Germany/E 40
USA 64

IDENTITY FORMATION
Finland/Finnish 78
Finland/Swedish 75
Other Nordic countries 67
Germany/W 59
Germany/E 68
USA 76

ACHIEVEMENT AND OPPORTUNITY
Finland/Finnish 85
Finland/Swedish 82
Other Nordic countries 74
Germany/W 58
Germany/E 63
USA 79

NEGATIVE AFFECT
Finland/Finnish 32
Finland/Swedish 22
Other Nordic countries 20
Germany/W 29
Germany/E 29
USA 23

■Finland/Finnish ▨Finland/Swedish ▧Nordic countries 1) ⊟Germany/W ☐Germany/E ▦USA
1) Iceland, Norway, Denmark

SOURCE: IEA Reading Literacy Study, Finnish National Study data.

218

of teacher-student relations. In these domains, Swedish-speaking students' attitudes were more similar to the views of the students in the other Nordic countries and in the United States. By contrast, the peer relations, social identity, and social status in class were assessed in both Finnish school systems similarly as in the United States and more positively than in the other Nordic countries or Germany. Likewise, the importance of achievement and opportunity was seen more clearly in Finland in both school systems and in the United States than in the other Nordic countries and Germany.

6.   Conclusions

The results of the assessment on the quality of school life indicate many similarities as well as some differences in the quality profiles in the Finnish- and Swedish-speaking schools in Finland. School life was experienced as inspiring or depressing in almost the same domains in both Finnish school systems and all compared countries. General school satisfaction was stronger than negative attitudes toward school. Furthermore, the students had a fairly clear idea of how to work, achieve, and succeed in school, and they also saw the importance of the school for the growth of their social identity.

Some diversity among Finnish school systems as well as among the compared countries, however, appeared both in general profiles and within all quality domains. In Finnish school systems, diversity was most obvious in teacher-student relations as well as in general school satisfaction and dissatisfaction. In these respects the Swedish-speaking schools in Finland resembled the other Nordic and the U.S. schools. The Finnish-speaking schools, however, corresponded in these domains to the German schools.

In the other domains—status in class, social identity, and achievement orientation—the Swedish- and Finnish-speaking schools were more alike and resembled the U.S. rather than the Nordic or German schools. In these domains, the German schools, particularly in Western states, had an exceptionally low quality of school life.

In all, the findings suggest that the quality of school life in the Swedish-speaking schools in Finland is more positive than in the Finnish-speaking schools. The culture of the Swedish-speaking schools seems to have many characteristics similar to the other Nordic schools. Particularly, relations between teachers and students proved warmer and more trustful in the Swedish-speaking school system in the same manner as in the Nordic schools. In other studies it has been proved that the teacher-student relationship is crucial to the general school satisfaction (Hoffman 1991; Linnakylä 1995). We also have to keep in mind that the parents of the Swedish-speaking students have a higher educational background and a better socioeconomic status; they are more often academically educated than the Finnish-speakers' parents (Brunell and Linnakylä 1994). This may have an effect on the students' school motivation, status in class, and quality of school life.

However, compared to the students in other countries, the Finnish students in both systems found the school as a place for peer relations and for their own social growth. Moreover, the Finnish students had a particularly clear idea of how to work and succeed in school. In this respect the Finnish schools even exceeded the U.S. schools.

Dissatisfaction towards school, however, is still strong in Finland in the Finnish-speaking schools. Even though the students find learning in general quite enjoyable and they seem to realize the relevance of schooling and achieving in order to succeed, they still do not particularly like school nor especially the kind of tasks it sets.

An important research task is to find the reasons for this relatively strong negativity in the Finnish-speaking school culture. With a better insight into this phenomenon, we would be in a better position to do something about this pattern of negativity and to create a more positive attitude towards school, especially towards learning tasks, and to improve relationship between students and teachers. In this respect, the Swedish-speaking schools and the other Nordic and U.S. schools could be used to model some changes for the Finnish-speaking schools.

On the other hand, we must remember that the Finnish-speaking comprehensive school has done rather well in achieving good academic learning standards (Elley 1994; Keeves 1992). Perhaps we have made our Finnish-speaking schools into a demanding but depressing learning environment (cf. Lundberg and Linnakylä 1992). Perhaps teacher-centeredness and external control are still so strong that our students cannot see teachers as encouraging mentors. Maybe the German and Baltic traditions in the Finnish-speaking schools are stronger than in the Swedish-speaking schools, which have always had close connections to the Scandinavian school culture (Iisalo 1991).

How could we develop our Finnish-speaking schools into more positive, cooperative, and enjoyable environments for learning and growing without risking high achievement and good peer relations between students? Could teaching methods that emphasize the students' own experiences and interests, as well as cooperative learning and joint responsibility, be part of the solution? Could the teacher be looking more for the students' strengths and talents rather than their weaknesses and mistakes? Should we, accordingly, develop our assessment methods by favoring personal performance and portfolios rather than normative tests? Should we break the tradition of school subjects and integrate our curriculum more closely with the issues and problems of real life and students' own culture? There are many questions, but there are also many opportunities to explore for those who develop our schools. How actively these opportunities are tried out is, of course, up to each school and each individual teacher, but it is also a challenge for comparative research, calling for broad-minded interdisciplinary effort and cooperation with the Swedish-speaking, other Nordic, and U.S. schools.

Dissatisfaction can, of course, be fruitful and act as agent for change to create a new Finnish school where academic achievement will still be excellent and where students as well as teachers will experience joy in learning, working, and growing together.

References

Ainley, J. (1986). *Influences on student views of the quality of school life*. Paper presented in the Conference of the Australian Association for Research in Education. Melbourne.

Ainley, J., and Bourke, S. (1989). *Student views of primary schooling*. Hawthorn, Vic.: ACER .

Brunell, V., and Linnakylä, P. (1994). Swedish speakers' literacy in the Finnish society. *Journal of Reading*, 37(5), 368-375.

Csikszentmihalyi, M. (1990). *Flow. The psychology of optimal experience*. New York: Harper and Row.

Deci, E.L. (1975). *Intrinsic motivation*. New York: Plenum Press.

Elley, W. (1994). *The IEA Study of Reading Literacy: Achievement and instruction in thirty-two school systems*. Oxford: Pergamon.

Fraser B.J. (1986). *Classroom environment*. London: Croom Helm.

Fägerlind, I., and Munck, I. (1981). *Attitudes towards school and education in seven countries*. Reports, 52. University of Stockholm. Institute of International Education.

Gage, N.L., and Berliner, D.C. (1988). *Educational psychology*. Boston: Houghton Mifflin.

Gerson, E.M. (1976). On quality of life. *American Sociological Review,* 41, 793-806.

Hoffman, J.V. (1991). Teacher and school effects in learning to read. In R. Barr, M.L. Kamil, P. Mosenthal, and P.D. Pearson (eds.). *Handbook of reading research, Vol. II,* 911-950, New York: Longman.

Husen, T. (1973). *Svensk skola i internationell belysning*. [Swedish school in international view]. Stockholm: Almqvist and Wiksell.

Iisalo, T. (1991). *Kouluopetuksen vaiheita*. [History of school teaching] Helsinki: Otava.

Keeves, J.P. (1992). *Learning science in a changing world. Cross-national studies of science achievement: 1970 to 1984*. The Hague: The International Association for the Evaluation of Educational Achievement.

Land, K.C., and Spilerman, S. (eds.). (1975). *Social indicator models*. New York: Russell Sage Foundation.

Linnakylä, P. (1993). Exploring the secret of Finnish reading literacy achievement. *Scandinavian Journal of Educational Research,* 37(1), 63-74.

Linnakylä, P. (1995). Quality of school life in the Finnish comprehensive school. A comparative view. *Scandinavian Journal of Educational Research,* 39(3).

Lundberg, I., and Linnakylä, P. (1992). *Teaching reading around the world*. The Hague: The International Association for the Evaluation of Educational Achievement.

Schleicher, A., and Siniscalco, M. (1991). *The quality of school life.* Unpublished manual. University of Hamburg. International Coordination Center of the IEA Reading Literacy Study.

Weiner, B. (1986). *An attributional theory of motivation and emotion.* New York: Springer-Verlag.

Williams, T., and Batten, M. (1981). *The quality of school life.* ACER Research Monograph No. 12. Hawthorn, Vic.: ACER.

Analysis of the Williams and Batten Questionnaire on the Quality of School Life in Spain

Guillermo A. Gil
Instituto Nacional de Calidad y Evaluación, Spain

1. Introduction

The aim of this paper is to examine the suitability of the Quality of School Life scale developed by Williams and Batten (1981) for describing education in Spain. A number of analyses were performed for the following purposes:

1. Examining the usefulness of the scale translated to Spanish with pupils engaged in the eighth course of the General Basic Education (equivalent to eighth grade), with the view to comparing the emergent factors and the assignment of the questionnaire's items to these factors found by Williams and Batten in their study.

2. Ascertaining the equivalence of the measure when translated into the four languages of Spain (Castilian—the predominant language, Catalonian, Galician, and Valencian).

3. Estimating the reliability of the test as a whole and of the separate subscales.

4. Estimating the relationships between an overall measure of the Quality of School Life scale and reading performance and other variables of interest.

The data on which these analyses are based were collected through the IEA's International Reading Literacy Study.

2. Williams and Batten's Quality of School Life Scale

The Williams and Batten Quality of School Life scale was developed initally in the early 1980s by administering a questionnaire on two successive occasions using two different samples of Australian pupils. When it was first administered, a version with 71 items was used; a reduced version with 42 items was used the second time. Factor analysis was employed to identify the latent structure of those items and to refine the item pool by eliminating those that made little contribution to the main clusters of items identified. The analysis provided evidence for six theoretical constructs. It also showed the validity of the several scales (defined as the correlation between the item composite and the associated constructs) to be about .90. The authors concluded that their model, with slight modifications, fit the data adequately. The final measure was based on items that identified six factors.

The questionnaire is based on 29 questions to which the pupils reply in terms of a 4-point agree-disagree Likert scale. The questionnaire takes the form of an initial statement *(School is a place where...)*, a short paragraph of instructions, and finally the list of statements.

The six underlying factors of the model, are as follows:

1. **General Affect**. Five items: (3) I really like to go; (21) I feel happy; (22) I find that learning is a lot of fun; (23) I get enjoyment from being there; (28) I feel great.

3.   **Status**. Five items: (5) I feel important; (8) People have confidence in me; (10) People come to me for help; (13) I know that people think a lot of me; (15) People look up to me.

4.   **Identity**. Five items: (4) Mixing with other people helps me to understand myself; (6) I learn to get along with other people; (19) I learn a lot about myself; (25) I get to know myself better; (29) I have learned to accept other people as they are.

5.   **Teachers**. Five items: (2) Teachers are fair and just; (7) Teachers help me do my best; (9) Teachers treat me fairly in class; (14) Teachers give me the marks I deserve; (20) Teachers listen to what I say.

6.   **Opportunity**. Five items: (1) I know how to cope with the work; (17) I know I can reach a satisfactory standard in my work; (18) I know the sorts of things I can do well; (24) I get satisfaction from the school work I do; (26) I know I can do well enough to be successful.

The final results obtained by Williams and Batten from the factor analysis are shown in Table 1. The reliability of the scale was calculated using Heise and Bohnstead's Omega coefficient. The results obtained for the subscales were .83 for general affect, .72 for negative affect, .86 for status, .74 for identity, .79 for teachers, and .76 for opportunity.

3.   Study of the Quality of School Life Scale in Spain

3.1   Sample

In implementing this study, the questionnaire on the Quality of School Life was administered to eighth grade pupils aged 13-15. In the context of the IEA Reading Literacy Study, that population was deemed appropriate for the study of reading achievement and for the analysis of the effects of the school, family, and personal variables affecting it, since this is the final stage of basic education and nearly all children of this age are still at school.

To select the sample, a nonproportional allocation technique was employed in those autonomous communities that have responsibilities in the field of education, and a proportional technique was used in the territory for which the Ministry of Education and Science is responsible. Accordingly, the sample as a whole took the form of a mixed proportional/nonproportional sample design. In distributing the sample, the reference features taken were the control of the school (state/private) and the size of the community (over 20,000 inhabitants, between 20,000 and 100,000 inhabitants, and over 100,000 inhabitants). The distribution of the sample selected is as shown in Table 2.

In addition, the questionnaire was administered to samples of pupils from Spanish autonomous communities having their own language—Catalonia, Valencia, and Galicia. Students in 34 schools were tested in each of these autonomous communities for a total of 3,147 students tested in these vernacular languages—1,099 in Catalonian, 936 in Galician, and 1,112 in Valencian.

Table 1. Factor analysis: Results of the analysis of the Williams and Batten questionnaire

Factor	Item	Statements	CA FA	h^2	*
GENERAL AFFECT (G)	3	I really like to go	.56	.46	
	21	I feel happy	.58	.57	
	22	I find that learning is a lot of fun	.56	.50	O
	23	I get enjoyment from being there	.68	.63	
	28	I feel great	.63	.60	
NEGATIVE AFFECT (N)	11	I feel lonely	.58	.39	
	12	I feel restless	.43	.44	G
	16	I feel depressed	.70	.59	
	27	I get upset	.52	.30	
STATUS (S)	5	I feel important	.43	.42	G
	8	People have confidence in me	.46	.38	
	10	People come to me for help	.50	.35	
	13	I know that people think a lot of me	.65	.56	
	15	People look up to me	.71	.55	G
IDENTITY (I)	4	Mixing with other people helps me to understand myself	.54	.40	
	6	I learn to get along with other people	.52	.39	
	19	I learn a lot about myself	.58	.48	
	25	I get to know myself better	.63	.54	
	29	I have learnt to accept other people as they are	.44	.26	
TEACHERS (T)	2	Teachers are fair and just	.67	.51	
	7	Teachers help me to do my best	.54	.42	
	9	Teachers treat me fairly in class	.77	.65	
	14	Teachers give me the marks I deserve	.60	.40	
	20	Teachers listen to what I say	.61	.49	
OPPORTUNITY (O)	1	I know how to cope with the work	.46	.30	
	17	I know I can reach a satisfactory standard in my work	.67	.54	
	18	I know the sorts of things I can do well	.48	.30	
	24	I get satisfaction from the school work I do	.41	.40	G
	26	I know I can do well enough to be successful	.71	.58	

CA FA = Factorial weight.

h^2 = Communality.

* = Departures from simple structure; loadings greater than 0.4 on factors identified.

SOURCE: Williams, T., and Batten, M. (1981). *The Quality of School Life*. Hawthorn, Vic.: Australian Council for Educational Research.

Table 2. Sample of the study: Eighth grade

Autonomous communities	Schools	Students
ANDALUSIA	37	1,096
CANARY ISLANDS	38	1,036
CATALONIA	39	1,121
GALICIA	38	1,041
BASQUE COUNTRY	36	1,018
VALENCIA	35	1,050
MEC*	55	1,644
NAVARRE	40	1,024
TOTAL	318	9,030

*Autonomous communities administered by the Ministry of Education and Science.
SOURCE: IEA Reading Literacy Study, Spanish National Study data, Spanish Ministry of Education and Science, 1991.

3.2   Results

3.2.1   Underlying Factors in the Questionnaire

Principal Components Analysis was used to elicit the latent structure of these data in the Castilian sample. Analogous analyses were undertaken using the data obtained from Catalonian, Galician, and Valencian samples in order to ascertain the equivalence of the latent structures in the four different languages. The eigenvalue-one criterion was used to select the numbers of factors to be rotated. An oblimin rotation was used since the theoretical assumption was that the factors would be correlated.

From the total Castilian sample, six factors were identified (corresponding very closely with the Williams and Batten factors shown in Table 1). After analyzing the content of each item allocated to each factor, it was deemed advisable to rename the factors, since the terminology employed by Williams and Batten did not seem to be wholly appropriate in Castilian. The idea underlying the sets of factor items was expressed in Castilian in this way:

Original name in English	New name in English	New name in Castilian
GENERAL AFFECT	POSITIVE FEELINGS	SENTIMIENTOS POSITIVOS
NEGATIVE AFFECT	NEGATIVE FEELINGS	SENTIMIENTOS NEGATIVOS
STATUS	SELF-ESTEEM	AUTOESTIMA
IDENTITY	LIVING TOGETHER	CONVIVENCIA
TEACHERS	RELATION WITH THE TEACHERS	RELACIONES CON EL PROFESORADO
OPPORTUNITY	SELF-CONFIDENCE	AUTOCONFIANZA

The results of the factor analysis for the sample in Castilian are shown in Table 3. Correlations among factors ranged between -.36 and .32, thus giving support to the assumption that correlations among factors do exist. With respect to the assignment of the items to the factors of the Williams and Batten model, 27 of the 29 items loaded in the same way. In the case of the two items not corresponding to expectations, item 1 showed a low factor loading, and item 24 did not load on the same factor with which it was associated in the original model. In view of these results, it can be concluded in general terms that the model of Williams and Batten is suitable, because the match between its factor structure and that obtained through analysis of the scale in Castilian was confirmed. Nevertheless, it was deemed advisable to place item 24 in the Positive Feelings factor rather than regarding it as part of the Self-Confidence factor, and this was done for the subsequent analyses for this study.

Subsequently, similar analyses were undertaken with samples of pupils responding to the Catalonian, Galician, and Valencian translations of the questionnaire. The results obtained are reported in Tables 4, 5, and 6 and reveal slight differences in the assignment of items to the factor structure as compared with the test in Castilian. The origin of these differences might lie in the translation process, which may have introduced some different nuances of meaning. It was therefore deemed advisable to carry out a third series of factor analyses using the students from the autonomous communities of Galicia, Catalonia, and Valencia tested in Castilian. The assignment of factors to questionnaire items as given by the results of these factor analyses are shown in Tables 7, 8, and 9. The results of these additional analyses are summarized in Tables 10 and 11 and are discussed taking the results obtained in the factor analysis of the sample tested in Castilian as the point of reference, since the most reliable results are those from that sample of 8,485 pupils. From these results it can be judged that the test possesses indicators for the six factors found by Williams and Batten in the original version. In light of these analyses, it would seem to be appropriate to define the Castilian version of Williams and Batten's Quality of School Life scale as having 28 items, with item 24 being regarded as part of the Positive Feelings factor and item 1 being omitted.

- The factor corresponding to **Negative Feelings** (comprising items 11, 12, 16, and 27) and the **Relations with the Teachers** factor (comprising items 2, 7, 9, 14, and 20) showed the same factor structure in all samples—those tested in Castilian and those tested in the native languages of Galicia, Catalonia, and Valencia (see Table 10).

- The **Self-Esteem** factor (comprising items 5, 8, 10, 13, and 15) revealed an identical factor structure for all the samples tested in Castilian and for the sample tested in Valencian (see Table 11).

- The **Living Together** factor (items 4, 6, 19, 25, and 29) showed an identical factor structure for the general sample tested in Castilian and for the Galician and Valencian samples tested in the Castilian language (see Table 11).

- The **Positive Feelings** factor (items 3, 21, 22, 23, 24, and 28) showed an identical factor structure in the general sample tested in Castilian, in the Valencian sample tested in Valencian, and in the Galician sample tested in the Castilian language (see Tables 10 and 11).

- The **Self-Confidence** factor (items 17, 18 and 26) revealed an identical factor structure for the sample tested in Castilian, the Catalonian sample tested in Catalonian, and the Galician sample tested in the Castilian language (see Tables 10 and 11).

Table 3. Factor analysis: Sample tested in Castilian (N= 8,485)

Factor	Item	Statements	CA FA	h²	*
POSITIVE FEELINGS (P)	3	I really like to go	-.75	.57	
	21	I feel happy	-.47	.50	
	22	I find that learning is a lot of fun	-.69	.57	
	23	I get enjoyment from being there	-.79	.70	
	24	I get satisfaction for the school work I do	-.64	.60	
	28	I feel great	-.44	.49	
NEGATIVE FEELINGS (N)	11	I feel lonely	.73	.56	
	12	I feel restless	.75	.55	
	16	I feel depressed	.78	.61	
	27	I feel upset	.74	.58	
SELF-ESTEEM (SE)	5	I feel important	.46	.34	
	8	People have confidence in me	.67	.53	
	10	People come to me for help	.58	.38	
	13	I know that people think a lot of me	.65	.44	
	15	People look up to me	.69	.52	
LIVING TOGETHER (L)	4	Mixing with other people helps me to understand myself	-.81	.60	
	6	I learn to get along with other people	-.70	.54	
	19	I learn a lot about myself	-.62	.53	
	25	I get to know myself better	-.68	.59	
	29	I have learnt to accept other people as they are	-.40	.34	
RELATIONS WITH THE TEACHERS (T)	2	Teachers are fair and just	.73	.57	
	7	Teachers help me to do my best	.68	.58	
	9	Teachers treat me fairly in class	.74	.64	
	14	Teachers give me the marks I deserve	.70	.53	
	20	Teachers listen to what I say	.66	.53	
SELF-CONFIDENCE (SC)	1	I know how to cope with the work	.26	.24	
	17	I know I can reach a satisfactory standard in my work	.79	.63	
	18	I know the sorts of things I can do well	.71	.58	
	26	I know I can do well enough to be successful	.72	.55	

CA FA = Factorial weight.

h² = Communality.

* = Loading greater than 0.4 on second factor indicated.

SOURCE: IEA Reading Literacy Study, Spanish National Study data, Spanish Ministry of Education and Science, 1991.

Table 4. Factor analysis: Catalonian sample tested in Catalonian (N=1,099)

Factor	Item	Statements	CA FA	h²	*
POSITIVE FEELINGS (P)	3	I really like to go	-.85	.71	
	22	I think that learning is a lot of fun	-.72	.59	
	23	I get enjoyment from being there	-.89	.76	
	24	I get satisfaction from the school work I do	-.46	.50	
NEGATIVE FEELINGS (N)	11	I feel lonely	.76	.61	
	12	I feel restless	.69	.52	
	16	I feel depressed	.83	.69	
	27	I feel upset	.76	.63	
SELF-ESTEEM (SE)	5	I feel important	.75	.54	
	13	I know that people think a lot of me	.79	.59	
	15	People look up to me	.61	.46	
LIVING TOGETHER (L)	4	Mixing with other people helps me to understand myself	-.68	.52	
	6	I learn to get along with other people	-.72	.60	
	8	People have confidence in me	-.45	.48	
	10	People come to me for help	-.42	.53	
RELATIONS WITH THE TEACHERS (T)	2	Teachers are fair and just	-.78	.64	
	7	Teachers help me to do my best	-.62	.50	
	9	Teachers treat me fairly in class	-.83	.67	
	14	Teachers give me the marks I deserve	-.64	.48	
	20	Teachers listen to what I say	-.76	.60	
SELF-CONFIDENCE (SC)	1	I know how to cope with my work	.36	.47	
	17	I know I can get a satisfactory standard in my work	.81	.68	
	18	I know the sorts of things I can do well	.63	.56	
	26	I know I can do well enough to be successful	.79	.66	
LIVING TOGETHER GENERAL (LG)	19	I learn a lot about myself	.41	.52	SE
	21	I feel happy	.45	.61	
	25	I get to know myself better	.44	.51	
	28	I feel great	.46	.60	
	29	I have learnt to accept other people as they are	.49	.44	

CA FA = Factorial weight.

h² = Communality.

* = Loading greater than 0.4 on second factor indicated.

SOURCE: IEA Reading Literacy Study, Spanish National Study data, Spanish Ministry of Education and Science, 1991.

Table 5. Factor analysis: Galician sample tested in Galician (N=936)

Factor	Item	Statements	CA FA	h²	*
POSITIVE FEELINGS (P)	3	I really like to go	-.75	.53	
	22	I find that learning is a lot of fun	-.72	.60	
	23	I get enjoyment for being there	-.71	.67	
	24	I get satisfaction from the school work I do	-.70	.55	
	25	I get to know my self better	-.36	.47	
NEGATIVE FEELINGS (N)	11	I feel lonely	.73	.62	
	12	I feel restless	.80	.64	
	16	I feel depressed	.72	.56	
	27	I feel upset	.69	.50	
SELF-ESTEEM (SE)	8	People have confidence in me	-.54	.51	
	10	People come to me for help	-.78	.62	
	13	I know that people think a lot of me	-.50	.49	
	15	People look up to me	-.56	.58	SE 2
LIVING TOGETHER (L)	4	Mixing with other people help me to understand myself	.39	.40	
	6	I learn to get along with other people	.44	.45	
	21	I feel happy	.38	.56	
	28	I feel great	.45	.61	
	29	I have learnt to accept other people us they are	.64	.52	
RELATIONS WITH THE TEACHERS (T)	2	Teachers are fair and just	-.74	.60	
	7	Teachers help me to do my best	-.72	.59	
	9	Teachers treat me fairly in class	-.70	.58	
	14	Teachers give me the marks I deserve	-.71	.57	
	20	Teachers listen to what I say	-.68	.57	
SELF-CONFIDENCE (SC)	1	I know how to cope with the work	.62	.42	
	17	I know I can reach a satisfactory standard in my work	.71	.51	
	18	I know the sorts of things I can do well	.68	.55	
	19	I learn a lot about myself	.62	.49	
	26	I know I can do well enough to be successful	.58	.47	
SELF-ESTEEM.2 (SE2)	5	I feel important	.79	.65	

CA FA = Factorial weight.

h² = Communality.

* = Loading greater than 0.4 on second factor indicated.

SOURCE: IEA Reading Literacy Study, Spanish National Study data, Spanish Ministry of Education and Science, 1991.

Table 6. Factor analysis: Valencian sample tested in Valencian (N=1,112)

Factor	Item	Statements	CA FA	h^2	*
POSITIVE FEELINGS (P)	3	I really like to go	.75	.61	
	21	I feel happy	.43	.50	
	22	I find that learning is a lot of fun	.64	.56	
	23	I get enjoyment for being there	.84	.73	
	24	I get satisfaction from the school work I do	.74	.68	
	28	I feel great	.43	.52	
NEGATIVE FEELINGS (N)	11	I feel lonely	.76	.57	
	12	I feel restless	.75	.55	
	16	I feel depressed	.74	.57	
	27	I feel upset	.68	.52	
SELF-ESTEEM (SE)	5	I feel important	.53	.41	P
	8	People have confidence in me	.57	.48	
	10	People come to me for help	.59	.38	
	13	I know that people think a lot of me	.56	.41	
	15	People look up to me	.63	.46	
LIVING TOGETHER (L)	4	Mixing with other people helps me to understand myself	-.71	.54	
	6	I learn to get along with other people	-.62	.52	
	19	I learn a lot about myself	-.59	.53	
	25	I get to know myself better	-.73	.63	
RELATIONS WITH THE TEACHERS (T)	2	Teachers are fair and just	-.69	.55	
	7	Teachers help me do my best	-.75	.60	
	9	Teachers treat me fairly in class	-.74	.63	
	14	Teachers give me the marks I deserve	-.69	.53	
	20	Teachers listen to what I say	-.69	.58	
SELF-CONFIDENCE (SC)	1	I know how to cope with my work	.34	.34	
	17	I know I can reach a satisfactory standard in my work	.83	.67	
	18	I know the sort of things I can do well	.64	.60	
	26	I know I can do well enough to be successful	.67	.50	
	29	I have learnt to accept other people as they are	.40	.39	

CA FA = Factorial weight.
h^2 = Communality.
* = Loading greater than 0.4 on second factor indicated.
SOURCE: IEA Reading Literacy Study, Spanish National Study data, Spanish Ministry of Education and Science, 1991.

Table 7. Factor analysis: Catalonian sample tested in Castilian (N=1,121)

Factor	Item	Statements	CA FA	h²	*
POSITIVE FEELINGS (P)	3	I really like to go	-.77	.58	
	22	I find that learning is a lot of fun	-.73	.61	
	23	I get enjoyment from being there	-.78	.70	
	24	I get satisfaction from the school work I do	-.68	.60	
NEGATIVE FEELINGS (N)	11	I feel lonely	.78	.64	
	12	I feel restless	.78	.63	
	16	I feel depressed	.73	.58	
	27	I feel upset	.70	.61	
SELF-ESTEEM (SE)	5	I feel important	.35	.46	
	8	People have confidence in me	.66	.52	
	10	People come to me for help	.60	.46	
	13	I know that people think a lot of me	.66	.49	
	15	People look up to me	.73	.60	
LIVING TOGETHER (L)	4	Mixing with other people helps me to understand myself	-.77	.57	
	6	I learn to get along with other people	-.64	.51	
	19	I learn a lot about myself	-.58	.55	
	25	I get to know myself better	-.69	.62	
RELATIONS WITH THE TEACHERS (T)	2	Teachers are fair and just	.67	.56	
	7	Teachers help me to do my best	.70	.60	
	9	Teachers treat me fairly in class	.71	.66	
	14	Teachers give me the marks I deserve	.67	.55	
	20	Teachers listen to what I say	.62	.55	
SELF-CONFIDENCE (SC)	1	I know how to cope with my work	.45	.35	
	17	I know I can reach a satisfactory standard in my work	.80	.66	
	18	I know the sorts of things I can do well	.71	.59	
	26	I know I can do well enough to be successful	.72	.54	
LIVING TOGETHER GENERAL (LG)	21	I feel happy	-.57	.68	
	28	I feel great	-.55	.66	
	29	I have learnt to accept other people as they are	-.39	.43	

CA FA = Factorial weight.

h² = Communality.

* = Loading greater than 0.4 on second factor indicated.

SOURCE: IEA Reading Literacy Study, Spanish National Study data, Spanish Ministry of Education and Science, 1991.

Table 8. Factor analysis: Galician sample tested in Castilian (N = 1,041)

Factor	Item	Statements	CA FA	h²	*
POSITIVE FEELINGS (P)	3	I really like to go	.69	.55	
	21	I feel happy	.47	.57	
	22	I find that learning is a lot of fun	.60	.54	
	23	I get enjoyment from being there	.79	.72	
	24	I get satisfaction from the school work I do	.68	.63	
	28	I feel great	.41	.55	
NEGATIVE FEELINGS (N)	11	I feel lonely	.77	.64	
	12	I feel restless	.74	.56	
	16	I feel depressed	.74	.54	
	27	I feel upset	.69	.51	
SELF-ESTEEM (SE)	5	I feel important	.39	.39	P
	8	People have confidence in me	.68	.53	
	10	People come to me for help	.60	.37	
	13	I know that people think a lot of me	.64	.46	
	15	People look up to me	.66	.47	
LIVING TOGETHER (L)	4	Mixing with other people helps me to understand myself	-.71	.54	
	6	I learn to get along with other people	-.69	.55	
	19	I learn a lot about myself	-.59	.56	
	25	I get to know myself better	-.72	.62	
	29	I have learnt to accept other people as they are	-.34	.32	
RELATIONS WITH THE TEACHERS (T)	2	Teachers are fair and just	-.70	.54	
	7	Teachers help me to do my best	-.69	.59	
	9	Teachers treat me fairly in class	-.72	.64	
	14	Teachers give me the marks I deserve	-.70	.56	
	20	Teachers listen to what I say	-.64	.57	
SELF-CONFIDENCE (SC)	1	I know how to cope with the work	.17	.25	SE
	17	I know I can reach a satisfactory standard in my work	.76	.62	
	18	I know the sorts of things I can do well	.69	.57	
	26	I know I can do well enough to be successful	.68	.52	

CA FA = Factorial weight.
h² = Communality.
* = Loading greater than 0.4 on second factor indicated.
SOURCE: IEA Reading Literacy Study, Spanish National Study data, Spanish Ministry of Education and Science, 1991.

Table 9. Factor analysis: Valencian sample tested in Castilian (N=1,050)

Factor	Item	Statements	CA FA	h²	*
POSITIVE FEELINGS (P)	3	I really like to go	-.76	.59	
	22	I find that learning is a lot of fun	-.65	.58	
	23	I get enjoyment from being there	-.80	.72	
	24	I get satisfaction with the school work I do	-.64	.64	
NEGATIVE FEELINGS (N)	11	I feel lonely	.77	.72	
	12	I feel restless	.74	.56	
	16	I feel depressed	.76	.62	
	27	I feel upset	.70	.65	
SELF-ESTEEM (SE)	5	I feel important	.56	.38	P
	8	People have confidence in me	.68	.56	
	10	People come to me for help	.55	.62	
	13	I know that people think a lot of me	.67	.56	
	15	People look up to me	.67	.62	
LIVING TOGETHER (L)	4	Mixing with other people helps me to understand myself	.83	.66	
	6	I learn to get along with other people	.69	.59	
	19	I learn a lot about myself	.53	.52	
	25	I get to know myself better	.58	.53	
	29	I have learnt to accept other people as they are	.43	.41	
RELATIONS WITH THE TEACHERS (R)	2	Teachers are fair and just	-.75	.58	
	7	Teachers help me to do my best	-.72	.61	
	9	Teachers treat me fairly in class	-.81	.71	
	14	Teachers give me the marks I deserve	-.70	.52	
	20	Teachers listen to what I say	-.70	.65	
SELF-CONFIDENCE (SC)	1	I know how to cope with my work	.15	.30	
	17	I know I can reach a satisfactory standard in my work	.50	.51	
	18	I know the sorts of things I can do well	.45	.51	
	21	I feel happy	.42	.62	P
	26	I know I can do well enough to be successful	.66	.55	
	28	I feel great	.42	.55	

CA FA = Factorial weight.

h² = Communality.

* = Loading greater than 0.4 on second factor indicated.

SOURCE: IEA Reading Literacy Study, Spanish National Study data, Spanish Ministry of Education and Science, 1991.

Table 10. **Factor analysis: Samples tested in Castilian and samples tested in Catalonian, Galician, and Valencian, by items associated with each subscale**

Language	Negative Feelings	Relations with the Teachers	Self-Esteem	Living Together	Living Together, General	Positive Feelings	Self-Confidence	N
Castilian . .	11,12,16,27	2,7,9, 14,20	5,8,10,13,15	4,6,19,25,29		3,21,22,23, 24,28	17,18,26	8,485
Catalonian .	11,12,16,27	2,7,9,14, 20	5,13,15	4,6,8,10	19,21,25,28, 29	3,22,23,24	17,18,26	1,099
Galician* . .	11,12,16,27	2,7,9,14, 20	8,10,13,15	(4),6,(21),28, 29		3,22,23,24,(25)	1,17,18,19, 26	936
Valencian .	11,12,16,27	2,7,9,14, 20	5,8,10,13,15	4,6,19,25		3,21,22,23,24, 28	17,18,26,29	1,112

*Item 5 was considered separately. This item had significance by itself (see Table 5).
NOTE: Figures in parentheses indicate items with loadings greater than 0.3 but less than 0.4.
SOURCE: IEA Reading Literacy Study, Spanish National Study data, Spanish Ministry of Education and Science, 1991.

Table 11. **Factor analysis: Samples tested in Castilian in Catalonia, Galicia, Valencia, and in the other autonomous communities, by items associated with each subscale**

Region	Negative Feelings	Relations with the Teachers	Self-Esteem	Living Together	Living Together, General	Positive Feelings	Self-Confidence	N
Whole . . .	11,12,16,27	2,7,9, 14,20	5,8,10,13, 15	4,6,19,25, 29		3,21,22,23, 24,28	17,18,26	8,485
Catalonia .	11,12,16,27	2,7,9,14, 20	(5),8,10,13, 15	4,6,19,25	21,28,(29)	3,22,23,24	1,17,18,26	1,121
Galicia . . .	11,12,16,27	2,7,9,14, 20	(5),8,10,13, 15	4,6,19,25, (29)		3,21,22,23, 24,28	17,18,26	1,041
Valencia . .	11,12,16,27	2,7,9,14, 20	5,8,10,13, 15	4,6,19,25, 29		3,22,23,24	17,18,21, 26,28	1,050

NOTE: Figures in parentheses indicate items with loadings greater than 0.3 but less than 0.4.
SOURCE: IEA Reading Literacy Study, Spanish National Study data, Spanish Ministry of Education and Science, 1991.

In relation to the samples tested in the vernacular languages of the autonomous communities, some variations were found. For example, a variation in the sample tested in Catalonian was that items 8 and 10, usually associated with the Self-Esteem factor, were associated with the Living Together factor. Items 19, 21, 25, 28 and 29 formed a new factor, which was labeled "Living Together, General" (see Table 4). A variation in the sample tested in Galician was that the item 5, usually incorporated to the Self-Esteem factor, arose as an isolated item. Another variation in this sample was that items 21 and 28, associated normally with the Positive Feelings factor, appeared under the Living Together factor. Similarly, item 19 became associated with the Self-Confidence factor instead of with the Living Together factor (see Table 5). In the sample tested in Valencian, item 29, usually associated with the Living Together factor, was associated with the Self-Confidence factor (see Table 6).

These variations in the results may be due in part to the process of translation, since they did not arise when the same samples were tested in Castilian, nor did they arise in the general nationwide sample tested in Castilian. It seems plausible, therefore, that these results can be explained in terms of problems connected with shifts in the meaning of the items through translation.

Other variations also appeared in the analysis of the data for the samples of Catalonia, Galicia, and Valencia tested in Castilian. In the Valencian sample, items 21 and 28, normally associated with Positive Feelings, were instead associated with the Self-Confidence factor. This departure from expectation would not appear to be particularly significant since it only arose in that sample. A second departure from the general model arose in the Catalonian sample, where items 21, 28, and 29 formed a group around the new factor, Living Together, General.

It is interesting to note that, in general, most of the variation observed in the different analyses relate to the items placed in the final part of the questionnaire, both for the populations tested in Castilian and for the populations tested in the language of each of the autonomous communities.

3.2.2 Reliability

The reliability of the scale as a whole and of the various subscales was estimated, both for the sample tested in Castilian and for the samples tested in the languages of Catalonia, Galicia, and Valencia. The reliability of the scale for each sample was calculated through Cronbach's α coefficient. The reliability for the national sample tested in Castilian was .85 for the scale as a whole and values lying between .66 and 83 for the subscales. For the samples from the autonomous communities tested in Galician, Catalonian, and Valencian, the reliabilities were estimated to lie between .87 and .83 for the scale as a whole and between .62 and .85 for the subscales. It can be concluded then that the test was highly reliable for the scale as a whole and adequate for the individual subscales.

On the basis of the results of the factor analysis, another estimate of reliability was carried out without taking into account the effect of item 1, although eliminating this item did not affect the results. The same reliability estimates were obtained for the national sample tested in Castilian in the calculations based on 28 items as in those based on 29 items, except for the Self-Confidence factor for which the reliability increased from .67 to .69. This result shows that item 1 can be eliminated from the test without any loss of reliability. The results in terms of reliability rates, both for the national sample and for the autonomous community samples, are shown in Tables 12 and 13.

Table 12. Reliability: National sample tested in Castilian

Subscale	α
COMPLETE SCALE	.85
POSITIVE FEELINGS	.83
NEGATIVE FEELINGS	.77
SELF-ESTEEM	.66
LIVING TOGETHER	.77
RELATIONS WITH THE TEACHERS	.83
SELF-CONFIDENCE	.67

SOURCE: IEA Reading Literacy Study, Spanish National Study data, Spanish Ministry of Education and Science, 1991.

Table 13. Reliability: Samples tested in Catalonian, Galician, and Valencian

Subscale	Galician	Catalonian	Valencian
COMPLETE SCALE	.83	.84	.87
POSITIVE FEELINGS	.77	.81	.85
NEGATIVE FEELINGS	.72	.79	.73
SELF-ESTEEM	.62	.68	.63
LIVING TOGETHER	.68	.70	.77
RELATIONS WITH THE TEACHERS	.82	.79	.82
SELF-CONFIDENCE	.67	.74	.73

SOURCE: IEA Reading Literacy Study, Spanish National Study data, Spanish Ministry of Education and Science, 1991.

3.2.3   The Relationship Between Quality of School Life and Other Variables in the Educational Context

In order to exemplify some applications of the scale, the relationship between some variables in the school environment and the factor weightings obtained by the pupils on the Quality of School Life scale were estimated. For this purpose, a factor score derived from all 28 items of the final scale were estimated. This factor score was calculated by multiplying the points given in each pupil's reply to each item by its factor weighting in the first factor of the unrotated factor matrix. The scores were rescaled to have a mean of zero. While the use of a single score such as this is useful on a summary measure, it is also possible to use different factor scores for each one of the six obtained factors. Variables may show different relationships across the six subscales.

The variables analyzed were obtained from pupil or teacher questionnaires. For the purposes of this section, one-way analysis of variance was used to calculate the significance of the differences obtained, even though multivariate analyses would be more appropriate given the correlation existing between many of these variables.

237

For example, the girls scored slightly higher than the boys in the Quality of School Life scale (F=317,00; d.f.=1,8458; p≤.0000). Without taking other variables into account, it could be said that the girls rate life in school more positively than do boys.

In the same way, in analyzing the variable "subsequent study expectations," which was evaluated in the student questionnaire through the question, "For how many years more do you expect to go on studying after you've finished this year?", we found that the Quality of School Life Scale score increased in step with the number of years over which the pupils expected to carry on studying, there being a significant relationship between these two variables (F=36,223; d.f.=6,8373; p≤.0000).

When attention was turned to the variable "time spent on homework," a uniform progression was likewise noted; hence, in a seven-step scale (from "None" to "Over 5 hours"), the greater the time devoted by the pupils to homework the higher the score on the Quality of School Life scale (F=31,47; d.f.=6,3658; p≤.0000).

Studying the variable "time spent watching television outside school" also proved interesting in that the less time the pupils spent watching television at home, the higher their scores in the scale (F=10.86; d.f.=6.8436; p≤.0000). This makes sense when we consider the relationship between frequency and quantity of homework and the time spent watching television.

In analyzing the variable "age of pupils," which ranged between 12 years 5 months and 16 years 9 months, three age bands were laid down, and it was shown that the pupils in the higher age band obtained a lower score in the Quality of School Life scale. This result is largely a function of pupils having had to repeat years, since 60.7 percent of pupils in the third band, the highest in terms of age, had been obliged to repeat one school year, and 15.73 percent had repeated two school years. Naturally, these variables were interrelated, since the score obtained in the Quality of School Life scale was also directly linked to a pupil's status as a repeater (F=27.85;d.f.= 2.7954; p≤.0000).

Finally, the relationship between the scale score and some variables concerning the pupils' reading performance were analyzed. In the IEA Reading Literacy Study, overall scores for pupils' reading performance with different kinds of texts—narrative, expository, and documents—were estimated. It was noted that the higher the pupils' scores in the Quality of School Life scale, the higher their scores in understanding written narrative texts (F=5.56; d.f.=3.8481; p≤.0008). However, the relationship between the score obtained in understanding expository texts and documents and the score obtained in the Quality of School Life scale did not turn out to be statistically significant (F=2.33; d.f.=3.8481; p=0.0724 and F=0.06; d.f.=3.8431; p=0.9784, respectively).

4.   Discussion of Results and Conclusions

The Williams and Batten scale appears to be an appropriate instrument for estimating the quality of life for pupils in a school context and for evaluating the relationship between significant factors in the educational context.

However, before any further development occurs, it would be advisable to pilot test and analyze factorially the translated tests, since text translation problems may have been responsible in part for the differences between the results obtained for the national sample tested in Castilian and those obtained for the samples tested in Catalonian, Galician, and Valencian. It is also possible that some cultural differences may underlie some of the differences found, and this possibility needs further examination.

Second, the Quality of Life Questionnaire is a measure in which, in the questionnaire's current form, the factor of the pupils' forgetting about the context could result. The test is headed by the statement "School is a place where ...," after which come six lines of instructions, and finally a list with the 29 items of the test. The heading is not repeated at any stage, and so when the student is answering the last items of the test, he or she may no longer remember whether the item is referring to life at school or to his or her personal life in general.

The recasting of certain items to include the header statement as a reminder would be advisable, since it has emerged from this study that some of the items worded in a general way, with no explicit reference to school, are those that depart most from expectation (items 4, 5, 6, 8, 10, 11, 12, 13, 15, 16, 19, 21, 25, 27, 28 and 29), while those worded in more specific terms related to the school life reveal greater correspondence with the original model (items 1, 2, 3, 7, 9, 14, 17, 18, 20, 22, 23, 24 and 26). Within the group of general items, there is a subgroup concerning negative feelings that behaves in the same way in all the studies examined (items 11, 12, 16, and 17).

Reference

Williams, T., and Batten, M. (1981). *The quality of school life.* Hawthorn, Victoria: Australian Council for Educational Research.

☆ U.S. GOVERNMENT PRINTING OFFICE:1997-422-400/60535

ISBN 0-16-048957-1

90000